Harvard Studies in Urban History

Series Editors
Stephan Thernstrom
Charles Tilly

Peasants and Strangers

Italians, Rumanians, and Slovaks
in an American City, 1890–1950

Josef J. Barton

Harvard University Press   Cambridge, Massachusetts   1975

In memory of Anna Mikulenčak (1868–1971)

Země pak nebude prodávána v manství; nebo má jest země a vy jste příchozí a podruzi u mne.

The land shall not be sold for ever; for the land is mine; for ye are strangers and sojourners with me.
   —Leviticus 25:23

Preface

This book is about the particular experiences of three immigrant groups — Italians, Rumanians, and Slovaks — in a specific
American industrial metropolis, Cleveland. I have attempted to
follow individuals and families through a number of experiences,
the sum of which made them into an ethnic community. The
agricultural villages of southern and eastern Europe, from which
these newcomers journeyed, imposed certain stringencies and encouraged certain aspirations. Patterns of migration selected particular people and led them to settle in particular locales. The choices
of immigrant leaders and the development of local associations
shaped the life of the new community. Rearing children, learning
to labor in an industrial economy, and watching their sons and
daughters leave the household and form their own families — these
events too reveal the diverse meanings which urban life had for the
immigrants and for the second generation. This is not a book about
the immigrant as the representative American, then, but about
the immigrant as a different American. It is an effort to grasp the
particular experiences of immigrants, from the time they left the
old world village to the time their children started their own
households, and to relate these phases of immigrant life to the
emergence and transformation of ethnic communities.

In writing an essay of this sort, I have acquired a great many debts. I owe most of my ideas of how to go about the task to John Higham and Timothy Smith. John Briggs shared his time, his ideas, and his research. Stephan Thernstrom gave the manuscript a thorough reading, and I have profited from his advice. I must thank Oksana Dragan, William Galush, Yeshayahu Jelinek, Tom G. Kessinger, Roman Kochan, Shaw Livermore, Jr., Mark Stolarik, Rudolph Susel, and Sam Bass Warner, Jr., for helpful discussions of particular problems. Francesco Nocito, Zosim Oancea, Ioan Popa, Johan Hegedus, and hundreds of other informants who preferred to remain anonymous shared their memories with me. And for courtesies extended in the course of research, I thank the staff of the University of Minnesota Immigrant Archives and the staffs of the libraries of Johns Hopkins University and the University of Virginia.

The Fund for the Advancement of Education and the University of Virginia generously provided financial support.

My family has contributed in many ways. Elsie and Josef A. Barton gave me more than I can thank them for. Jane Dupree Barton read many versions of each chapter and edited the manuscript. The book is hers as much as mine.

I regret that Anna Mikulenčak did not live to see this book. It's a long way from pulling beets in Moravia and Slovakia, but she would have understood what I have written about.

Charlottesville, Virginia
July 1974

Contents

Tables

Peasants and Strangers

Introduction

Ilie Martin Selișteanul, the founder of the largest mutual benefit association for Rumanian immigrants in the United States, was born in Seliște, a large village of Rumanian and Saxon peasants, the son of an agricultural laborer. While still a young man, Martin taught himself to read and write Hungarian and Rumanian. In 1900 he left Seliște for Martin's Ferry, Ohio, where he set up a store and taught himself English. During the next few years he organized the Union of Rumanian Societies in America, beginning in Cleveland, and set up a fund for nationalist activities in the Hungarian principality of Transylvania. At the same time he relished lecturing to school children — in English — on the strenuous life of Theodore Roosevelt.[1] In 1905 he established a printing press, and in his preface to his Rumanian-language history of the United States, which he published a year later, he wrote: "Nothing is more valuable to a man than to study the history of his own country."[2] After six years in America Martin returned to Seliște and spent the rest of his life organizing savings banks in the communities surrounding his native village.

This sketch of Ilie Martin's life illustrates some aspects of American immigration that have too often been ignored. Martin was socially mobile before he left his village, his cultural ties were plural, and his migration served not to sever his connections with

1

his village but rather to enhance his position there. Yet most students of immigration have assumed that brute poverty or agricultural crisis pushed peasants out of their homelands, they have pictured the dogged determination of newcomers to preserve their traditional culture, and they have taken too literally Oscar Handlin's beautiful epithet, the uprooted.

One of the important reasons that certain aspects of immigration have been neglected is, as John Higham has recently suggested, the conception of immigration as a *rite de passage* to an American identity.[3] In this view, the immigrant's entrance into American society is the quintessential act of mobility in a nation of mobile men, and his subsequent life traces the career of the representative American. Thus in his two classics, *Boston's Immigrants* and *The Uprooted*,[4] Oscar Handlin begins his story with the rupture of a corporate community, proceeds with the migration of a people to a wholly new social system, and then shows a partial reconstruction within a new social form — the voluntary association — which fulfills the particular needs of urban newcomers.[5] According to Handlin, the immigrant's response to his deracination is the achievement of small-scale communities in the modern city; and the voluntary character of group life defines the limits of collective action.[6]

Immigration was significant in this inclusive sense, but it was also a major force for change and differentiation in American society. Marcus Lee Hansen, whose perspectives have been ignored in favor of more expansive conceptions of the meaning of immigration, pointed out thirty years ago that mass migration was "the result of the break-up of something old and it was the preliminary of something new. It was a sign of change and it hastened change." The pace and level of change differed from group to group, but there was one aspect of the transition from the Old to the New World that seemed to characterize every group: the bulk of the immigrants, Hansen observed, "merely hoped to preserve what they had — not alone property, but a status in society which was uncertain at home."[7] Enhancement of one's current status or achievement of a new one was a regular component of the process of arrival and settlement.[8]

The multiple levels of immigrant adjustment to American life require a conceptual scheme sensitive to the various sources of ethnic differences. John Higham's effort to specify the social meaning of ethnicity in a comparative perspective emphasizes the shifting lines of cleavage between immigrant and native. The essential fact about immigrant groups is their instability. Ethnic groups undergo a steady attrition as growing proportions of the second and third generations marry outside the group and cease to be identified with it. The erosion of the second and third generations' ties greatly reduces the group's importance as an ethnic minority. "Those who lose meaningful contact with their immigrant origins," Higham writes, "become absorbed in the Anglo-American community; and this inflow continually widens its limits. That is why Americans have likened their society, not too inaccurately, to a melting pot."[9] The unstable nature of ethnic loyalties and the constant transformation of group identities make the task of conceptualization one of the most important in the study of immigration.[10]

The following facts about American immigration between 1880 and 1924 illustrate the outlines of the conceptual problem. The most important fact is that assimilation was possible in the United States because the Quota Acts of 1921 and the Immigration Restriction Act of 1924 sharply reduced the flow of new immigrants from southern and eastern Europe. The number of new arrivals fell drastically after 1924, and that pattern remained fixed until the Immigration Act of 1965. In Argentina and Brazil and in Australia and Canada, on the other hand, a heavy flow of immigrants continued after 1920.[11] The constant immigration in these countries meant that intermarriage never steadily absorbed immigrant generations into the receiving society, since new arrivals periodically heightened the sense of ethnic separateness in already settled communities.[12] In the United States, however, the sudden reduction of immigration in 1924 enabled assimilation to proceed generation by generation.

In addition, various patterns of economic adjustment had a major impact on the social mobility of the second generation. The major currents of nineteenth-century migration flowed from highly stratified societies to more open societies. But as the United States became more economically diversified and socially stratified in the late nineteenth century, the composition and recruitment of international migration changed decisively. As the sons of British, German, and Irish immigrants gained some footing in skilled and white-collar jobs, all new arrivals from these countries faced fierce competition, particularly if they were unskilled. Hence there was an important change in the occupational distribution of immigrants from these three countries after the turn of the century, as the proportion of unskilled immigrants fell and the proportion of skilled rose rapidly. The enormous flow of unskilled labor from southern and eastern Europe at the end of the nineteenth century, in turn, replenished the supply of manual workers who had come earlier from Britian, Germany, and Ireland.

The long-run consequence of this change in the composition of immigration was the emergence of a relationship between immigrant generations and social mobility. When second-generation northern and western European groups claimed a place of their own in prestigious occupations, a reservoir of common labor was needed to fill manual jobs. Far from being a threat to the middle-class aspirations of the children of mid-nineteenth-century immigrants, the new arrivals facilitated their maturation. The scope of social mobility in the first generation of southern and eastern European immigrants was thus restricted to the occupational roles and means of assimilation defined by the dominant Anglo-

American community. But there remained ample opportunity for advancement from one generation to another. It was in the second generation that twentieth-century immigrants broke decisively from their entrance status. And this break was so sharp that by 1950 the sons of immigrants had become more mobile than members of the Anglo-American charter group.[13]

An approach to the social history of American immigration must account, then, for this varying relationship between ethnicity and social status during the course of assimilation. Early popular theories of assimilation employed the image of the melting pot to illustrate the stages of immigrant absorption. The melting pot served as a symbol of an amalgamated society which the immigrants entered as they acquired an American civic culture yet retained traditional private loyalties. But two more recent studies sought to show that the outcome of the melting pot was not amalgamation but a continual renewal of ethnic ties. Will Herberg's *Protestant, Catholic, Jew* signaled an important reinterpretation of the sequential nature of assimilation.[14] Herberg showed how the heterogeneous groups in the receiving society absorbed the ethnic loyalties of the second and third generation and allowed the transfer of old loyalties to new social forms. Nathan Glazer and Daniel Patrick Moynihan demonstrated in *Beyond the Melting Pot* that the ethnic group was no mere survival of the age of mass migration but a new social form.[15] Their vigorous rendering of New York City's ethnic mosaic illustrated the way in which the political and social aspirations of newcomers were articulated within ethnic groups. Both these books emphasized that, far from disappearing, ethnic groups would reappear in American society in different forms. Both led to the expectation of a continued relationship between ethnicity and social status but also pointed out that the strength of this connection might vary according to a variety of factors — the objective aspects of immigrant origins, the subjective role of community associations, and the incidence of group conflict. Yet neither account spelled out an adequate paradigm of those changing relationships.[16]

What is needed is a model of immigrant assimilation that accounts for the persistence of the relation between ethnicity and social status while it allows for the strength of assimilative forces.[17] This can best be done on a local level, where the number of variables can be controlled but the complexity of the process of immigrant arrival and adjustment can be analyzed. Here, at the level of the community, the relationship between patterns of migration and the establishment of ethnic groups can be seen clearly and the process of assimilation brought into sharp focus.

Where there are no hindrances to movement, migration proceeds according to a regular sequence of stages. In the earliest stage, the pioneer emigrant, motivated largely by private aspirations for a better life, journeys alone to a new society in search of a new position. A successful pioneer may communicate with family and friends at home and persuade them to follow him. The second stage is the development of a minor stream of migrants from one particular place to another. If this intermediate stage establishes a settlement, then a mass migration follows as villagers are carried forward by a pervasive social momentum. This third stage typically produces large urban settlements where immigrants form ethnic groups by establishing societies, parishes, and newspapers.[18] Migration within well-defined streams is important because settlements acquire many of their social characteristics according to how migrants leave their homelands and arrive at their destinations. Traditional ties, for instance, are likely to persist in an immigrant settlement recruited largely from one village or district, while a settlement drawing its population from a variety of locations typically develops a broader identity.

Although this migration sequence largely concerns free peasant movement and the early stages of settlement, the model can systematically relate various types of settlement to different stages of migration, assess the influence of numbers, and link the various categories of migration to the structure of the societies of origin and reception. However, a second paradigm is needed for relating an array of assimilation variables to the slow process of ethnic integration. Milton Gordon's effort to construct a typology of variables provides a useful scheme for American immigration.[19] Gordon identifies several assimilation variables, the two most important being change in cultural patterns, or acculturation, and entrance into primary-level association with members of the charter society, or structural assimilation. Three hypotheses systematically relate these variables to each other: (1) acculturation is likely to be the first type of assimilation to occur when an ethnic group arrives on the scene; (2) acculturation may occur even when assimilation takes place on no other level; and (3) once entrance into primary-group associations, or structural assimilation, has gone forward, all other types of assimilation will follow. These hypotheses constitute a double theory: a fixed, temporal sequence typically swings into action when primary-group association takes place; and, in the absence of primary-group assimilation, a number of processes may occur, if at all, simultaneously and independently. The key to understanding the process of ethnic absorption, then, is structural assimilation — that is, the entrance of immigrants and their children into personal relationships with members of the host society. The result of such assimilation is the disappearance of the ethnic group as a separate entity and the muting of its distinctive values.[20]

These paradigms of the process of arrival and assimilation suggest a hypothetical sketch of the development and subsequent absorption of ethnic groups in a local setting. Since migration begins and proceeds selectively, one must examine the working of selection at both origin and destination. The migration streams that develop from this selective process control the social composition of the early settlement and also determine the extent to which new arrivals are exposed to the assimilative forces of the city. In the American city the process of migration ceases to have direct influence on the social composition or demographic characteristics of the community after the first decade of settlement, so one must next bring into focus the array of assimilative factors. A systematic analysis of the absorptive influences touching the immigrants and their children — the alterations of traditional behavior, the opportunities for social mobility, the participation in personal relationships with members of the larger society — provides a means of gauging the pace and level of change.

In my study I have approached five aspects of immigration. First, what was the relationship between social structure and emigration in the societies of origin? Second, what was the importance of different patterns of migration in the social adjustment of newcomers? Third, how did ethnic settlements succeed in developing distinctive communities and values? Fourth, what meaning did ethnic origins have for the process of social mobility in an American city? And finally, was assimilation a cumulative process, proceeding from generation to generation in regular stages?

In order to determine the answers, I have explored the migration of Roman Catholic Italians, Byzantine Rite Catholic and Eastern Orthodox Rumanians, and Roman Catholic Slovaks from their homeland villages to the urban setting of Cleveland. Chapter 1 sketches the social history of Cleveland from 1890 to 1950, for the structure of the city was a crucial facet of the process of assimilation. Those aspects of the city that bore most strongly on the lives of the immigrants and their children — the composition of the population, the occupational hierarchy, the residential structure, and the educational institutions — are discussed in some detail. Chapter 2 focuses on the European origins of the immigrants, particularly on the relationship between the structure of rural society and patterns of emigration. Chapter 3 offers an overview of patterns of migration and attempts to gauge the social meaning of migration. Chapter 4 traces the emergence of self-conscious ethnic communities. Chapters 5 through 7 follow the careers of the first and second generation in an attempt to judge the impact of social mobility and intermarriage on the communities. The conclusion assesses the relationship between ethnicity and social status in a comparative perspective. The overall effort, then, is to locate the social meaning of ethnicity in an urban setting.

The three groups with which the study deals — Italians, Rumanians, and Slovaks — incorporate a range of experiences which should illuminate those of other immigrant groups of similar size and composition. The largest group, the Italians, is comparable in size to the Poles. The Slovaks, a middle-sized group, resemble the Hungarians in size. The Rumanian group exemplifies the experiences of smaller groups, such as the Greeks and Syrians.[21]

The samples forming the basis of the study were drawn from parish records in the cases of the Italians and Rumanians and from both fraternal insurance and parish records in the case of the Slovaks. The Italian sample is composed of all Italian adults who married in Italian Catholic parishes in Cleveland between 1889 and 1914, the Rumanian, of all Rumanian adults who married in Byzantine Rite and Greek Orthodox parishes between 1905 and 1915. The Slovak sample was drawn from all parish marriages between 1888 and 1914 and from all membership applications to Cleveland lodges of the First Catholic Slovak Union.

In all three cases, the samples consist of reconstitutions of the families of adult immigrants who married in the United States. This reconstitution was based on parish and fraternal lodge records and was checked against school censuses and public marriage and birth records.[22] The families in the samples thus satisfy a minimal definition of ethnic group membership — marriage in an ethnic parish, baptism of children in an ethnic church, membership in an ethnic lodge. The bias of the samples is toward immigrants who participated at least minimally in the organized life of the community. But this skew is what is required in an exploratory study, for it provides a baseline from which to observe the adaptation and assimilation of the first and second generations. Hence the limitations inherent in the composition of the sample are more than compensated for by the information I have gained about the social characteristics of ethnic groups and immigrant families.[23]

The samples thus exemplify the immigrants who married in the United States and their children. These immigrants usually entered the American labor market before marriage; they most often chose a spouse within the ethnic community, although many young men must have found a wife in the homeland on return visits; and their first children were born in America. The children of these marriages attended similar schools, often entered the labor market contemporaneously, and experienced many of the same difficulties in making their way in an urban society. The character of the experiences of both the immigrants and their children developed as first the fathers and then the sons underwent the slow process of ethnic integration.[24] Thus neither the three groups nor the city is statistically representative of every immigrant group or every city. Yet the exploration of the experiences of Italians and Rumanians and Slovaks in the burgeoning city of Cleveland indicates in some measure the experiences of contemporary immigrant groups in urban America.[25]

1 The Growth of a City

Cleveland was a mercantile city in 1850, not unlike two other cities on the Great Lakes, Detroit and Chicago. Commercial enterprises occupied the choice sites along the Cuyahoga River. As stores and warehouses pushed private dwellings away from the central district, the city began to annex the outlying areas. By 1854 Cleveland had incorporated the portion of the city that would make up the core in 1930, and by 1891 the boundaries were drawn at the limits that would mark the beginning of the city's residential ring in 1930.

Between 1850 and 1880, when railroads brought coal and iron ore together, the city's economy was transformed. The Britt Iron and Steel Company opened Cleveland's first rolling mill in 1854; during the following two decades hundreds of foundries, blast furnaces, and rolling mills were built, and secondary construction followed these heavy installations. Cleveland was well situated with respect to both Lake Superior ore and Pennsylvania coal. The development of the fuel-conserving Bessemer and open-hearth processes lowered the coal requirements for a ton of steel from an average of five to eight tons in 1850 to two tons or less by the close of the 1930s. Cleveland thus had an advantage over Pittsburgh, and the advantage was not confined to steel alone but extended to petroleum refining as well — it was in Cleveland that Rockefeller opened his largest refinery in 1865. Pennsylvania remained the top producer of crude oil, but Cleveland quickly became a major refining center during the 1880s.[1] Thus Cleveland rose to industrial prominence on the eve of the great migration of Germans and Czechs in the 1880s and the huge influx of eastern and southern Europeans between 1890 and 1914.

This economic transformation worked remarkable changes in the city landscape. Where pasture had still supported cattle in the 1850s oil refineries and foundries now squatted along the river valley. By 1880 the Cuyahoga River, which had flowed peacefully and cleanly a generation before, was choked with barges, tugs, and an oil film. From the heights on the west bank of the river, Willard Glazier described the scene in 1880:

> There are copper smelting, iron rolling, and iron manufacturing works, lumber yards, paper mills, breweries, flour mills, nail works, pork-packing establishments, and the multitudinous industries of a great manufacturing city, which depends largely upon these industries for its prosperity. The scene at night, from this same elevated position, is picturesque in the extreme. The whole valley shows a black background, lit up with a thousand points of light from factories, foundries, and steamboats, which are multiplied into two thousand as they are reflected in the Cuyahoga, which looks like a silver ribbon flowing through the blackness.[2]

A London *Times* correspondent who traveled through the city a few years later found the same view impressive — he described a dozen railways spreading their arms through the districts of the city. By the time of his visit, the city had built a great stone bridge over the Cuyahoga Valley, from which the traveler peered down into "the black hives bordering the river, where the grimy yet profitable business is conducted that has done so much toward making Cleveland progressive and wealthy."[3]

The growth of Cleveland from a mercantile city into an industrial metropolis changed the patterns of its inhabitants' lives. In 1880 the city counted only a tenth of its inhabitants foreign-born; this figure had swelled to more than a third by 1910. Less than 2 percent of the city was black in 1910; by 1950 the proportion had grown to 20 percent. Work patterns changed also — what was a city of laborers and merchants in 1880 included in its labor force more than one-fifth clerical and sales workers by 1950. The motley sources of its population growth and the diversification of its occupational structure created new social patterns, the most important of which was the residential segregation of ethnic, racial, and occupational groups. The laggard response of public institutions to the growing number of urban problems meant that private institutions were extremely important. The family, the residential neighborhood, the voluntary association — these were the principal agencies of social control and reform between 1890 and 1950.[4] These characteristics defined the New World for the immigrants and structured the course of their lives.

The city grew unevenly between 1890 and 1950. In 1890 the city counted 260,000 residents; sixty years later the population was 900,000. The most rapid spurt of growth within the core of the city (the old mercantile city, the area of which was defined by the 1854 city limits) came in the two decades after 1900, when the average decennial growth rate was over 40 percent. The population of the core reached its peak in 1930 and remained constant to mid-century. Cleveland was the nation's sixth largest core city in 1910 and has remained fifth or sixth since then.

Even after the population growth of the core slowed, the population of the metropolitan area (holding land area constant) continued to increase rapidly. This increase was due to the fact that the residential ring, which began a very rapid expansion in 1900, almost doubled its population during the twenties and continued to grow rapidly into the fifties.[5]

Migration was the principal reason for Cleveland's extraordinary growth. Between 1890 and 1930 the arrival of foreign-born migrants accounted for a third of the average decennial growth, migrants from all sources for more than half. White migration to Cleveland fell drastically in the depression decade, and from 1930 to 1950 many whites left Cleveland. But the city continued to grow because black immigration increased dramatically after 1910. The city's growth from 1890 to 1950 resulted, then, largely from two great migrations, the first of southern and eastern Europeans between 1890 and 1920, the second of southern blacks between 1910 and 1950.[6]

The industrial base of Cleveland's economy provided a great range of manufacturing employment. In 1910 more than an eighth of the active population labored at industrial tasks. But there was already a significant number who had white-collar occupations. The story of the next forty years was the rapid decline of the number of laborers and the steady growth of the number of clerks. By 1950 almost a quarter of the work force sat at a desk or stood behind a sales counter, while only 7 percent spent their lives at industrial labor. Cleveland followed closely the pattern that Colin Clark considers typical of advanced economies — the devotion of more and more effort to tertiary employment and the consequent diminution of the laboring sectors of the work force.[7]

The sources of this change were the long-range decline in heavy industry's share of the labor force and the lessening importance of building and clothing. The steadily increasing employment in wholesale and retail trade and in professional and technical occupations absorbed much of the growing population after 1930. The outcome, then, was to change Cleveland from a predominantly manufacturing to a nonmanufacturing city, to shift the population from manual jobs to white-collar callings.

The effect of this transition was to open new positions in the occupational hierarchy. When immigrants arrived in Cleveland at the turn of the century, the easiest jobs to find were common labor. But these jobs were poorly paid and fraught with insecurity. In 1900 unskilled laborers risked a great deal of short-term unemployment of one to six months, a risk they shared with most of the working class. But they also encountered long-term unemployment of seven to twelve months, which semiskilled and skilled workers avoided. The wages of industrial laborers placed them on the bottom of the occupational hierarchy, for in 1910 their mean annual earnings ranged between $400 and $500. The hourly rate for unskilled labor remained below forty cents until 1937, when it began a slow, steady rise to one dollar in 1948. Despite this increase, unskilled labor continued to be a risky employment.

Within the working class there was a group of occupations, however, that provided significantly more steady and more remunerative employment. Semiskilled and skilled occupations accounted for about a third of all jobs in Cleveland during the first half of the century. While both operatives and skilled workers were exposed to short-term unemployment, the risk of long-term unemployment was greatly reduced. Moreover, wages improved steadily between 1910 and 1950. The important change within this sector of labor was the increase in the semiskilled classification, for operatives amounted to more than a fifth of all workers by 1950. The growing number of operatives reflected an increase in the division of tasks and in the use of assembly methods and induced a relative decline in the number of both unskilled laborers and craftsmen.

The major change in the labor force, however, was in white-collar employment. The tremendous expansion of wholesale and retail jobs and the growth in clerical occupations opened up new occupations to the children of the working class. What few data there are on unemployment among nonmanual employees indicates that the risk of joblessness was significantly lower than among manual laborers in 1900, in the early depression in 1930, and in the midst of the depression in 1935. The movement to white-collar employment thus represented not only a gain in wages but also greater job security. This long-term shift in Cleveland's work force from laboring to semiskilled and nonmanual occupations meant that the children of immigrants who had entered laboring jobs at the turn of the century could look forward to opportunities in semiskilled and white-collar occupations.

One of the most remarkable characteristics of modern American cities is the congeries of segregated neighborhoods in which urban dwellers live out their lives. This pattern is of recent origin, as Sam Bass Warner, Jr., has shown for Boston and Philadelphia.[8] Residential segregation was one important result of the transition from the mercantile city to the industrial metropolis. Changes in modes of transportation and in patterns of private housing defined the new neighborhoods in which the American city accommodated its heterogeneous population.

Mercantile Cleveland in 1880 was a small city, and walking was the primary way of getting to work. The grand streets to the east — Euclid, Superior, Prospect — were dominated by the houses of the city's rich, while the cross streets were lined with the small homes of proprietors and clerks. Behind these homes ran sixty miles of alleys crowded with the dwellings of Cleveland's workers. Many laborers' huts perched on the peripheries of the city and along the shores of Lake Erie, close to small shops and factories. For most clerks and workers, and even for many of the rich, the place of work was within walking distance.

The electrification of streetcars in 1889 drastically changed this pattern. The first routes ran east and west, following the old lines of horse-drawn streetcars. But in 1903, as the demand for commuting facilities grew, the first crosstown rails were laid; a network of connecting lines was completed by 1911. In 1918 more than half the residents of the core of the city rode a streetcar to work, most of whom spent between thirty minutes and an hour hanging on a strap. Over half these riders traveled one to three miles to reach downtown office buildings or the fifty factory sites where two hundred or more employees worked.[9]

This system served as an adequate mode of transportation until about 1925, when new demands for transportation were the result of the growing specialization of downtown Cleveland and the decentralization of the city. The difficulty of transferring from one line to another and the length of the journey downtown from the residential ring eight or nine miles distant pointed to a need for more rapid transportation. There was a brief flurry of interest in rapid transit systems, but the automobile won out in Cleveland as it did in every other American city. By 1927, 35 percent of the people who daily entered the central business district arrived by automobile. Two years later, on the eve of the depression, there were already ninety cars for every hundred families in the city. Although the majority of people within the core of the city continued to ride streetcars to work well into the 1930s, the residents of the more affluent ring quickly adopted the automobile. By 1934 two of every three automobiles in Cleveland were owned by middle-class families in the residential suburbs. The downtown became more and more a destination for automobile traffic and a place of work for the suburban resident. At the end of World War II, the destination of more than one-third of the people who daily left the residential ring was downtown Cleveland. Thus the growing use of the automobile after 1920 greatly enlarged the residential area within a half hour's journey of downtown and completed the transformation of residential patterns which had begun with the introduction of electric streetcars.[10]

These transitions in transportation facilitated the creation of the modern core and ring of Cleveland. The development of a series of concentric circles of residence, graded by ethnicity and income, was one of the major social changes of the industrial metropolis. This phenomenon began in the inner city, where aging structures and growing demand from recently arrived immigrants for cheap housing led landlords to subdivide two- and three-story houses into two-family dwellings. This stock of old housing was the private means of dealing with a major public problem, the housing of new arrivals, and the public agencies of the city sanctioned this means by appropriately amending zoning laws. Tenements never assumed the same importance in Cleveland that they did in New York, since the number of old subdivided houses was adequate to accommodate the newcomers.[11]

The residential ring of the city began to appear at the turn of the century. The extension of streetcar lines to the east opened up East Cleveland, Glenville, and Collinwood in 1900, while the southern and western suburbs were linked to downtown five years later. Suburban developers clearly recognized that what the working- and middle-class resident wanted was "an out-of-town house, . . . still within twenty-five minutes or half an hour's ride from his business." In these residential areas "the air [was] pure, the environment quiet, free from unsanitary conditions, and the living cheap."[12] The rural ideal informed not only middle-class communities, with their bird lovers' associations and their folk festivals celebrating a lost past, but also working-class neighborhoods. As subdivision went forward in each neighborhood, especially after 1910, the controlling institutions were neighborhood savings and loan companies and local real estate developers. The men who made loans and built houses shared the cultural ideals of the people looking for residences. Hence the dominant activity in the real estate market was the construction and sale of one- and two-family houses, while tenement and apartment construction lagged far behind. The result of an unrestrained market and the activities of small lenders and builders was a weave of small patterns creating the ring and core of modern Cleveland.[13]

The social geography that emerged from these patterns of activity was a discontinuous series of residential neighborhoods segregated by ethnic origin and income. Hence during the period of heavy immigration the city was fragmented into ethnic and economic districts. Table 1 shows that in 1910 the recent arrivals from Italy and Russia were clearly concentrated within the core of the city; the same was true of the black community. Occupational groups were also beginning to exhibit patterns of residential segre-

Table 1. Percentage of ethnic and occupational groups residing in Cleveland's core and ring.

	1910		1950	
	Core[a]	Ring	Core[a]	Ring
Total population	37.9	62.1	40.6	59.4
Ethnic groups				
Blacks	78.2	21.8	76.9	23.1
Foreign-born	43.4	56.6	32.9	67.1
German	29.6	70.4	—	—
Irish	55.0	45.0	—	—
Italian	56.2	43.8	23.6	76.4
Polish	—	—	29.9	70.1
Russian	62.3	37.7	27.2	72.8
Number	(560,663)		(914,808)	
Occupational groups				
Professionals	42.5	57.5	30.9	69.1
Proprietors and managers	46.5	53.5	30.1	69.9
Clerical and sales workers	49.4	50.6	32.9	67.1
Skilled workers	47.5	52.5	34.5	65.5
Laborers	64.9	35.1	57.9	42.1
Number	(1,598)		(390,424)	

Sources: The 1910 data for ethnic groups are from U.S. Bureau of the Census, *Thirteenth Census, 1910: Statistics for Ohio*, pp. 633–634. The 1910 data for occupational groups were determined from a systematic sample of the listings in the *Cleveland City Directory* for 1910. The 1950 data for both groups are from U.S. Bureau of the Census, *Seventeenth Census, 1950: Population*, vol. III, *Census Tract Statistics*, chap. 12.

[a]The core is the area of the city annexed as of 1854.

gation. Professionals had already begun to desert the core and were
followed closely by businessmen and even by skilled workers, leaving the central city with its old housing to laborers.

The situation at mid-century represented the logical outcome
of private efforts to meet public problems. Most professionals and
businessmen lived in the residential ring of the city, most domes-
tics and laborers in the core. As immigrant groups began to move
up into skilled and clerical occupations, they too escaped into a
residential zone about five miles from the central city, which was
left to the burgeoning black population. By 1950 Cleveland exhibited the typical social patterns of the older cities of the East and
the north central states: the poor and black remained within the
inner city, while the affluent and white dispersed throughout the
residential ring.[14]

As revealing as a simple division of the city's residences into
core and ring can be, an even more important consideration is residential segregation, especially since the ethnic ghetto is one of the
general themes in the study of immigration. The extent of residential segregation in Cleveland provides a striking confirmation
of the existence of the ethnic ghetto as well as an important quali-
fication of this theme. As table 2 indicates, in 1910 Italian and
Russian immigrants and blacks were significantly segregated from
the rest of the city, while Irish and German immigrants experienced much less marked separation from their neighbors.[15] The
foreign-born in general were not very segregated; rather they
tended to scatter among the districts of the city. The immigrant
ghetto was a new institution in the city, a segregated neighborhood
which grew in response to the huge influx of immigrants after
1890. As the indices for 1930 and 1950 indicate, Italians and Poles
began to disperse through the city after immigration halted, although most large groups of recent arrivals continued to be significantly segregated into the 1950s.

The concentration of cheap housing indicates the main reason

Table 2. Indices of segregation, Cleveland.

1910	Index no.	1930	Index no.	1950	Index no.
FB Italians	86.9			Blacks	85.3
		Blacks	78.4		
Blacks	70.4				
		Rentals, $100+	65.2		
		Rentals, under $15	63.7	Rentals, $100+	64.8
		FB Russians	59.5		
		FB Italians	53.6		
		FB Poles	51.5		
FB Russians	47.8			FB Russians	49.2
				FB Italians	48.4
				FB Poles	48.0
				Rentals, under $19	45.5
		Rentals, $50–99	37.5		
		Rentals, $15–29	32.0		
Professionals	30.1				
FB Irish	27.4			Rentals, $50–99	28.5
				Rentals, $20–29	23.9
FB Germans	22.4			Professionals	23.0
		Rentals, $30–49 (the median)	19.2	Laborers	21.4
				Owner-occupied homes	19.5
Clerical and sales workers	15.8	Owner-occupied homes	18.3	FB whites	17.6
FB whites	14.1	FB whites	13.9	Clerical and sales workers	15.1
Laborers	9.9			Rentals, $30–49 (the median)	13.9

Sources: The 1910 indices for foreign-born Germans and Irish are based on data from U.S. Bureau of the Census, *Thirteenth Census, 1910: Statistics for Ohio*, pp. 633–634; the 1910 indices for other ethnic groups and 1930 indices for occupational groups, from Howard Whipple Green, *Population Characteristics by Census Tracts* (Cleveland, 1934); the 1910 indices for occupational groups, from a systematic sample of listings in the *Cleveland City Directory* for 1910 ($N = 1,598$). All other indices are based on data from U.S. Bureau of the Census, *Seventeenth Census, 1950: Population*, vol. III, *Census Tract Statistics*, chap. 12. All indices are calculated on census tracts except those for Germans and Irish in 1910.

[a]FB = foreign-born.

for the ghetto. Low rentals were clustered quite markedly in 1930 and 1950, in about the same degree as the foreign-born Italians, Poles, and Russians. The indices show the modern metropolitan pattern — the high concentration of low skills, low rents, and blacks and newly arrived immigrants.[16]

The task of accommodating the immigrants to urban life fell to Cleveland's public institutions and private associations, since neither big business nor big government could deal with the problem. The heterogeneous population, the diversifying work force, and the fragmented residential patterns all weakened the large metropolitan institutions and restricted efforts at accommodation to the small-scale environment of the local community. The classic private mode of social control in the big city was the voluntary society, which represented both an assertion of group identity and a tentative adjustment to the industrial metropolis.

Private associations usually began within the immigrant groups themselves. As soon as there was a significant number of a particular ethnic group in the city, it would establish a network of voluntary associations "to order well the community," as a German Lutheran congreation put it in 1848.[17] These associations, which proliferated among German and Irish immigrants in the 1850s, and then among Czech and Hungarian arrivals in the 1870s and 1880s, gave an appearance of stability to the mercantile city. After their formation, many federations were organized as a means of consolidating disparate segments in each immigrant group.[18] As immigrants began to obtain prestigious positions in Cleveland, their associations became vehicles for attaining commensurate places in the cultural life of the city. Growing numbers of cultural groups appeared in the 1890s to celebrate Irish, German, Czech, and Hungarian culture; these societies came to dominate much of the cultural life of the city in the early 1900s.[19] Thus while the native-born had praised an exceptional immigrant in the 1880s "for ele-

ability which plagued public education, the settlements could experiment with free kindergartens, industrial schools, summer schools, evening schools, and trade schools. The typical pattern was the settlement house's experimentation with a new program — such as the training of new teachers in the classrooms of the core of the city — which the public schools eventually adopted.[25]

As these programs came under official sponsorship, the function of public schools expanded. A mass educational system emerged, responsive in specific ways to the needs of immigrants, the result of a mixture of the requirements of the state and the voluntary reforms of private groups. The public schools made periodic efforts to meet the needs of adult immigrants who wanted to learn English. Night schools were established in several public schools in 1850 and continued to function until they petered out in the 1870s. It was in the 1890s, during a renovation of many municipal institutions, that the public schools again organized adult evening schools. At least thirty were operating in the city in 1891. Funds were always difficult to come by, but the schools continued to operate. That they met a real need is evident, for learning English was an important job skill for the immigrant. The business community began to support them; an educational commission reported in 1906 that most employers saw evening schools "as an integral part of a well conceived plan of public education."[26]

More important than these efforts, however, were the attempts to adapt public schools to the needs of the immigrants' children. Such programs were always under financial constraints which limited the range of experimentation. From the late 1860s to the 1920s, for instance, the number of children per room was between fifty and sixty. Despite these limitations, the same years that saw the adoption of night schools on a large scale also saw the establishment of free kindergartens (1896), the introduction of night elementary schools for working children (1902), and the beginning of summer schools on both elementary and secondary levels (1903). These innovations became a permanent part of the public school system and gained broad support from immigrant groups, merchants, and industrialists.

The relationship between private innovations and public institutions reached an important point during World War I. The Americanization movement, which acquired momentum from the patriotic enthusiasm of the first months of the war, provided a focus for the disparate energies of a variety of voluntary groups; the result was a reform thrust concentrating on the provision of evening language and trade schools. At the same time, Cleveland teachers began to acquire a sense of their professional identity in the heady early years of progressive education.[27] Granted, the main emphasis of Americanization was on English and civics, but the net result was the establishment of a close relationship between public schools and private community agencies.[28]

The experimentation of the settlement houses and the professionalization of teachers combined with the Americanization campaign to produce a context in which public schools could institutionalize the many innovations in community education. Public schools continued to be hampered by small budgets and administrative restraints, but the innovations made by private agencies between 1895 and 1915 became a permanent part of Cleveland public education.[29] What developed, then, was a professional group of innovators within the public schools who maintained close ties with settlement houses and community agencies through the 1920s. So long as this link persisted, public schools could adapt to the changing needs of the city. But in the 1930s the relationship between private and public agencies weakened, and the schools of the central city began to suffer under the weight of a bureaucratic administration.[30]

The institutions of the city, both public and private, served as intermediaries to newcomers only in specialized ways. Public schools were successful only insofar as they were able to absorb private innovations. The voluntary association thus remained the most important agency, for it provided a way for immigrant communities to claim a permanent position in the city. The impact of public agencies, then, was to shore up those private associations which were the genius of the American city. As these agencies performed their limited but crucial function, they slowly helped newcomers to accommodate themselves to Cleveland.[31]

2 Origins

Emigration was an alternative to restricted opportunities in traditional agrarian societies. As the pioneer historians of Italian and Hungarian emigration perceived, the huge movement of people from rural southern Italy, Rumania, and Slovakia between 1890 and 1913 was largely toward economic goals.[1] In these regions, there was little differentiation between economic and familial activities within more or less self-sufficient households. When faced with hardship, a large proportion of the members of rural households chose emigration as an alternative to the old order. In other regions of these same societies, where improved transportation, expanding markets, and capital-intensive farming had led to some modernization of agriculture, cultivators turned to radical organizations whose intent was to transform society. Thus areas dominated by household agriculture produced heavy emigration, a familistic response to economic problems, while those in which commercial agriculture prevailed underwent a militantly political reaction to economic stress.[2]

Cleveland's emigrants came from areas of peasant farming in Slovakia (now a federated region of Czechoslovakia), the principality of Transylvania (now a region of Rumania), and southern Italy and Sicily. Today these areas remain predominantly agricultural (although modern industry has begun to penetrate the countryside), and enough of the old society remains to encourage returned emigrants to imagine that they can take up where they left off. Yet mass emigration was a sign of important changes in the villages and it hastened those changes.

Land had become an alienable property in all regions of Hungary and Italy by the mid-1860s. As the tangled skein of feudal land usage unwound, much land passed into the hands of the cultivators, but nowhere did the disintegration of the old order result in an equalitarian system of small owner-operators; rather, in southern Italy, Transylvania, and Slovakia, the redistribution of property broadened the membership in the middle and upper strata of property holders (more than it did in central Italy or in the Hungarian heartland).[3]

The process of property redistribution created distinctive regional class structures. On the Tisza Plain of Hungary, for instance, a new property regime emerged during the nineteenth century. As railroads penetrated the plains and urban markets developed, the new proprietors began to develop a market agriculture. Cereal culture spread through the region, and the subsequent diffusion of more productive agricultural methods drove out marginal peasant producers. Agricultural production thus became organized largely within capital-intensive units. The same development characterized the Transdanubian Hills and the regions between the Danube and the Tisza. Hence an agricultural society emerged in which a class of capitalist farmers dominated agricultural production, while a relatively small group of peasants eked out a living on the margins of a market economy.[4]

In central Italy, Apulia, and the interior of Sicily, agricultural property was similarly concentrated in the hands of an entrepreneurial element. In Tuscany, Umbria, Emilia-Romagna, and the Marches, proprietors furnished both capital and management to a well-integrated system of tenant farming. Cultivators were organized under the direction of managers and foremen who were

actively interested in allocating resources among the operations
and in marketing products. In Apulia the large scale of operations
meant that a distinct class of agricultural entrepreneurs developed
during the nineteenth century (but cultivators worked as day laborers in seasonal gangs, rather than as tenant farmers). And in Sicily's
interior as well large estates dominated the small holdings of
peasants. The *latifondo*, as a famous Sicilian proprietor wrote in
1895, imposed an "agricultural unity" on cultivators as well as on
an expanse of land.[5] Hence in each of these areas a hierarchical
social structure resulted from the very unequal property distribution and the two discrete classes of proprietors and cultivators.[6]

These Hungarian and Italian cultivators were not so much candidates for emigration as recruits for militant agricultural unions. As
John S. MacDonald has shown in the case of Italy, the regions of
capital-intensive agriculture and hierarchical social structure were
areas in which the Socialist party of the Red Crescent was able to
gain a solid hold in the early twentieth century.[7] It was among the
cultivators of the interior, who did not have a stake in the land,
that the Sicilian Fasci found their adherents. Their revolt began, as
a Sicilian novelist wrote, the day the cultivator's sons realized that
the land their father worked would not be their own.[8]

Similarly, agricultural organization in the Tisza Plain, the Transdanubian Hills, and the Hungarian heartland between the Danube
and the Tisza formed a great class of landless agricultural laborers.
More than half of these cultivators were employed on large operations of 40 hectares or more. Thus the structure of agricultural
relationships consisted largely of proprietor-laborer contracts.
Every attempt on the part of the proprietors to force contractual
obligations on the laborers led to a militant response by the latter.
The conflict intensified after 1891, and by 1897 socialist agricultural unions began to stage great strikes throughout the Tisza
Plain. The movement spread into the other two regions at the turn
of the century.[9] In none of these distinctive regions of Italy and

Hungary did emigration develop into the mass movements which characterized Slovakia, Transylvania, and southern Italy.[10]

Rural populations chose emigration as an alternative to the old order in the regions that were characterized by relatively broad distribution of property and mixed agricultural systems. The redistribution of property and the development of commercial agriculture had gone far enough in the Italian deep south, as the historian Domenico Demarco has written, to create a countryside in which small and large properties, all labor-intensive operations, were ranged side by side.[11] Stefano Jacini's great *Inchiesta agraria* thoroughly documented this characteristic of southern Italy in the early 1880s, but most historians of Italian emigration have gone on reciting the litany of landless laborers, overpopulation, and oppressive landlords. As recently as 1948, Giuseppe Medici found it necessary, at the conclusion of his long study of land tenure in post–World War II Italy, to dispel again the notion of southern Italy as the classical land of latifundia. His analysis effectively did away with "such legendary ideas as the predominance in Southern Italy and Sicily of large and very large properties," for he showed that "small operating-ownership [was] widespread and assert[ed] itself decisively in the tree-planted coastal lands," as well as in areas of primitive farming systems. Medici concluded that medium and large holdings were more typical of Tuscany and Umbria than of Sicily, and that small owner-operators were present in significantly lower proportions in central than in southern Italy. The dominant characteristic of southern Italian agriculture, then, was the dispersal of various types of holdings over the countryside.[12]

As Italian migration passed from the pioneer stage to the mass movement of the early twentieth century, the deep south experienced the highest incidence of emigration. These regions, under relatively backward agricultural conditions, were very low in per capita income. Table 3 shows the strong correlation between low per capita income and emigration. These income figures mean very little in themselves, however, for they reflect not the relative wel-

Table 3. Emigration, income, and property concentration in central and southern Italy.

	(1) Transoceanic emigrants, 1902–13 (per 1000 inhabitants)	(2) Average per capita income, 1928 (hundreds of lire)[a]	(3) Rural property concentration index, 1921[b]
Regions			
Calabria	368	16	2.7
Basilicata	340	18	3.2
Abruzzi	338	17	1.4
Sicily	263	18	3.7
Marches	164	20	7.9
Apulia	118	18	5.0
Umbria	52	25	6.8
Tuscany	52	28	9.0
Emilia-Romagna	39	27	10.8
Correlation with emigration (Spearman's rank-order)[c]		−0.86	−0.78

Sources: Column 1, Commissariato Generale dell'Emigrazione, *Annuario dell'emigrazione italiana, 1876–1925* (Rome, 1927); column 2, Associazione per lo Sviluppo Industriale del Mezzogiorno (SVIMEZ), *Statistiche sul Mezzogiorno d'Italia, 1861–1953* (Rome, 1954), p. 683; column 3, Istituto Nazionale di Economia Agraria, *Inchiesta sulla piccola proprietà coltivatrice formatasi nel dopoguerra*, 15 vols. (Rome, 1931–38), XV, 311.

[a]1938 values.

[b]Assessed agricultural income per family of owner-operators, minus assessed agricultural income per family engaged in any form of agriculture.

[c]The critical value of r_s, at a significance level of 0.05, is 0.60.

fare of various sectors of the population but rather regional levels of economic development. The third column of the table provides an index of relative inequality of income in the form of a measure of the concentration of rural property. The striking pattern that emerges from the ranking of emigration rates alongside a measure of property concentration is that migration rates were highest in regions where property was least concentrated. These regions were poorest in terms of per capita income, which indicates agricultural backwardness; in the same regions, nevertheless, property was widely distributed among peasants. Thus emigration developed into a mass movement where rural society was characterized by subtle gradations in income and status, as in the deep south and the Sicilian coastlands, rather than by deep class cleavages, as in central Italy, Apulia, and the Sicilian interior.

In the kingdom of Hungary as well migration occurred most frequently in regions where the rural population had very low incomes but enjoyed relatively broad property rights. The Hungarian demographer Gusztáv Thirring noticed as early as 1904 that Slovaks who were leaving the county of Šariš were better off in terms of property than most Hungarians.[13] Eastern Slovakia, the Banat, and Transylvania ranked high in the median area of agricultural operations, as table 4 shows. This fact, however, reflects not a predominance of large holdings but a broader distribution of holdings through the middle sector of the peasantry and the apportionment of the land among a variety of uses — farms, meadows, gardens, vineyards, and woodlands.[14] The parallel strips of the peasants bordered the small farm of a proprietor, and open meadow furnished grazing land for all households.[15]

The social organization of farm labor reflected the traditional form of agricultural operations in eastern Slovakia, the Banat, and Transylvania. In all regions of Hungary, a sizable proportion of those employed in agriculture were day laborers — from about one-fourth in Transylvania to nearly 40 percent in the Hungarian heartland between the Danube and the Tisza. It was not, however, the relative size of the laboring segment of the agricultural work force that was associated with emigration. Rather, the important fact was the inclusion of laborers within small agricultural

Table 4. Emigration and agricultural organization in the kingdom of Hungary.[a]

Regions	(1) Emigrants, 1904–13, per 1000 inhabitants[b]	(2) Median area of operations, 1900 (ha)	(3) Estates over 100 ha, 1895 (% of arable land)	(4) Laborers, 1900 (per 1000 persons in agriculture)	(5) Laborers on farms under 50 yokes[c] (per 1000 laborers)	(6) Income inequality[d]
Eastern Slovakia	148	2.8	29.2	312	436	3.85
Banat	77	2.6	22.8	343	444	[28.02]
Transylvania	65	3.3	19.1	228	610	6.07
Western Slovakia	53	2.6	37.4	251	324	10.33
Tisza Plain	45	2.5	38.9	280	420	8.10
Transdanubian Hills	43	2.2	47.4	246	240	16.65
Danube-Tisza Interfluve	26	1.8	42.1	395	294	13.05
Correlation with emigration (Spearman's rank-order)[e]	+0.87	-0.82	-0.04	+0.78	-0.60

Sources: Column 1, *Magyar statisztikai evkönyv*, 1904–13; columns 2–5, Tibor Kolossa, "Statistische Untersuchung der sozialen Struktur der Agrarbevolkerung in den Landern der österreichisch-ungarischen Monarchie (um 1900)," in *Die Agrarfrage in der österreichisch-ungarischen Monarchie (1900–1914)* (Bucharest, 1965), pp. 153, 160, 164, 167; column 6, Kolossa, "The Social Structure of the Peasant Class in Austria-Hungary: Statistical Sources and Methods of Research," *East European Quarterly*, 3 (1970), 428.

[a] Excluding Croatia (because the military frontier introduces a complicating factor).

[b] Hungarian statistics on emigration become dependable only in 1904.

[c] 1 cadastral yoke = 0.576 ha.

[d] This is a complex measure of relative inequality of income between operations and combines average net income in guldens per cadastral item and median area of operations. If the Banat is excluded, $r_s = -0.89$.

[e] The critical value of r_s, at a significance level of 0.05, is 0.71.

operations. Where most laborers and servants lived on large operations, emigration did not develop into a mass movement. But where laborers resided in the households of small farmers, as was the case in Slovakia, the Banat, and Transylvania, emigration reached very high levels.

The three regions of heavy emigration were characterized, then, by a social structure in which a few large proprietors formed the upper stratum. The membership in the second stratum of middling farmers was broader for it was here that the alienation of ancient estates had an important impact on agricultural organization. An even larger group of small owner-operators who produced enough for their own households and a small surplus for the town markets occupied a third stratum. Finally, a sizable group of laborers made up the largest segment of the agricultural labor force, a large proportion of whom possessed a recognized status as residents of farming and peasant households. Traditional agricultural practices and relatively broadly distributed property muted inequalities of income in Slovakia and Transylvania. Farther west, across the Tisza in the Hungarian heartland, class cleavages were sharper. The Banat was the significant exception to this generalization, for here the tremendous expansion of mechanized cereal growing makes income inequality a misleading index of agricultural organization.[16] If the Banat is excluded on the grounds of the irrelevancy of this particular measure of income distribution, the correlation between income inequality and emigration becomes very strong indeed. As in the Italian deep south, in Hungary emigration most strongly affected the regions where agricultural development was most backward but where equality of misery characterized the society.

These regions of heavy emigration had distinctive social structures characterized by a high degree of integration within households and local communities and a great deal of fragmentation among them. These were regions in which, in normal times, the wide diffusion of property rights tethered young men to peasant society. But emigration was a sign of change, and it hastened change. While disaggregation of peasant society went forward at different speeds in different places, everywhere the characteristic result was the deserted village.[17]

The emergence of distinctive regional patterns of land tenure was evident to a government commission that traveled through most of Sicily in 1875 and 1876. The commission felt that the bulk of the testimony it had taken and the statistics it had collected clearly indicated that more than 20,000 inhabitants of the island had become proprietors since 1860 alone. Even though complaints from artisans, peasants, and laborers filled the pages of the junta's transcript, the members regarded Sicilian peasants as not nearly so destitute as the rice growers of Lombardy or the shepherds of the Roman hinterland. The junta concluded its report on a theme which informed most accounts of Sicily before 1914: the growth of a large sector of smallholders, whom it called *borghesia*, was effecting a transformation of the island's agricultural and proprietarial structures.[18] Baron Sidney Sonnino adopted the junta's conclusions after independent study and tried to sum up agrarian relationships in the coastal regions of Sicily. In these areas, he wrote,

> one can say that the social conditions of the peasantry are somewhat superior to those on the rest of the Island. Economically, what with the great extension and variety of tree culture, the peasant enjoys greater security in his tenure; and socially, his relations to other classes, if not cordial, at least exhibit a larger sentiment of civil equality. Here the greater division of property, and varied types of agriculture which are poorly adapted to leases and subleases, have contributed to reducing the role of the intermediary between the proprietor and the cultivator, and, by creating broader contacts between the two classes, have tempered somewhat the harshness of struggle.[19]

The labor and love which smallholders invested in their miniscule fields testified to the importance of land in this society. A succession of inquirers, from Baron Sonnino in 1876 to Giuseppe Lorenzoni in 1906, discovered that the world which the peasants had made depended on the accessibility of land. The Society of Agricultural Laborers of San Cataldo, a village in the province of Caltanissetta, informed Lorenzoni in 1906 that when large proprietors must break up their estates "the population will spring up where no one now lives, the land will be cultivated more productively, public security will be maintained, and the improvement will redound to the whole Sicilian economy."[20]

Such effusive statements indicate the pervasive meaning of property in these agricultural regions. What is most impressive is the persistent surfacing of this theme in the volumes of the *Inchiesta agraria* of the 1880s and the *Inchiesta parlamentare* of the first decade of the twentieth century. On page after page one encounters the same testimony — the diffusion of property rights in the coastal areas of Sicily and the efforts of men without means to come into property.[21] This was the kind of society that produced the old peasant whom Giuseppe Lorenzoni encountered on a back-country road in Palermo province. The old man offered the following account of his life since his son had emigrated to America: "Signore, we are no longer in the old days, when one returned home at night with a pitchfork on one's shoulders. Now things are getting better. The *signori* used to be on horseback, but now we shall mount."[22]

The same theme emerges in accounts of other areas of heavy Italian emigration — Basilicata, the Abruzzi and Calabria. In each area, the report runs thus: the broad distribution of land, the emergence of smallholders, and the consequent provision of households for each generation. The resultant holdings were typically very small, but the point here is that a particular kind of agrarian society appeared, in which broadly diffused property rights assured each generation of some hope of inclusion in the proprietarial peasantry.[23]

A similar analysis can be made of the Rumanian villages of Transylvania and the Slovak counties of northern Hungary, although neither case is so well documented as the Italian. George Barit, a Rumanian social critic and historian, wrote an impassioned series of essays in 1882 and 1883 on the relationship between the Rumanian peasants of Transylvania and the land. Barit's main argument was that the proportion of land owned by Rumanian peasants was shrinking; yet he clearly realized that property rights remained broadly distributed within the peasant sector.[24] Indeed, official statistics indicate that the share of small properties rose between 1895 and 1919 (although the figures for the latter date are questionable). This diffusion of property rights characterized every area of Transylvania except the Banat, where, as pointed out earlier, the rapid mechanization of cereal agriculture led to a concentration of land within a smaller and smaller circle of owners.[25]

Landholding among Slovak peasants widened somewhat after the 1850s. Here again one is confronted by the lack of information on landholding patterns, but a series of studies by Julius Mésáros on agrarian problems in the second half of the nineteenth century indicate that land tenure in Slovakia resembled that in Italy's deep south and in Transylvania. The alienation of estates and of communal lands created new estates in several villages of eastern Slovakia, but it also formed a new group of middle peasants. There is some indication that disproportionate numbers of Hungarian peasants may have entered this middle group, but clearly many Slovaks enjoyed membership as well.[26] In the four eastern counties of Slovakia — Abov, Šariš, Spiš, and Zemplín — the same process was at work. Nowhere, of course, did the changes produce an equality of property ownership. But in these four counties, which were the region of heaviest emigration between 1890 and 1914, the process of change went further than elsewhere in Slovakia.[27]

Although property rights were widespread, not eveyone owned property. In the Italian deep south, Transylvania, and Slovakia, a very large sector of the rural population was composed of cultivators who shared in the produce of the land but never owned property themselves. In southern Italy, tenant farming (*mezzadria*) and sharecropping (*colonia parziaria*) emerged as the usual forms of contract between proprietors and cultivators. In the areas of heaviest emigration (coastal Sicily and the mountains of Basilicata and of the Abruzzi) sharecropping appears to have been the dominant form of contract after 1880.[28] Cultivators under participation contracts formed an intermediary group between peasant landowners and agricultural laborers, for they were, as a Sicilian agriculturist called them in 1894, a "petite bourgeoisie without means."[29] As Baron Sonnino concluded, the modified forms of share contract which he discovered in coastal Sicily served as a halfway house to ownership. The laborer who purchased a mule could then expect to get a scrap of soil under a participation contract and, having the mule and the land, could begin saving to buy his own field.[30]

Tenant farming and sharecropping were probably less important in Transylvania and Slovakia; nevertheless, they formed an important part of tenure arrangements. The gradual redistribution of land within the middle ranges of property owners after 1850 created a large group of Slovak sharecroppers who cultivated the land. In some areas, such as Trenčian county, the custom of long-term leases established an agriculture whose stability approached that usually associated with peasant ownership.[31] Similarly, participation contracts much like those in Italian tenant farming developed extensively in traditional agricultural regions of Transylvania, although it is by no means clear what particular crops they were used for. Share contracts provided an avenue to eventual ownership, or at least to a usufruct arrangement, and consequently promised the sons of cultivators some place in the peasantry.[32]

The distinctive characteristic of the regions of heavy emigration, then, was a diffusion of property rights, which normally provided households for the sons of cultivators. The practice of partible inheritance in all these areas continued to fragment land and to distribute property rights, which tied men to their village. And within this system was a second set of relationships to the land, the sharing in the land's produce through participation contracts, which both gave the landless cultivator some stake in the land and provided a means to acquire property.[33]

Another aspect of these agrarian societies which should be examined here is the role of credit institutions. One of the persistent complaints appearing in immigrant newspapers is that usury became more widespread during the last quarter of the nineteenth century. The proportion of peasant debts owed to individuals is not known, but the development of savings banks in the emigration regions of Italy and Transylvania tends to make the accuracy of the complaint doubtful. The Junta for Inquiry into the Condition of Sicily, for instance, reported that credit institutions were spreading throughout the island — a judgment which appears also in the Jacini Inquiry of 1882 and the Lorenzoni Commission of 1907.[34] In Rumania as well, savings banks emerged as important credit institutions in the early 1880s and gained strength throughout the 1890s.[35] The significant aspect of these institutions was their penetration into different village social groups. A sampling of the histories of some widely scattered savings banks in Sicily and the county of Sibiu in Transylvania reveals the participation of every social group from middling peasants to day laborers.[36] The provision that these banks made for mortgage credit prevented any widespread structural changes in ownership that might have resulted had usury been common.

The sources of emigration must be sought, then, not simply in the agricultural structure but in the social structure of particular regions as well. The broad distribution of property rights, the emergence of intermediate forms of tenure, the growth of communal credit agencies — all these factors supported a peasant agriculture. Emigration was symptomatic not of a general crisis in peasant agriculture but of the growing imbalance between the needs of peasant households and the opportunities for nonagricultural employment. What had contributed to the stability of peasant communities before the 1870s was the close connection between agriculture and household industry. But everywhere the slow decline of artisan manufacturing restricted the peasant's resources. Unable to find a piece of land in already crowded villages, young men and women who once would have become apprentices and artisans abandoned the land altogether. And as their chances of finding work in the village narrowed, they emigrated and joined a world market of labor.[37]

It was through the local community that the peasants were integrated into agrarian society, that laborers found their daily employment, and that artisans disposed of their products. Thus a discussion of the origins of emigration must include an analysis of the local setting, and of the ties binding rural subsocieties of laborers, peasants, and artisans to the whole.[38]

Italian, Rumanian, and Slovak villages in the regions of heavy emigration shared some basic relationships to the land. The countryside around them was taken up in a variety of uses — farms, gardens, orchards, and meadows. The form of settlement in this mixed landscape was largely the nuclear village, either along some roadway or, as in Transylvania, along the banks of a stream. In both Slovakia and Transylvania, a few villages with a green common remained, relics of the integration of various land uses under a feudal regime. The right of public privilege extended to southern Italian and Sicilian villages the use of forest lands, meadows, and springs.[39]

The inhabitants of these villages belonged to part-cultures — that is, they belonged in significant ways to the agrarian society around them and to urban centers. Village communities, then, were open in the sense that various segments of the population continuously interacted with the outside world and tied their fortunes to its

demands. The villages of the province of Messina, on the northern
Sicilian coast, for example, participated actively in an extensive
network of agricultural fairs. These were functional meeting places
where peasants could sell products or locate markets, artisans
could dispose of their wares, and laborers could hear of available
jobs. In 1898 alone, a peasant almanac announced 283 fairs in
Sicily, and these did not include the hundreds of local markets
convened weekly.[40] Baron Sonnino caught the essential features
of local labor markets in a moving passage:

> One sees, every morning before dawn, a crowd of men and boys
> pushing into the square of every town, each one armed with a
> hoe; this is the labor market, and these are the laborers, who
> await whoever might come to rent their arms by the day or
> week. . . . Those who gain employment only for the day will
> return home at night; but if the job is for the week and the dis-
> tance is great, then they will sleep perhaps in the courtyard of
> the big house, or under a lean-to in the middle of the fields, or
> under the arc of the sky.[41]

The artisans of Rumanian villages in the Carpathian foothills
depended upon periodic forays to the markets of small towns like
Cisnădie or Seliște or small cities like Sibiu or Făgăraș for opportunities to sell their wares. Itinerant Slovak craftsmen were an
extreme instance of the mobility of the villagers, for the chronicle
of the village of Jarabine, in Spiš county, tells of tinkers who went
as far afield as Rumania, Bulgaria, Serbia, Turkey, Russia, and
Poland.[42] These villages were not bounded communities with clear-
cut limits; rather, their very persistence depended on contact and
exchange with the larger society.

The relative openness of these villages led to a good deal of population interchange with surrounding communities. Again, what
strikes one here is the remarkable incidence of contact with neighboring villages. (Because of the concentration of anthropologists and
sociologists on the southern Italian family, this important aspect of

the village world has been ignored.)[43] In the small mountain village of Alcara Li Fusi, Messina, for instance, about 7 percent of marriages contracted between 1891 and 1901 involved one partner from another Sicilian village. An additional 15 percent of Alcara's households were formed by parents who had moved into the village from other communities within a radius of 15 kilometers. Thus on the eve of the great migration of *alcarese* to Cleveland, more than one-fifth of the village's households had at least one member from outside the village. Similarly, one-tenth of the households of Villavellelonga, a mountain community south of the Fucino Basin in the Abruzzi, were headed by men from the semicircle of small agricultural villages that ringed the rich basin. Both Alcara and Villavallelonga were set at the end of difficult roads which climbed to the narrow tops of deep valleys, yet both experienced a high incidence of in-migration.[44]

The coastal village of Sant'Agata di Militello, about 7 kilometers from Alcara, had an even more diverse population. In 1860 Sant'-Agata was an inconsequential village of 1,800 inhabitants and a few fishing boats. But the railroad from Palermo to Messina opened up new urban markets in the 1860s and created a boom town, and by 1901 it had grown to over 7,000 inhabitants. In 1871 over two-thirds of Sant'Agata's households sheltered at least one adult from outside the village. Nearly a third of all households, in fact, were composed of families who had moved into the community from other towns as far away as Trapani, on the west coast of Sicily. According to an analysis of marriage registers, the influx of new-comers continued into the late 1890s. This population movement spilled over into the neighboring village of Militello Rosmarino, 3 kilometers distant. Even though Militello was a declining agricultural village and was losing population at the rate of 3 percent yearly, more than 7 percent of the marriages between 1891 and 1901 involved partners from another village.[45]

Some Slovak villages seem to have been characterized by the

same pattern of interchange, although I have information for only two villages, both within the orbits of small administrative centers in eastern Slovakia. While only 5 percent of one village's marriages involved a partner from outside the village, nearly half of the marriages in the other village included a spouse from outside the community. Recent studies of peasant mobility in the nineteenth century, which show a remarkable amount of population movement in areas which would furnish most of the emigration, lend support to my general argument.[46]

In the case of Rumanian villages in Transylvania, the social meaning of population movement can be explored more fully. The striking pattern that emerges in an analysis of emigration and population interchange is the close relationship between out-marriage and out-migration. Column 2 of table 5 gives the rates of out-marriage for eleven villages in the county of Sibiu.[47] If emigration rates are ranked with the rates of marriage to a partner outside the village, the resulting correlation is quite impressive. This suggests that the search for marriage partners outside the native village reflected the villagers' willingness to make the final break with the bonds of community and leave for America. Between 30 and 50 percent of the young men and women of the villages of Daia Şaseascǎ, Sibiel, Galeş, and Tilişca found a spouse outside their native villages between 1870 and 1900. A few years later, another generation left these same villages for America at an annual rate of twenty, thirty, and even forty per thousand inhabitants.

The villagers' desires to improve their condition found concrete expression in geographical mobility.[48] In the case of Rumanian villages in the Carpathian foothills south of Sibiu, the seasonal migration of whole families of shepherds had long acquainted the villagers with the economic rationale for migration.[49] Between 1870 and 1890, the three sheep-raising villages of Galeş, Sǎcel, and Sibiel gained between 20 and 40 percent of their shepherds through migration. Most of the newcomers arrived from villages within a

Table 5. Emigration and marriage patterns in the county of Sibiu, Rumania.

	(1)	(2)	(3)
		Marriages with one partner	
	Average annual emigrants, 1907–10 (per 1000 inhabitants)	born outside village, 1870–1900 (% of marriages)	Religious intermarriage, 1870–1900 (% of marriages)
Villages			
Daia Şasească	40	49	19
Sibiel	38	35	5
Orlat	29	19	12
Galeş	28	43	4
Tilişca	23	30	—
Gura-Rîului	20	11	13
Talmacel	20	18	7
Sadu	16	11	0
Poplaca	8	10	3
Chirpăr	7	42	8
Porambacul de sus	0	10	10
Correlation with emigration (Spearman's rank-order)[a]		+0.66	+0.33

Sources: Column 1, Passport register, Sibiu, Arhivele Statului, fond Comitat; columns 2 and 3, for all villages except Sibiel, Arhivele Statului, Colecţia Starea Civilă, for Sibiel, marriage registers in parish archives.
[a]Critical value of r_s, at a significance level of 0.05, is 0.56.

15-kilometer radius, but at least one in ten came from the lowlands of the Danube delta in the old kingdom of Rumania. The neighboring village of Talmăcel, whose inhabitants lived largely by exploiting a coal mine, experienced similar levels of migration. Most of the skilled artisans — cobblers, blacksmiths, and masons — were recent arrivals in the village. In all four villages, moreover, there was as well a surprisingly large proportion of day laborers who had

migrated from surrounding villages.[50] This fragmentary information suggests, then, that geographical mobility was a common experience among a wide variety of social groups.

A similar picture emerges from a close look at the populations
of two very different Italian villages, Sant'Agata di Militello, in
Sicily, and Villavallelonga, in the Abruzzi. The heads of new families entering Sant'Agata between 1860 and 1870 were divided
almost equally into laborers, artisans, and fishermen and merchants.
Migration to the mountain village of Villavallelonga was much less
diversified, since the occupational structure of this essentially agricultural town was much simpler than that of Sant'Agata. Yet about
half the newcomers possessed some skill, while the other half were
largely agricultural laborers. These data indicate that migration
between villages affected every social group in the coastal region
of Sicily and the mountains of the Abruzzi as well.[51]

The point here is that on the eve of emigration, the families of
origin of the emigrant generation had already experienced important changes wrought by migration. Some fragmentary data on the
intergenerational social mobility of the emigrants' fathers in Sant'
Agata adds to the impression of change.[52] Between 10 and 20
percent of all three of the important village social groups — laborers, artisans, and fishermen — enjoyed some gains between 1870
and 1900. Of the six agricultural laborers who can be traced over
the thirty-year period, for instance, at least one was able to purchase a mule and thus gain some security as the holder of a participation contract. One-fifth of the artisans in the small sample
either eventually set up their own retail shops or acquired clerical
skills. If social mobility was as characteristic an experience as this
admittedly inadequate sketch suggests, one could expect the sons
of these men to be eager for improvement.[53]

Indirect evidence of upward mobility, or of efforts to provide
avenues to upward mobility, strengthens the impression of slow
but pervasive change. The opening of a night school in Alcara Li

Fusi in 1881 brought fifty-seven men to classes, twenty-seven of whom were day laborers. The school was run under the auspices of the communal government for a few years, but it petered out in 1887. In 1892, however, the newly formed Agrarian Society of Alcara reestablished the trade school and supported it for more than ten years.[54] Similar movements for the establishment of night and trade schools surfaced in a wide variety of villages. In 1890, for instance, all the villages in the province of Caltanissetta had some type of adult education program. Changing patterns of apprenticeship and new skill requirements moved many artisan societies to establish trade schools. The efforts of town and agricultural laborers to institute evening schools, under private or public auspices, convey the sense of urgency with which many groups must have viewed the establishment of new avenues of upward mobility.[55] This indirect evidence indicates, then, that these village worlds were undergoing slow but pervasive change.

The same element of change pervaded, I suggest, the maturation of the generation born between 1870 and 1890, the birth cohort that furnished the bulk of emigrants after 1900. Fifty children between the ages of six and fourteen entered the first form in Alcara Li Fusi in the fall of 1887, thirty of whom were the children of joiners and carpenters. Seventeen of the artisans' children dropped out over the next three years, so only thirteen remained in school in the spring of 1890. Of these thirteen, seven finally made it to the second form that spring, while four managed to graduate from the third form. These fortunate four were eligible to go on to the secondary school at Militello Rosmarino, and perhaps eventually to the lycée in Patti. Thirty-four children of peasant households began the first form in 1898 at Villapriolo, a tiny village in Caltanissetta. At the end of the year, twenty-six had disappeared from the records, four failed to advance to the second form, two were promoted to the second form, and two boys, nine and eleven, passed the final exams allowing them to enter the fourth form.[56] The experiences of children of peasant and artisan households in the villages of Militello Rosmarino, Valledalmo, and Villarosa were essentially the same. The impression this leaves is of a very slow trickle of young men of this generation who acquired the skills necessary for entrance into retail business or clerkship.[57]

The situation was similar for the same generation in Rumanian villages. One finds a great deal of emphasis in both Greek Orthodox and Byzantine Rite Catholic religious journals on education as a means of enforcing the authority of the peasant households.[58] The experience of children from shepherds' households in Sibiel bore out this perception. One of the early schools, founded in 1857, was actually a means of training children for the church choir. But after 1869 an academic school regularly met in the village. Nevertheless, in each year between 1869 and 1890, more than 20 percent of the shepherds' children of school age did not attend school, while only a few children graduated from the village school and went on to secondary schools in the nearby towns of Orlat or Seliște and perhaps eventually to the gymnasium in Sibiu.[59]

Rather than look for the causes of emigration in a general crisis of peasant agriculture, I have sought here to document the persistence of some elements of traditional agriculture and to trace the slow transformation of peasant society. The emigrants leaving for Cleveland from Alcara Li Fusi, Sant'Agata, and Termini Imerese, like those from Rumanian or Slovak villages, included large numbers of men from every social group — from day laborers to artisans to small merchants.[60] They left for a new land not merely to escape the misery of the village but to survive threats to an old way of life. That many peasants and craftsmen and storekeepers stayed in Cleveland testified to the passing of their hopes to restore a waning peasant world.

3 Migration and Settlement

The emigrants left their villages and their homelands as solitary individuals, as members of kin groups, and as links in migration chains. From Militello Rosmarino and Alcara Li Fusi, Sicilians hiked down the steep mountains to Sant'Agata, where they boarded trains for Palermo or Messina or Naples. There they waited to sail to America, many spending their time learning to read and write in state and charity schools or seeking help from the St. Raphael Society for the Protection of Sicilian Emigrants.[1] When a ship finally put into port, it might already be half-filled with Galician Poles, Montenegrins, and Slovenes who had boarded at Trieste.[2]

Others had far to go to reach the ships. Rumanian villagers from Sibiel, Selişte, and Orlat walked the four or five kilometers to the railroad that ran to Sibiu, and then made the interminable journey to Bremen or Hanover (or later, after 1910, to Trieste.)[3] As the train moved northwest through the Alföld and onto the Tisza Plain, Hungarian peasants from the great heath farmsteads (*pusztas*) crowded the stops along the way. At Košice, on the margin of the great Hungarian plains and the Slovak Hills, a big crowd of Slovaks waited to entrain — bound, like the rest, for Bremen or Hanover. Among both the Slovaks and Rumanians, someone usually spoke German and so made the way easier with German or Austrian officials. So there they were, aboard a Pester Lloyd steamer or the *Martha Washington*, putting out to sea after years on the land.

Migration to Cleveland flowed mainly within well-defined steams; more than three-quarters of the Italians, Rumanians, and Slovaks proceeded along well-traveled courses to specific destinations in the city. These streams created ethnic concentrations in Cleveland, and ethnic settlements eventually emerged from these concentrations, largely through the operation of three factors. First, the pattern of migration itself — the predominance of immigrants from a few villages or from a few districts — assured that most of the settlers would encounter familiar faces, dialects, and social customs. Second, arrivals from certain well-represented regions of the homelands early established demographic and social hegemonies in the settlements, partly because of their numerical superiority, but also because they tended to annex, through marriage or other means, significant numbers of migrants from sparsely represented regions. Third, in the case of the Italians traditional cultural loyalties to village, district, and region asserted themselves in a favorable demographic context during the lifetime of the first generation, while in the case of the Rumanians and Slovaks, intermarriage patterns provided a context in which a common folk culture overrode purely village and district loyalties and molded the newcomers into nationality settlements. These three factors were all associated with areas of origin and the process of selective migration from those areas.

The simple concept used here to describe the mechanism of selection is chain migration. Since the term is subject to a great many constructions, a working definition may be useful. Contemporary observers and historians often pointed to the important contributions of a few villages to Italian settlements in the United

States, and many adopted the image of a chain to describe the migration patterns that led to group settlement.[4] The report of the Commissioner-General for Immigration for 1907, for example, noted that letters and return visits of immigrants daily forged "endless chains . . . link by link" between the Old World village and the New World city.[5] This usage, while by far the most popular among historians of immigration, confines itself to one kind of migration. In the case of the immigrants considered here, migration from particular villages of origin to settlements in Cleveland was indeed the largest single movement. Nevertheless, a large proportion of Rumanians and Slovaks came from a common district rather than a common village. This was also a type of chain migration, but one in which district rather than village connections were important.[6]

Migration began when a man left a village for a new land, either as a solitary traveler or as a follower of some earlier pioneer. Many early Slovak emigrants, for instance, trailed Jewish craftsmen and tradesmen who had been going to America since the 1850s. When Emily Green Balch searched the county of Šariš in 1906 to find the area's earliest emigrant, she ran across a Slovak hatter who had gone to New York in 1880. But he had simply traced the route of a Jewish cloth dealer who had gone before.[7] German-speaking Saxons were typically the first to leave the villages in the Carpathian foothills of Rumania. By 1891 the Transylvanian Saxon settlement in Cleveland was large enough to sponsor a mutual benefit society and several clubs. This group settlement attracted a number of Rumanian peasants from the ethnically mixed villages near Sibiu, and thus the movement spread until it affected the Saxon and Rumanian populations of more than eighty villages in the area.[8] The ethnic diversity in Rumanian and Slovak villages made some inhabitants particularly fitted for solitary migration. The great mixture of peoples — even within a single village — exposed different segments of the population to different economic and social pressures and also provided some individuals with special resources. Thus the areas of earliest and heaviest migration in both Rumania and Slovakia were marginal districts, where Saxons and Szeklars shared a village with Rumanians, where Polish Jews and Hungarian peasants lived next to Slovaks.

Diversity was also great in Italy, where a wide variety of social types under specific stresses were the early solitary emigrants. The precipitous drop in the demand for Sicilian cotton after 1873 threw young spinners and weavers out of work and made them candidates for emigration. These young men had a skill, moreover, which gave them an advantage over the cotton choppers who were deprived of work by the same contracting market but whose skills were nowhere in great demand.[9] A shift in the precarious balance between proprietor and peasant might induce one group to emigrate while entrenching the position of the other. In the Abruzzi and Molise, in the early 1860s, cereal culture repeatedly failed, and small commercial farmers, who were forced to sell out because of declining marginal profits, began to emigrate. Since artisans depended on these farmers' demands for special services, they started to emigrate as well. The shepherds in the area, however, worked for the larger proprietors and thus enjoyed a favorable labor market as grazing areas extended into formerly cultivated fields.[10] Andrea Surdo, an artisan from Brindisi di Montagna, left Basilicata in 1880 after finding his traditional skills less and less productive. He returned in 1885 to discover the artisans of his own and neighboring villages eager to find some alternative to their customary employment.[11]

With many places of origin, migration to Cleveland never passed this pioneer stage of solitary movement. The arrival of a significant proportion of Cleveland's immigrants had an accidental character, as though the city attracted people from some places and not from others. As table 6 shows, about one-third of the Rumanians

Table 6. Distribution of Cleveland immigrants and places of origin according to migration patterns, 1888–1914 (percent).[a]

Migration pattern	Immigrants			Places of origin		
	It.	Rum.	Sl.	It.	Rum.	Sl.
By village						
Villages of solitary migration in districts of sparse migration (1–5 migrants)	19	29	34	62	58	55
Villages of solitary migration in districts of minor and major chain migration (1–5 migrants)	9	24	32	24	31	38
Minor village chains (6–20 migrants)	21	35	27	11	10	6
Major village chains (21+ migrants)	51	12	6	3	1	1
Number	(1,466)	(866)	(987)	(282)	(312)	(463)
By district						
Districts of sparse migration (1–20 migrants)	20	33	27	85	84	75
Minor district chain (21–100 migrants)	9	50	48	8	14	21
Major district chain (101+ migrants)	71	17	25	7	2	4
Number	(1,466)	(866)	(987)	(61)	(50)	(48)

Sources: Parish marriage registers, interviews, and naturalization records, Cuyahoga County Courthouse.
[a]Percents sometimes do not add to 100 because of rounding.

and Slovaks came from villages and districts that produced no chain movements to Cleveland. The native villages of solitary migrants from districts of sparse migration accounted for more than half the total villages of origin, and districts of sparse migration for more than three-fourths of the total migration districts. Solitary migration characterized a comparable proportion of Italian places of origin but made up a somewhat smaller proportion — about a fifth — of Italian arrivals in Cleveland. Altogether, about a fourth of the arrivals of the three groups migrated in a fashion in which neither village nor district connections were important.[12]

Another group of villages characterized by solitary migration, however, was located on the edges of minor and major districts of origin. The diffused migration from these villages accounted for a fourth of the Rumanian and a third of the Slovak arrivals. The hill villages south and west of the small administrative center of Făgăraş, for example, supplied a large proportion of the total Rumanian arrivals in Cleveland. Thirty percent of the immigrants from the three important districts in this region — Arpaşul-de-jos, Şercaia, and Făgăraş — came from villages near the margins of these areas, drawn along in twos and threes by the larger village streams. Dispersed district migration was even more important in the case of the Slovaks. The important migration area of the Košice Basin, in eastern Slovakia, furnished about 16 percent of the total arrivals. Half these immigrants came in groups of fewer than three members from the small villages in the foothills of the Ore Mountains and the Slovak Karst, in the margins of the two districts of the Košice and Moldava nad Bodvou. Essentially the same pattern developed in the major districts of Sabinov, Prešov, and Levoča, north and west of Košice. Migration from villages producing very few migrants made up a much smaller proportion of Italian arrivals — no more than 10 percent.

The most striking feature of the Italian migration was the predominance of large village chains. The median size of village streams was thirty persons, and fully a fourth arrived in chains of a hundred or more migrants. The median number of Rumanian migrants in village streams, on the other hand, was about five, and the median number of Slovaks was less than four. The significant contrast between the Italians and the other two groups appears most forcefully in the frequency with which Italians migrated in *major* village chains. One-half of the Italian arrivals moved from ten villages in southern Italy to major village concentrations in Cleveland. Three Rumanian villages produced important chains, accounting for only 12 percent of the total arrivals, while two major village chains produced a mere 6 percent of Slovak migrants.

Pioneer Italian migration to Cleveland thus developed into large-scale chain migration from both villages in particular and districts in general. Three-fourths of the Italian migrants moved within streams in which both village and district connections were significant. More importantly, half arrived in major village chains of twenty or more members. Chain migration succeeded solitary migration in relatively few Rumanian and Slovak villages. Fully a third of the Slovaks, and slightly fewer Rumanians, came to Cleveland from villages and districts where solitary migration was the rule. Another third of the Slovaks, and a fourth of the Rumanians, derived from districts where emigration was diffused among a great many villages. Thus concentrated chain migration was not a major factor in building either the Rumanian or the Slovak community.

This difference between the migration patterns of the Italians and those of the other two groups shows up in differences in the stability of the resulting ethnic settlements. The early concentrations of new arrivals in Cleveland were transient groupings: about one-third of newly wed Italians and Slovaks persisted for at least ten years in the city, while only 16 percent of the Rumanians survived the first decade after marriage.[13] A couple of examples convey clearly the impermanence of the early settlements. The tiny Slovak Calvinist community on the outskirts of Cleveland, which today seems so tightly knit with its marriages between cousins and its visits among neighbors, was established by families who had worked first in the Pennsylvania anthracite region, then had scattered through the small steel towns ringing Pittsburgh, and had finally settled in Cleveland.[14] The records of the Union of Rumanian Societies indicate that in 1916, the union's tenth anniversary, 10 percent of the members had moved between American cities at least once, while another 10 percent had returned to Rumania. Return migration reached such proportions that by 1920 only about 15 percent of the union's prewar membership remained in the United States.[15] The important period for the settlement's establishment, then, was during the first ten years after arrival.

Table 7 suggests a general pattern: Italian and Rumanian migrants who arrived in some form of chain migration were more likely to persist than solitary migrants, while this factor played no part in the Slovaks' decision to settle down. But more important is the contrast between the settlement patterns of the Italians and those of the Rumanians and Slovaks. More than a third of the Italians who had migrated in major village chains persisted longer than ten years after their arrival. By 1920 settlers who had arrived in major village chains made up two-thirds of the Italian immigrant community. These village settlements provided a measure of continuity and stability during the formative years of the Italian settlement which was lacking in the Rumanian and Slovak communities. The Italian immigrant community thus persisted not simply as a result of the predominance of major village chains but rather as a result of the impact of that migration pattern on the formation of settlements.[16]

These migration patterns produced a demographic context in which some places of origin enjoyed numerical superiority over others. The settlers sorted themselves into village, district, and regional groups and found that their ties to the homeland were

Table 7. Rates of persistence in Cleveland according to migration patterns (percent).

Migration pattern	Persisting 1910–19			Persisting 1920–29		
	It.	*Rum.*	*Sl.*	*It.*	*Rum.*	*Sl.*
Villages of solitary migration in districts of sparse migration	15	9	66	67	65	78
Villages of solitary migration in districts of minor and major chain migration	6	27	44	46	63	70
Minor village chains	20	29	8	72	66	67
Major village chains	66	19	0	66	37	—
All	28	16	38	65	61	75
Number (at beginning of decade)	(1,466)	(866)	(987)	(411)	(136)	(375)

Sources: Cleveland city directories, interviews, and death certificates in Cuyahoga County Courthouse.

crosscutting bonds. What was remarkable about the settlement of all three ethnic groups in Cleveland was the rarity of concentrations from restricted areas — a village group existing alone in a neighborhood or a nationality settlement persisting without any gathering of arrivals into village or district groups within it. Pure village, district, and regional groups accounted for no more than 10 percent of the immigrant communities, while mixed settlements composed 90 percent. The numerical dominance of certain places of origin, and the varieties of village, district, and regional connections within the ethnic settlements, sheltered the greater part of the immigrants from the direct impact of the city's culture and society.[17]

Among Italian places or origin, four districts — Patti and Palermo, in Sicily, and Benevento and Campobasso, in the Abruzzi — furnished 70 percent of the total arrivals; ten years later these same four districts accounted for 84 percent of the settlers. The other places of origin were widely scattered among fifty-seven other districts, none of which provided more than 2 percent of the total arrivals. Although Rumanian and Slovak migration was dispersed among more districts, eight Rumanian and eight Slovak districts furnished about 60 percent of each group's arrivals. All three ethnic groups, then, derived largely from a restricted number of homeland districts.

Two major regions — Sicily and the Abruzzi — dominated the Italian settlement in Cleveland. These two regions provided 90 percent of the migration and ten years later accounted for 97 percent of the settlers. Three similar Rumanian regions — the Carpathian foothills, the Transylvanian Plain, and the Bihor Massif — produced about 85 percent of the migration, while a single region of eastern Slovakia — Vychodoslovenska — furnished more than three-fourths of the arrivals.

But the difficulty in discerning the pattern of settlement is more than simply deciding where the boundary of a group fell (whether on village, district, regional, or nationality lines) and what proportion of the settlers were included in each group. A more sensitive test of group settlement is the spatial pattern of concentration, that is, whether villages, districts, and regions were segregated in some manner, or whether the settlements were mixed.

It is clear, first, that no village concentration settled by itself along some street or alley. Village groups characteristically dispersed among settlements deriving from their districts and regions. But there were some important differences on the regional level. Among the Italians, a sharp distinction emerged between the Sicilian and Abruzzi settlements. Five miles of the city separated their areas of first settlement, and over the next thirty years only 3 percent crossed over. Among the Rumanians there was no regional separation; rather, migrants from every region crowded together in a postage-stamp settlement in the western quarter of the city, from which few migrated to other parts of Cleveland. The Slovak pattern of settlement was somewhere between these two extremes. Slovak arrivals settled in at least five distinct areas of the central city, yet there were no discernible regional concentrations.[18]

The pattern of intermarriage within and across district and regional lines reinforced the development of these contrasting settlement patterns.[19] Within the numerically large regional groupings, intermarriage with other regions tended to lessen regional coherence and strengthen the nationality grouping, while a high rate of marriage within regional boundaries consolidated the regional grouping. Moreover, the partners chosen by those who did marry outside the group reveal the direction in which the immigrant group was moving — whether toward the consolidation of a regional grouping or toward the creation of a nationality settlement. Italians from the heavily represented regions had a low rate of marriage outside their region (between 3 and 7 percent), while

Slovaks and Rumanians from such regions had a consistently high rate (from a low of 11 percent to a high of 27 percent). The Italians settlement, then, was maintaining its regional groupings, while the Rumanian and Slovak settlements were becoming federations of regional groupings within nationality settlements.

One can see the divergence in the two intermarriage patterns more clearly if one begins with the smaller groupings. Eighty percent of Italian men and women from the well-represented districts married within their district, compared to 40 percent of those from less well-represented districts. When the former married outside their district, moreover, they almost always chose partners from the same region of origin. When the latter sought spouses outside their district, however, they chose partners from the two most heavily represented regions — the Abruzzi and Sicily — in 80 percent of the cases. Thus the direction of the intermarriages across both district and regional lines indicates a reinforcement of the dominant regions of Sicily and the Abruzzi.

Intermarriage rates within the Rumanian and Slovak communities, on the other hand, disclose a movement toward the transformation of regional groupings into nationality settlements. Twenty percent of both Rumanians and Slovaks from the dominant districts consistently married outside their district, while more than 30 percent of those from the smaller districts married outside. Rumanian marriages across district lines also crossed regional lines in 80 percent of the cases; the Slovaks experienced a comparable rate of marriage outside the region. These relatively high rates of marriage outside district and regional groupings consolidated the many local groups within a single cultural boundary.

These differences between the migration and settlement patterns of the Italians and those of the Rumanians and Slovaks produced demographic situations favoring the emergence of contrasting configurations of cultural loyalties. The fact that nearly three-fourths of the Italians arrived in village chains provided constituencies for village and regional organizations; the growth of these organizations testified to the persistence of local ties. By 1901 the five most powerful societies of the early settlement had been organized — Fraterna, Operaia, Fratellanza Siciliana, La Calabrese, and Cristoforo Colombo. Three of these (Operaia, Fratellanza Siciliana, and La Calabrese) had memberships drawn from particular homeland regions, while the other two societies remained throughout the life of the community the most important reminders of an Italian folk loyalty.[20] During the pioneer years of the Italian settlement, then, regional societies were the most important.

Village loyalties asserted themselves strongly, however, with the beginning of mass migration to Cleveland after 1900. One consequence of the heavy migration between 1900 and 1910 was the rapid multiplication of Italian societies, which reflected the peculiar pattern of village chain migration. Twenty-five of the thirty-five mutual benefit societies incorporated between 1903 and 1910 limited their membership to persons born in a particular village. Twenty-two also sponsored an annual festival in honor of the patron saint of their native village.[21] These societies and festivals reaffirmed ties to the homeland localities. The Sons of Labor, for instance, was a branch of a society of the same name in Militello Rosmarino. The secretary of the Cleveland organization, Pietro Filocco, a notary public and clerk, was the son of the notary of Militello, who was also the secretary of the parent organization. Many of the leaders of the San Nicolò Society, a group composed of immigrants born in Alcara Li Fusi, were either members of the Agrarian Society in the old village or the sons of members. Some of the *alcarese* kept their membership in the village society even though they lived in Cleveland.[22] The examples might be extended, but the point should be clear: the Cleveland societies connected in an immediate way with the immigrants' traditional loyalties. Thus the Sant'Agata Workers' Society announced in its constitution that only laborers from the homeland village could belong, "exactly as in the old society in Sant'Agata."[23]

In contrast to the persistence of local ties in the Italian community, broader folk loyalties characterized the formative stage of Slovak organizations. When Štefan Furdek founded the first explicitly Slovak Roman Catholic society in 1885, he named it after St. Stephen, the patron saint of Slovakia. The same emphasis on broadly religious and national loyalties appeared in the charters of the pioneer societies organized before 1900 — St. Joseph, St. George, St. Andrew, St. Martin, and some twenty others.[24] Fragmentary information about the membership of eighteen of these societies, which survives in the original applications for membership, indicates that only three lodges had a membership drawn primarily from one homeland region. The other fifteen lodges had no important concentrations of village or district groups.[25] Thus the integrating process that was at work in marriage and settlement patterns affected organizations as well.

A second major difference between the Slovak and the Italian organizations during the formative period was that local Slovak organizations contracted strong ties with Slovak groups elsewhere in the United States. Whenever a new society came into existence, it affiliated almost immediately with a larger group. Four months after the founding of the St. Joseph Society in Cleveland in 1889, for instance, eight similar associations from Pittsburgh, Wilkes-Barre, Minneapolis, and other cities sent delegates to the first convention of the Slovak Catholic Union. Thus a national Slovak society emerged simultaneously with local societies: it sanctioned new lodges, set forth programs, and claimed a devotion to the language of L'udovit Štur and the culture of the Matica Slovenská.[26] Almost every Slovak society in Cleveland about which any documentation remains belonged either to a regional organization — the Cleveland Slovak Union, for example — or to the Slovak Catholic Union, the National Slovak Society, or the Greek Catholic Association, to

name only the largest of nine national federations. Occasionally
a few immigrants might form a Šariš White Tie Association for the
purpose of presenting an annual ball, or they might organize a
circle whose aim was to bring together the shrinking number of
immigrants who still spoke a regional dialect well. But most organizations were part of broad federations.[27]

A similar situation predominated in the Rumanian community.
Hungarian officials and early immigrants both agreed in the assessment that religious loyalties overrode local ties in the Cleveland
settlement. A Hungarian consul who visited the city in 1903 found
the Greek Orthodox Rumanians a remarkably cohesive group,
while a Rumanian immigrant who arrived in the same year discovered few indications of serious challenges to the organizational
unity of the community.[28] It is apparent as well that when Rumanian immigrants began organizing societies and parishes in 1902,
national loyalties won out over local ties. Under the forceful leadership of Moise Balea, the first Rumanian Greek Orthodox priest
in America, the Rumanians were organized into folk rather than
village or district unions.[29] The origins of the members of the various societies that Balea helped to found show the operation of the
same integrating process that was present in the Slovak community.
There was no development of local societies during the formative
period of the community, nor have I found any evidence that this
kind of society was seriously proposed before 1908.[30]

The Cleveland Rumanian societies, like the Slovak ones, quickly
established a national organization, the Union of Rumanian Societies in America (1906). The important leaders of Cleveland lodges
were in every case also active in the national society, so that ties
to the national group were very strong. Greek Catholics formed a
similar federation three years later. In all these societies, the pre-
vailing loyalties were to homeland culture and confessional religion
rather than to specific localities.[31] The strength of these ties is evident in the story of a society of immigrants from Sebeş, a village in

western Sibiu county, which was formed in 1908. Ioan Santeiu, the founder, was active in the Greek Orthodox parish and in various societies, but he did not succeed in having the Society, Romîna sebeșană, accepted by the Union of Rumanian Societies. As its constituency drained away over the next decade, the society affiliated with one of the local union lodges and was finally absorbed by the lodge in 1925.[32] A similar fate met almost every other society that had ties to a particular locality, and only rarely did the Orthodox hierarchy feel it necessary to speak out against the incursion of local interests against the church's authority.[33]

I have argued here that migration patterns had a significant impact on the development of ethnic settlements. The distinctive aspect of Italian migration was the predominance of major village chains. The settlement emerging as a result of this migration pattern formed around a stable core population from ten villages in the Abruzzi and Sicily. Immigrants from these two regions established a hegemony in the settlement, and the marriage choices of the arrivals reinforced the dominant regional groups. The pattern of parochial cultural loyalties that characterized Italian organizations reflected the community's peculiar demographic structure.

The Rumanians and the Slovaks migrated in minor district streams, and village streams were much less important than in Italian migration. In both the Rumanian and Slovak settlements, efforts were made to maximize national rather than local ties, and mixed patterns of settlement and intermarriage across the boundaries of local groups facilitated these efforts. The resulting configuration of cultural loyalties was in sharp contrast to the Italian emphasis on village and regional organizations, for both Rumanian and Slovak societies oriented themselves strongly toward religious and national aims.

4 Ethnic Communities in the Making

As groups of immigrants began to form ethnic communities, they looked to traditional relations in the village as well as to the adjustments they would have to make in the American city. The typical means of assuring order in the village was the voluntary association, and since social activity took place within the household, the church, and the community proper, associations in the homeland were based on these groups.[1] In the urban context of the New World, however, social relations assumed more complex patterns, and associations grew more specialized in their functions and in the solidarities they expressed. They embodied criteria of social order for a people in a strange city — they furnished what Philip Gleason has called "a tangible organizational reality" within which the newcomer could identify himself and declare his solidarity with a people,[2] and they served as the means of adapting disparate groups to the life of the city.[3]

Mutual benefit associations are the best indication of the extent of social organization in peasant communities. In his thorough study of Sicily in 1876, Baron Sidney Sonnino found a variety of organizations in each village, from mutual benefit societies to savings banks and popular circulating libraries.[4] The government reports of the incorporation of mutual benefit societies show that during the 1860s and 1870s there was a great deal of formative activity in Sicilian villages — activity that increased during the hard times of the mid-1870s. In the early 1880s the tempo of organization again picked up, and by 1885 mutual benefit associations reached into every corner of the island. Suppression of the Fasci in 1894 somewhat stunted this growth, but by 1900 there remained a broad group of associations in nearly every village.[5] In particular areas, of course, the flurry of activity in the early 1880s was clearly more intense than official publications indicate. In the province of Palermo alone, for instance, there were fifty-six workers' societies in 1890. Nor was this type of organization confined to Sicily. The remarkably full records of local organizations in the province of Potenza show very extensive organizational efforts as early as the 1870s.[6]

In Rumanian and Slovak villages the parish furnished the basis for organization. Both Eastern Orthodox and Byzantine Rite Catholic parishes included a synod of laymen and priest, which supervised the expenditure of funds for parish education and poor relief. These arrangements were, moreover, written into the parochial constitution. The articles governing Orthodox parishes in Transylvania, for instance, specified that "all confessional, elementary, superior, and citizenship schools shall be under the jurisdiction of the parochial synod."[7] This code established religious and educational institutions in which various village groups could participate. This participation had limits, and it never extended to the political process; nonetheless, a number of bylaws and institutions sanctioned the participation of villagers in the religious and educational affairs of their community.[8]

The development of organizations concerned with one important aspect of Rumanian and Slovak village life — parish education — illustrates the process of participation. The records of the school fund in the Rumanian village of Sibiel show that most of the support for the school came from a collection taken every Sunday. Tenants on church land and a small endowment provided about a tenth of the income, but for the most part parishioners voted for the continuance of the school by dropping coins in the plate.[9] Villagers' questions about the administration of the fund reveal several social groupings; this was especially true, of course, of the ethnically mixed communities. Was the fund to be used only for the communal elementary school, or should the parish have a confessional school as well? Should Byzantine Rite children attend school with the Orthodox, or did they have to have their own school? Should manual training be included in the schools, or must artisans continue to depend on apprenticeship?[10] These divisions among religious and occupational groups and households led to a proliferation of village organizations.

In the southern Italian village, on the other hand, organizations grew out of the efforts of various elite groups. The most important rationale for the organizational efforts of proprietors, merchants, notaries, and so forth was a felt decline of deference — "a great fluidity of life," as one proprietor of the village of Lauria Superiore, Potenza, claimed, "an incessant shout, 'Forward! Forward!' which infects every soul." To combat the felt effects of this unsettling change, the notary of the same village urged "harmony, brotherhood, family unity, and as an essential base, mutual aid. . . ."[11] The activities of these organizations centered on cultural goals, one important aim being the raising of the cultural level of the villagers. Among civil employees and proprietors, this often took the form of mutual instruction in reading and writing, while among landed proprietors, many societies were created to diffuse knowledge of new crops and new methods of cultivation. These essentially conservative groups were also active in supporting work houses, orphanages, and pauper children's education. The organizations of the village elite thus formed to preserve the social hierarchy.[12]

Artisans formed similar associations. Among this group, too, the chief concern was to preserve an apparently threatened tradition.

The artisans' society of the town of Enna declared in 1876, for example, that its task was to assure the customary relationship between "the master and the workmen." Again, one of the important means of securing this relationship was through various educational efforts. Each society proposed to effect in some way the "moral and economic improvement" of the artisans and skilled workers. This concern went beyond the present, for the organizations generally stipulated that each member must send his sons to school or provide an apprenticeship for them. For men with a trade, as the declaration of a Sicilian society implied, the important problem was to defend their status and make sure that their sons followed in their footsteps.[13]

Agricultural workers were also involved in organizational activity. A group of peasants from Militello Rosmarino, Messina, declared to Giuseppe Lorenzoni in 1908 that a conspicuous aspect of the peasantry was the "sentiment of respect and obsequiousness toward the law and persons."[14] In 1892 the Agrarian Society of Alcara Li Fusi, a neighboring village of Militello Rosmarino, was composed of about an equal number of laborers, tenant cultivators, and peasant proprietors. This society defended the peasantry against the encroachment of *signori* on established rights and privileges such as customary grazing arrangements. But associational activities extended beyond these essentially defensive or restorative measures to other kinds of action. As I discussed in chapter 2, the societies organized savings banks, cooperative marketing unions, and night schools. In the emigration areas, these kinds of organizations were the typical forms of peasant associations well into the period of heavy migration.[15]

In Rumanian and Slovak communities as well the circle of organizations extended beyond the formal structure of the parish to embrace all village groups. Educational societies, for instance, set out to improve the literacy of young and old. In Reşinari, a large Rumanian village near the city of Sibiu, the Rumanian Society hoped to "encourage more men to read by providing a library and reading room." The members also paid monthly dues, which the local priest used to buy books for the Orthodox confessional school library. A women's sodality in Avrig and a choral society in Mercurea supported the establishment of similar reading rooms in their villages. Artisans and laborers organized reading or improvement societies, declaring their intention "to promote the intellectual, moral, and material interests of workers." Share-tenants' societies from seven villages around Seliṣte met in 1896 to establish agricultural schools that would teach their children new methods of growing crops for the market. Thus the impact of these societies exceeded the mere writing of constitutions. The most impressive evidence of this thrust into the village is the hundreds of local savings banks established by agricultural societies between 1880 and 1910.[16]

The rural communities, then, were laced with the strands of many associations. In Sibiel, a Rumanian village of 1,000 inhabitants, at least ten societies flourished between 1890 and 1910. Shepherds formed a mutual benefit society, peasant tenants an agricultural school, and the whole commune a savings bank which shortly before the war became a cooperative store and market. Young and old both had their religious sodalities, while students formed two youth societies. In Alcara Li Fusi, a Sicilian village of 1,800 inhabitants, a similar array of associations developed after 1890. Three religious sodalities, an evening school for agricultural laborers, a mutual aid society for "honest workingmen," and several agricultural societies assured residents membership in one or another association.[17]

If these societies served on the local level as the dominant means of association among village groups, they also linked the village to larger social structures. While the ties of the Rumanian and Slovak countryside to the city were the work of many hands, the role of the clergy was most important. The priesthood was the main link between Rumanian villages like Sibiel and urban centers like Sibiu, between the Slovak peasant community of Hermanovce and the religious and administrative city of Košice. In 1882 theology students at the Greek Orthodox Seminary in Sibiu, a major center of Orthodox culture in Transylvania, organized a society named for the great Metropolitan Andreiu Şaguna "to assist members to broaden their culture and to acquire pedagogical skills." One of the important aims of the society was to found parish schools and establish libraries in each village. The Şaguna Society expanded its membership in 1890 to include village teachers, and the society's activities subsequently focused on rural education. Byzantine Rite Catholic teachers also formed regional associations which, as in Reşinari in 1899, often supported efforts to establish village schools. Such organizations had a cumulative impact on the villages, for they not only founded a number of village schools but also contributed to the involvement of local associations in urban organizations. Associations of lay teachers in the county of Sibiu alone, for instance, counted over a hundred members by 1899, all of them village teachers.[18] Similar ties between local associations and more cosmopolitan organizations developed in Slovak villages after 1890, where local societies had the example of the Matica Slovenská to follow. Through the agency of priest and teacher, then, Rumanian and Slovak villages developed enduring ties to urban groups.[19]

In southern Italy many village associations were part of the Roman Catholic parish and thus acquired some connection with groups outside the village. But the ties were not nearly so strong as in the case of Slovak Catholic and Rumanian Orthodox parishes, for in Sicily and southern Italy the ties to urban groups and institutions were tenuous.[20] So these societies remained essentially local groups, the dominant form of coalition — "the best means of maintaining social order," as a peasant society of Valguanera proclaimed in 1901.[21]

The pioneer immigrants of the nineties came from peasant communities formed by the ties of traditional village groups. These early newcomers shaped the young settlements of the city, and their experience in creating an associational life responsive to urban conditions yet similar to the village became the model for mass arrivals after 1900. Entrance into Cleveland during the formative period of immigrant neighborhoods secured the pioneers preferential positions in the ethnic communities. Since the bulk of the immigrants arrived after the settlements had formed, later arrivals entered the communities on terms acceptable to the leaders.

The first important leader of the Slovak community was a Catholic priest, Štefan Furdek. He was born in Slovakia in 1855 and studied in Budapest, then at Nitra's famous seminary, and later at Charles University in Prague. In 1882 Bishop James Gilmour invited the young scholar to Cleveland, where he became assistant to a Czech priest and then established Our Lady of Lourdes, the city's largest Czech parish. Three years after his arrival he began to celebrate Mass for Slovaks at a Franciscan chapel, and in 1888 he founded the first Slovak parish in Cleveland.[22] During the first years of the Slovak immigrant community, then, a clerical leader established an ethnic parish as the institutional nucleus of organizational life.

In the young Italian community, on the other hand, the first important figure was a layman. Giuseppe Carabelli came to Cleveland in 1880 and quickly established a marble and granite works, which attracted a large group of stonecutters from the province of Campobasso. Carabelli set out early to order the Italian settlement. He asked a women's group in 1885 to organize a nursery and a kindergaten. The school rapidly grew into Alta House, a settlement house which by the early 1890s had become one of the main points of contact between the newcomers and Cleveland. Carabelli also played a major part in forming the first Italian mutual benefit society in 1888, the Italian Fraternal Society. This society served as the model for almost all of the early benevolent groups, and by the mid-1890s it functioned as the arbiter of associational life.[23] Carabelli went on to a successful business career and a term of service in the Ohio House of Representatives in 1910. He managed to cap his career by pushing a bill through the legislature proclaiming Columbus Day as an official holiday.

In the Rumanian community the first leader was a saloon-keeper, the characteristic immigrant entrepreneur. Mihail Bârza arrived in Cleveland in 1888, set up a large saloon, and initiated several organizational efforts. Bârza and another saloon owner, Pavel Borzea, founded the first Rumanian mutual benefit society in Cleveland in 1902. Both continued to exercise leadership well into the next decade.[24]

One sees in the biographies of these first leaders early instances of the effort to develop urban associations. In the Slovak community, the main strands of organization were secured in the parish, and the network of group relationships formed a pattern of religious affiliations. In the case of both the Rumanians and the Italians, organizations were begun by self-made men, by merchants and storekeepers who exemplified a modest realization of the myth of success.

Slovak clerical and lay leaders ordered the community by means of a network of parishes and mutual benefit societies. A few of the early pioneers joined with Czech and Polish immigrants to form an organization in 1865, but by 1878 the Bohemian Benevolent Association had absorbed this group. Many of the first leaders were saloonkeepers and petty merchants with taverns and shops on the edges of the Czech, German, and Polish communities. Ján Roskoš, from Hermanovce, in Zemplín county; Ján Ondrej, from Drinova, Šariš; Jozef Dovalovsky, from a tiny village in Spiš — all came to Cleveland before 1880.[25] These pioneers began movements from their own and neighboring villages which

by the turn of the century had carried hundreds of their country-
men to the city. Ondrej, Dovalovsky, and others established mutual
benefit societies; these associations acquired regional characteristics
as a consequence of their founders' ties to particular homeland
districts and to other immigrant families from the same localities.
The fact that a society's members spoke a regional dialect and
came from a particular district drew in migrants from similar backgrounds. Leaders cultivated these traditional bonds in order to
provide a measure of stability in the membership. But these early
Slovak leaders were also innovators. Their business and clerical
roles brought them into contact with other immigrant groups and
with the charter society early in the community's life.[26] They
stood between immigrant newcomers and the larger community
as mediators in the formative years.

The early organizational ventures of the Slovak community
were conducted by mobile men. A long apprenticeship or a technical education were the primary avenues of mobility in Slovakia,
but the immigrant community opened new outlets for men of
artisan and clerical origins. Juraj Onda, for instance, left his native
village of Čel'ovoc, Zemplín, shortly after completing elementary
school. He studied cabinetmaking first in Košiče, later in Budapest.
He and his brother Andrej made their way to Cleveland in 1885.
Juraj was a founding member of the St. Joseph Society, the first
Slovak society in Cleveland, and served as president during its first
four years. Ján Miller, the son of a day laborer, came to Cleveland
about 1885 also. He opened a saloon shortly afterward, and by
1899 he owned a chain of taverns in the largest Slovak settlements
of Ohio and Pennsylvania. He was also a founding member of
several local and national societies. Jakub Gruss began work in a
Cleveland steel mill in 1880, first as a stoker, then as a molder, and
finally as a foreman. Though more modestly successful than either
Onda or Miller, he and his brother Tomaš participated in the for-

mation of several associations bringing together the Slovak iron-
workers who lived in the little houses on Corwin and Berg streets.[27]

Among this group of early Slovak leaders there were also physicians, lawyers, teachers, and newspaper editors — immigrant intellectuals educated in Košice, Prešov, Budapest, and Paris. Štefan
Kubašak, for instance, studied at a Paris lycée, taught school in
Slovakia, and then emigrated to Cleveland in 1890. He subsequently organized several societies in Cleveland, as did other teachers. The physician Miloslav Francisci, together with Furdek and
several other Cleveland leaders, organized the Matica (literally,
"queen bee") in 1893. An academy modeled after the parent
organization in St. Martin, this establishment's cultural activities
reached into every Slovak organization, particularly into the priesthood. The Society of Slovak Priests declared, at its first convention
in 1895, that every priest had to become a supporting member of
the Matica. Like the immigrant priests, the Slovak intellectuals
arrived with their attitudes well formed and firmly convinced of
their role as cultural arbiters. Like their Italian counterparts, they
claimed a higher social position because of their superior education.[28]

The early Italian community developed along traditional lines.
Most of the early leaders were self-made men, but they sought to
reconstruct old village associations. Salvatore Di Nardo, the first
of a large family to come from Alcara Li Fusi, Messina, settled in
Cleveland in 1879. As more of his kinsmen and townsfolk arrived,
he established the feast of his village's patron saint in 1897 and
in 1907 organized a village society among immigrants from Alcara.
Pietro Oddo brought his family from Alimena, Palermo, in 1900.
Having persuaded half the band he had led in the village to come
with him, he became the first of a long line of bandleaders from
Alimena. He too helped form a saint's festival and presided at the
first meeting of a village society of *alimenese*. Oddo's nephew,

Francesco Russo, followed in 1905. He had studied music under
his uncle in the village and had led the military band of an infan-
try regiment. As soon as he arrived in Cleveland he organized a
band and shortly afterward he set up a music school. He was perhaps the most conservative of Italian cultural leaders in the city
and insisted on the necessity of instilling *civiltà* in the younger
generation. Russo's advertising was a fascinating collection of slo-
gans. He promised to "teach anyone to play any instrument in
six months" or even three, and at the same time "to free the inner
world from barbarism and pernicious vice." For all his traditional
concerns, Russo became a link among many of the village groups
by forming and conducting village bands.[29]

Organizing activity continued through the 1890s. A group of
small merchants formed the Sicilian Fraternal Society in 1896, the
same year that several laborers established the Italian Workers'
Society. Some of the more prominent immigrants, among them a
teacher, a shop foreman, and a fruit wholesaler, organized a broadly based society named for Columbus in 1897. In 1901 immigrants
from the Calabrian provinces formed a regional benevolent association. By the latter year the five most important societies in Cleveland had been organized — Fraterna, Operaia, Fratellanza Siciliana,
La Calabrese, and Cristoforo Colombo.[30]

The Italian founding fathers often developed business firms or
professional practices while exercising leadership in various associations. Before the onset of mass migration to Cleveland they were
the arbiters of associational life in the small colony. Gaetano Caito
could draw on both kinship and organizational resources in his
position as leader in several societies. He and two of his brothers
ran R. G. Caito & Company, a wholesale grocery firm. Two of the
brothers, Gaetano and Giuseppe, had married into a Sicilian merchant family that had arrived in Cleveland in 1890. Michele Marco
Giuseppe, a lawyer, Cosimo Catalano, a banker, and several other
leaders had the same advantages of early arrival in the city and

strong ties to other families. The cumulative resources of business or professional prominence, participation in the immigrant community's formation, and kinship bonds to other families created a group of men who could expect deference from the colony. Most of the leaders of Cleveland's Italians, and of similar settlements in Pittsburgh, San Francisco, and Boston, came from this group.[31]

The Roman Catholic parish played little part in these formative years. The paucity of documents supports no more than a tentative sketch, but clearly the Italian experience was very different from the Slovak one. The earliest priests were members of the Congregation of Saint Charles Barromeo, an organization founded by Bishop Giovanni Battista Scalabrini of Piacenza. His avowed model was the great German missionary society, the St. Raphaels Verein. But the impact of the congregation among Italian immigrants never approached that of the Verein or of the Ludwigs-Mission Verein, a similar Austrian society.

Two Italian parishes were formed in the late 1880s and early 1890s. Antonio Gibelli was priest at Holy Rosary parish between 1894 and 1907, but though present during the formative years of the community he participated very little in organizational activity. The relationship between priest and laymen was one of persistent tension. The lay leaders in Cleveland developed no working relationship with the parish in the Italian community's early years, in striking contrast with those in Boston, Pittsburgh, and other cities.[32]

The early Rumanian associations were also formed by characteristically mobile men; they had moved about the Old Kingdom of Rumania and the kingdom of Hungary in search of opportunity. Like Ilie Martin — laborer, storekeeper, and self-taught writer — they were ambitious young men for whom migration to the United States was of a piece with their seeking of new chances in the homeland. Pantelimon Chima, who was president of several societies during his career, was born in a tiny village in the county of

Făgăraș, served an apprenticeship in a print shop in the Old King-dom of Rumania between the ages of thirteen and seventeen, then moved to Bucharest to work in the composition room of a famous literary review. After arriving in the United States in 1905 at the age of nineteen, Chima found his first job in a factory but soon went into business for himself and became a successful merchant.

Self-made men like Chima played the major role in the early organization of the Rumanian community. As one man remarked in 1906, during the first meeting of a new society in Cleveland, the leaders' task was "to found societies such as this in order to serve as examples to other Rumanians." "The time has come," wrote another early leader, "to shake off our lethargy and, by forming associations, to act as examples for the rest of the Ruman-ians in this country." One of the earliest immigrants in Cleveland recalled in 1907 that all these men had a clear sense of participat-ing in the "founding era" of a community.[33]

The clergy played a secondary role in the formative years of the Rumanian settlement. Orthodox and Byzantine Rite Catholic priests participated largely as editors of newspapers and interpre-ters of the religious aspects of immigrant associations. The first Orthodox priest in Cleveland, Moise Balea, began a newspaper in 1906, the year of the founding of the Union of Rumanian Soci-eties in America. Balea had come to Cleveland upon the petition of lay leaders to the Orthodox Consistory of Sibiu. When he arrived in 1905 he found several mutual benefit societies and a parish com-mittee already in existence. During his tenure, and the tenure of his successors, the Orthodox clergy devoted themselves to editing a newspaper and to participating in the dedicatory ceremonies of benefit societies.[34] The experience of Epaminonda Lucaciu, the first Byzantine Rite priest in Cleveland, closely paralleled that of Balea. The early participation of laymen in the founding of the parish, and the dependence of the church on the members of mutual benefit societies, set the pattern for two decades.[35] Hence,

even though the clergy remained an important group in the Rumanian community, they no longer held the dominant position
which they had occupied in the Transylvanian village. In the urban
context of immigrant communities, Rumanian religious organizations became dependent upon the leadership of voluntary associations.

The predominance of lay leadership in the Rumanian community shaped the structure of immigrant associations, for the initiative in expanding the organized community came from the laymen.
The first mutual benefit society in Cleveland, Carpaṭina, helped to
form the Rumanian Club in 1904. Both these societies, in turn,
spawned other associations. In 1909 a Hungarian consul reported
after a long stay in Cleveland that at least two-thirds of the Rumanian immigrants belonged to some ethnic association. A growing
density of organizational life was apparent after 1910. Organizations radiated from the original mutual benefit societies like the
spokes of a wheel; the new organizations were differentiated in
function, yet closely linked to the hub of activity. Choirs and
theater groups, for instance, segregated the young according to age
and sex while providing formal training in the Rumanian language.
Family organizations stressed the Orthodox image of the patri-
archal father. Self-improvement societies offered the worker the
means of literacy.[36] Between 1910 and 1920, then, the network
of local clubs came to affiliate most Rumanian immigrants with
the formally organized community.

Enduring features of immigrant communities emerged during the
formative period. In the early Slovak community, the parish served
as the center of ethnic affiliations, and as masses of newcomers
arrived after 1900 religious ties continued to structure the community, for the pattern of affiliations remained basically un-
changed. In the Italian and Rumanian communities, on the other
hand, the dominant motif of the early settlements was the ascen-

dancy of self-made men. After 1900, however, this pattern was altered in significant ways. The old Italian elite was displaced by young men eager to make their modest success the model for the community. They began to stress the cultural life of immigrant Italians and thus acquired a vehicle for reordering the community. Out of these concerns grew the effort of Italian associations to reconcile tradition and mobility. For the Rumanians as well the task was to adapt traditional cultural values to a new and unsettling society where achievement was the prevalent theme, and voluntary associations served this purpose.

A strong alliance between the ethnic parish and voluntary societies had already developed in Cleveland when Štefan Furdek formed the first explicitly Slovak society (the St. Stephan Society) in 1885, at the same time that he began to hold Mass for Slovaks. Some of the early officers, however, had close connections with Czech Catholics, and in 1899 the group affiliated with the Central Czech Union, a national benevolent association.[37]

Meanwhile the process of organization continued. The St. Joseph Society, the most important of the Cleveland Slovak societies, was founded in 1889. Štefan Furdek again played a central role; he was joined by an ironworker, a grocer, a cabinetmaker, and three manual laborers. The ironworker, Jakub Gruss, was the first vice-president, and he held several important offices during the society's formative period. Other pioneer organizations were formed before 1900 — St. George, St. Andrew, St. Martin, and twenty other Catholic societies. Laborers accounted for about 80 percent of the first officers. Entrepreneurs and proprietors were much less important, accounting for no more than 10 percent; lawyers, doctors, and a few clerks made up the remaining 10 percent.[38] The recruitment of leaders reflected participation in the parish rather than the ascendancy of mobile immigrants.

The cooperation of priests and laymen was also important in the emergence of national organizations. Four months after the founding of the St. Joseph Society in Cleveland, eight similar associations in Pittsburgh, Wilkes-Barre, Minneapolis, and other cities sent delegates to the first convention of the Catholic Slovak Union in Cleveland. Furdek was the most important leader, but Catholic priests from other cities who had roles similar to Furdek's were also instrumental in forming the union. Raymond Wider, born in Silesia, fluent in Polish, German, and Czech as well as Slovak, was elected president of the union in 1893. Ján Zavadan, a professor of theology before he left Slovakia in 1892, also played an important part in the union's formative years. But the clergy did not dominate the proceedings, although it had the major voice in planning the organization's direction. The first president and all but one of the first elected officials were laymen, and the laymen decided to what extent the organizational aims would be fulfilled.[39]

There was continual interplay between local and national or regional organizations. Several Catholic and Lutheran Slovaks established the Republican Club in 1893, thereby declaring their intention to join a reform movement in Cleveland politics. The club dropped its political aims in the late 1890s and became instead a nationalist association, the Cleveland Slovak Union. By 1900 it counted ten Catholic and Lutheran lodges among its membership. Two other regional associations, the Passaic Slovak Union and the Pennsylvania Roman and Greek Catholic Brotherhood, developed along similar lines. On the national level there were the Catholic Slovak Union, the National Slovak Society, the Greek Catholic Association — to name only the largest — and five other federations.[40]

At the end of this formative period Jakub Molitoris, a Cleveland Slovak who had observed the community's development since 1894, said at the tenth anniversary of the founding of the First Catholic Slovak Union:

Today we Slovak Catholics must be proud that our small association has grown into such a large union. We must thank God
for providing a leader like Štefan Furdek. . . . He stood like a tall
oak among us and thus was able to lead us and to infuse us with
his character and spirit. And because every Slovak Catholic has
always respected him, our union has been able to improve the
life and health of wretched Slovaks. When we have good leaders,
only then will we be able to rise and dream of higher things.[41]

Other Slovak communities shared this confidence. A Philadelphia
layman described how Slovaks had organized eleven societies in the
city during 1898 and noted that only a political club was lacking.
Letters from Passaic, Newark, Pittsburgh, and even the very young
settlements in Indiana Harbor and Joliet conveyed the same impression of a stable community.[42] The most important element in
this confidence was the interweaving of religious motives and
cultural aspirations which immigrant associations had carried out
between 1895 and 1900. A broadside from a congregation illustrates this powerful mixture:

All the progress which our Slovak people have enjoyed origi-
nated in the diligent work of the faithful. Slovaks! You must
realize that every founding of a church advances the Slovak
name and the cultural progress of the Slovak people, and thus
should thrill the heart of every true Slovak.[43]

The relationship between Catholic parishes and ethnic associations was strengthened after the turn of the century. In the late
1890s the Society of Slovak Priests had begun working toward a
popular federation of Slovak Catholics. Their efforts came to
fruition on both the local and national levels in the great congresses at Philadelphia in 1905 and at Wilkes-Barre in 1906. Like
the German *Katholikentage* after which they were modeled, these
popular meetings served to confirm the fusion of parish and association. Following the success of the congresses, the clergy orga-

nized the Slovak Catholic Federation in 1911, which remained a symbol of the interplay of religion and ethnicity into the 1920s.[44]

While mass migration reinforced the structure of the Slovak community, new arrivals eroded the social base of the early Italian community and limited the influence of the pioneers. One major consequence of the heavy migration between 1900 and 1920, as I have already indicated, was a rapid multiplication of Italian societies. This astonishing growth, which produced over fifty societies between 1900 and 1912, reflected a new heterogeneity of geographical origins and social status among the new arrivals. Three of every four mutual benefit societies incorporated between 1903 and 1910 limited their membership to persons born in a particular locality, and half admitted only persons from a particular occupation. The local societies usually sponsored an annual festival in honor of the patron saint of the homeland village. Thus these new societies connected in an immediate way with the immigrants' traditional loyalties. Here is, then, the clearest evidence of the native village as the reference for the reconstitution of cultural and organizational ties in an American city.

A parade, a panegyric to the patron saint, an evening with old friends, served to restore the village's moral order in an urban setting.[45] Yet the perambulation of the urban parish stretched along streets lined with strangers from other villages, rather than within a well-known precinct. Members of associations were mobile: they might move to Cincinnati or Detroit, to be replaced by others who had first migrated to Pittsburgh or Youngstown. Memberships often split, as when Achille Di Bartolo and Vincenzo Coniglio struggled over the Alcara society's existence in 1909. Di Bartolo took half the members with him and formed a new Alcara society, many of whose members were born in Forli del Sannio, a village hundreds of miles from Alcara Li Fusi. Immigrants might continue to call themselves *alcarese* or *santagatese*, but the old ties became tenuous in the urban setting. Through a syncretic process, specific loyalties combined into a diffuse attachment to whatever patron saints or local societies one found in the city district.[46]

As Italian organizations proliferated after 1900, a new leadership developed as well. The new men were likely to have matured in some American city, and they often had acquired secondary education and professional training in American schools. Their leadership depended on their ability to voice the concerns of an Italian community rapidly becoming part of a larger urban society rather than those of a colony living on the city's periphery. They developed a brokerage style, a cultural leadership aimed at mediation between the ethnic group and the host society.[47]

A few examples convey characteristic features of the new leaders' careers. Vincenzo Nicola left Montenero Val Cocchiara, Campobasso, in 1881 for Ulrichsville, Ohio, where he reared a large family. His son, Benjamin, born in 1879, attended public schools in the town and graduated from Ohio State, where he received a law degree in 1900. He passed his bar exams and began to practice in Cleveland in 1904. That same year Fernando Melaragno and his cousin Olindo moved to Cleveland from Providence to found a newspaper, *La voce del popolo italiano*. Two of Fernando's brothers had established a cigar business in Cleveland in the 1880s, and a sister had married a Cleveland banker in 1890. Fernando Melaragno was no stranger to the city; he had come to Cleveland with his brothers in 1882 at the age of fourteen but returned to Italy in 1886 to study at the University of Naples. His cousin Olindo came to Ohio with his parents in 1887 and attended high school in Mechanicsburg. He moved west in 1890, working for a few years in Montana, then advancing from railroad laborer to division superintendent as he worked his way to San Francisco. When the two cousins established the newspaper, both had thus had wide experience of American society and many contacts with other Italian communities. And like Benjamin Nicola, Giuseppe Barricelli,

Francesco Aidala, and others, they had spent their formative years in the United States.[48]

The varied background of new leaders and the proliferation of societies brought about important changes in the Italian community. A simple analysis of leadership patterns in twenty-eight of the societies organized after 1903 suggests the dimensions of these changes. Three hundred sixty-four men held office in these societies between 1909 and 1910. Fifteen percent held office in both years; 40 percent of this group occupied positions in two or more societies. In the Spedaliere Circle, for instance, fifteen of the seventeen officers in 1909 were reelected in 1910. This literary circle was one of the last resorts of an old elite, like the Republican Social Club and the Italian Philanthropic Society. The activities of the old leaders thus had contracted to a small circle of covertly elitist social clubs. Only on Columbus Day did they take part in a public affair, and then only to restore a mythical unity to the community. In the village and workers' societies, on the other hand, the leadership turned over very rapidly. No more than 5 percent of the 1909 leadership remained in 1910; less than 1 percent of these served as officers in more than one society. Moreover, the officers in these new societies were mobile men, for more than three-quarters were formerly manual workers, having become small merchants or clerks since their arrival in Cleveland.[49]

The changing characteristics of Italian leadership were connected to a broad organizational reorientation of the community about 1910. The proliferation of local associations and the volatility of local leaders had eroded the old social basis of the Italian community, and now a new group of leaders set about to shape the community in a fundamentally different way. Three prominent entrepreneurs, Salvatore Lo Re, Giuseppe Zingales Botta, and Alfredo Oddo, founded the first lodge of the Sons of Italy in 1910. These men were Sicilians who had arrived in Cleveland after 1900. They were joined by Silvestro Tamburella, Michele Trivisonno, and Vincenzo Marcogiuseppe, professionals of peasant origins, in a general move to federate Italian societies. Tamburella organized the Dante Alighiere Cultural Circle in 1909, the most important indication of change in the community. It included, two years later, all of the twenty new leaders in the city.[50] The Dante Circle in Cleveland, like those in New York, Boston, San Francisco, and other cities, served as the means of introducing Italian into public schools and of achieving acceptance of public schooling in the Italian community. The Boston Dante Society, for instance, stated in its constitution that its purpose was "the diffusion of Italian language and culture by adopting the most efficacious measures — schools, libraries, educational circles, and reading rooms." The circle's intention was "principally to attract the new Italo-American generation into our orbit. . . ."[51] Efforts to raise the literacy of laborers, build new organizations, and use the public schools characterized these groups. The hopes that appeared most often in their constitutions were "material improvement" and "moral uplift."[52]

The aim of the Cleveland Dante Circle, Tamburella wrote in 1912, was a "systematization" of ethnic organizations. The community's leaders carried out their consolidation program through the Sons of Italy, however, since the social base of the Dante Circle proved too narrow. The national organization of the Sons of Italy declared in 1905, in its first constitution, that its purpose was "to promote the material and moral improvement of all American Italians." Nineteen hundred ten marked the beginning of its steady growth, both nationally and in Cleveland. Three years later there were three lodges in Cleveland, and by 1915 there were six.[53]

Giuseppe Zingales Botta emerged as the most important leader in this reorientation of the Italian community. Zingales Botta left Sant'Agata, Messina, in 1902, where his father had been a small storekeeper. He began his career in Cleveland as a waiter,

and by 1909 he had acquired a large restaurant and had invested
heavily in real estate. His name began to appear in every variety
of ethnic association in 1908, and by 1915 he was the most important of the young leaders. When he organized the Sant'Agata
Workers' Society in 1915 he brought together much of the traditional and the new in the Italian community. The society admitted
only laborers born in Sant'Agata "exactly as in the old village,"
the constitution declared. Yet Zingales Botta's description of the
group indicates clearly the emphasis placed on status: "We see
among the forty-five members who have joined the society to date
the colony's best and most intelligent element: all enjoy equal
estime, whether men of affairs or simple laborers." This uplift
culture fitted the needs of a changing community in which, as a
lawyer wrote, not only the professionals and merchants would
lead, but also those who manifested "a desire to obtain distinction,
or to advance the position they already have."[54]

The Sons of Italy made steady gains in spreading these expectations of mobility. Ten societies had affiliated with the order by
1910, when the Italian Fraternal Society, the oldest and most prestigious of the Cleveland organizations, joined the Sons of Italy.
Four other societies immediately followed. As the secretary of a
workers' mutual benefit association wrote, "the action of the Fraternal Society has led us to affiliate with the Order." By 1920 all
the village and regional societies formed between 1900 and 1912
had joined the Sons of Italy.[55] Hence in the early 1920s the Italian
community had become an amalgam of traditional ties to village
and region and new promises of mobility exemplified in the modest
successes of recent immigrants. This peculiarly mixed culture
formed the background for the new arrival's adjustment to the
city.

A similar transformation affected the Rumanian community in
the years of mass immigration. As mutual benefit societies responded to the needs of the new arrivals, a series of changes in the

recruitment of leaders altered the roles of the societies. From
the very beginning, both local and national societies had been interested in providing a means of recruiting and educating leaders.
But after 1910 this became one of their most important activities.
Participation in Rumanian associations became an avenue of
mobility and thus provided a model of achievement for the community.

The early leadership, as I have mentioned earlier, was drawn
from men who had been mobile in both Hungary and America. As
a priest remarked of these men in 1906, the migration and the
creation of a new community "made them more conscious of their
dignity; they doffed their shepherd's hats, sloughed off their old
habits, and adopted a more commercial spirit." But even then,
during the first flush of their discovery of a new range of action,
they became concerned about the welfare of the community. Ioan
Babor, a well-known entrepreneur in Cleveland and Youngstown,
noted at a banquet in 1906 that the leadership of the Cleveland societies "belonged to the hard-working middle class of the community —
men who will work with great zeal and sacrifice to create a national
culture." During the early years of local and national organizations, the attempt to establish an organizational basis for a nationalist culture had some support. Most Cleveland societies favored
the founding of newspapers and other cultural agencies such as
bookstores. The conviction of the local leaders that Cleveland was
the "center of Rumanian culture" added a sense of urgency. Thus
the Cleveland settlement led the way in organizing groups that
later structured the immigrant community — dramatic and cultural societies, women's sodalities, and societies for the second
generation.[56]

Contemporaries observed that this transition in organization
reflected changes in the pattern of recruitment of leaders. A Greek
Catholic priest wrote in 1906 that the typical immigrant "built a

house near his place of work, made monthly payments and, after two or three years, became a proprietor. Thus established, with a good salary, he forgot about his roots in the homeland." Within this context, as a bartender recalled in 1909, societies were largely concerned to assure support in times of sickness or accident. The effort to establish organizations on a firm basis overrode interest in maintaining a distinctive culture. But by 1909, a real estate agent noted, there were two different groups of leaders: "The young leaders are as interested in cultural organization as in mutual benefit societies, while the older men tend to be more interested in mutual benefit and religion." Another immigrant wrote that the immigrant community "had gained, by means of hard manual labor, a small fortune. . . . Now, we need to leave the life of the factory, the work in the shop, the standing at machines, and look for a more satisfying life."[57] This new life should begin, he went on, with a renewed emphasis on the ethnic culture — on books, newspapers, and libraries. And above all, the stress should fall on education, for it would prepare young men to lead the coming generation.[58]

These promises led to concrete action in organizing several varieties of new associations. On the local level, many societies formed cultural organizations that sought to include the second generation within the ethnic group. In the process they established evening and weekend schools offering instruction in Rumanian language and literature. The most significant change, however, was the increased emphasis on cultural activities within the mutual benefit societies themselves. In 1913 the Union of Rumanian Societies created a cultural fund which was to be used to help Rumanian students attend professional schools. Significantly, the first student to be sponsored by this fund became a prominent lawyer and was president of several societies between 1920 and 1928.[59] The union's sponsorship of students continued to expand in the 1920s until the program had such a broad impact that most local and national leaders were drawn from this group of educated young professionals.[60]

On the national level, these various organizations grew more interrelated. The Union of Rumanian Societies, founded in 1906, drew in the various associations which continued to form at the local scene. After a difficult period between 1907 and 1909, the union overcame the resistance to the penetration of national organizations into local settings. Moreover, it withstood a determined attempt on the part of Orthodox priests in 1912 to make the organization an arm of the church.[61] Hence, as lay leaders continued to organize mutual benefit societies on the local level, their relationships with national groups remained firm. The ties between new local organizations and the network of national organizations was reinforced in 1913, when the Rumanian-American Association was formed.

These impressive organizational efforts occurred between 1910 and 1920, when there was a great deal of return migration to Rumania and an even greater migration within the United States. As Rumanian immigrants moved about — from small industrial cities like Canton, Oberlin, and Zanesville to Cleveland and Detroit — they carried their ethnic affiliations with them. Thus the internal migration from small mill towns to industrial metropolises took place within the context of two national organizations, the Union of Rumanian Societies and the Rumanian-American Association. When local organizations were formed in the migration, they quickly affiliated with these national associations.[62]

After this period of flux in the 1910s, the two national organizations moved toward consolidation. The initiative for this movement came from within the ranks of lay leaders in 1923. Both Orthodox and Byzantine Rite priests offered some resistance to the consolidation, since it tended to make the associations even more secular,[63] but by 1926 enough momentum had been gained to overcome this problem, and the union was completed in 1928. After twenty-two years of organization, then, Rumanian societies remained essentially lay associations.[64]

The emergence of ethnic communities was in part a reconstitution of traditional models of order and in part an accommodation to the life of the city. Migration patterns limited the extent to which the Rumanian and Slovak communities could restore the old order, since the Cleveland settlements were drawn from hundreds of small villages. The Italian community, however, came largely from ten villages in the Abruzzi and Sicily; hence a pattern of particularistic cultural loyalties characterized the settlement. The process of arrival thus produced contrasting demographic situations for the development of ethnic communities.

The distinctive features of immigrant cultures grew out of the various ways in which voluntary associations adapted to urban society. The Slovak community maintained religious affiliations that defined membership in the ethnic group. Social life was an amalgam of religious and associational ties; the prevalent values were order and continuity. As one congregation declared, "the diligent work of the faithful" advanced the Slovak people. The community wove a pattern of stability for its members.

The Italian and Rumanian communities were quite different. Despite the strong localism of its associations, the Italian community developed a large group of young and mobile leaders after 1910. These leaders emphasized the continuity of associations with village life but also exemplified mobility and success. While associations represented old values in a new setting, the expectation of mobility also became an important feature of the Italian community. Rumanian associations possessed neither the traditional emphasis on religion nor the element of localism. The voluntary association itself became an avenue of mobility and institutional achievement.

These variations in orientation to urban life shaped the expectations of the immigrants. The Slovaks hoped for orderly lives within the confines of parish and organization, and mobility held little importance in this hope. The Italians expected to grasp at new opportunities without interrupting ties to their village origins. And the Rumanians enthusiastically embraced the promise of mobility. Their secular values and mobile leaders gave them a head start in making it in Cleveland.

5 Fathers and Sons: Trends in Social Mobility

A man's occupation is the most important index of his social status, as virtually every major theorist of social mobility has emphasized. Locating a man within an occupational hierarchy amounts roughly to specifying his social status — his job translates natural endowment, upbringing, and education into class, status, and power. And, as the English sociologist W. G. Runciman writes, "the most significant moves which the individual can make in all three dimensions will be by means of a change from one occupation to another."[1] I have therefore taken as a simple model of social mobility the change from one occupational stratum to another. The five strata I have adopted — high white-collar, low white-collar, skilled, semiskilled, and unskilled — are comprehensive enough to suggest important differences in life chances, yet narrow enough to report mobility in some detail.[2]

In exploring the occupational mobility of the Cleveland immigrants and their sons, I have had to use small samples throughout, oftentimes too tiny to yield any dependable information. However, the patterns I have observed indicate significant differences, even though rigorous tests of statistical significance have not everywhere been applied. My point here is to develop some relationship between group membership and opportunity, not to establish a close association in any one sample. Since my argument rests on the recurrence of patterns in different groups, the dismayingly small samples still provide a good start.

Andrea C. left Termini Imerese, Palermo, at the turn of the century. His passport listed Cleveland as his destination and described his occupation as *contadino* ("peasant tenant"). He began his career in the city as a day laborer in 1901; on this unsteady foundation he established a household in 1902 with Teresa S., also from Termini. Teresa bore him eight children between 1903 and 1919, seven of whom managed to reach at least the eighth grade. Andrea, meanwhile, began to drive a truck for an Italian grocery firm and acquired a modest home worth $3,700. But age began to tell, and in 1940 he was back at casual labor. The three sons could not improve on their father's career — two drove a truck for most of their lives, the third spent his life digging ditches.

Carmelo L. left Sant'Agata di Militello, Messina, sometime between 1905 and 1909. His father was a day laborer in the fields and had established a household on the outskirts of the village, among a small cluster of other members of the L. family. When Carmelo married Nicoletta Di V. in 1911 he lived near the center of Cleveland and worked as a casual laborer. In 1920 he was a splicer in a steel mill; ten years later he owned a grocery store and a $13,000 home in Shaker Heights. Both his children attended a parochial elementary school and graduated from public high school. His son Charles took over the business in 1940.

Rosario O. joined the emigration from Sant'Agata about the same time as Carmelo L. His father had been a sharecropper, but Rosario at some time acquired a cobbler's skills. Between 1910 and 1940 he stayed at his trade, moving at least five times in order to keep up with his customers as they moved away from the central city. His four children finished junior high school; only Sam, the youngest, went on to senior high school. Except for Sam, the children remained at home past their twenty-fifth birthday, working as laborers and seamstresses. Sam moved into a managerial position in a meat company. Their father, meanwhile, neither changed his job nor acquired any property.

From the neighboring village of Alcara Li Fusi came Vincenzo B., the son of an artisan. He established a barbershop in the heart of the central district, on Orange Street, shortly after his marriage to Maria G., from Sant'Agata, in 1906. By 1930 he had acquired $7,000 in property. The couple produced five sons, four of whom finished the ninth grade and went into skilled trades. The fifth, Biagio, ranked exactly in the middle of his class at Central High. After graduating he attended a pharmaceutical college in Cleveland. He subsequently moved to Chicago, where he established a profitable practice.

Salvatore G. was a cobbler's son from Termini Imerese. In 1906 he married a girl in Cleveland from a neighboring Italian village; four years later he established a small fruit stand on East Twenty-sixth. The stand grew over the next twenty years into the Cleveland Celery Market. In the meantime he had accumulated over $13,000 in real and personal property. None of his three sons finished high school, but each became an officer in his father's company — vice-president, secretary-treasurer, and manager. A fisherman's son from the same village, Giuseppe R., who married in the same year as Salvatore G., established a similar market on the west bank of the Cuyahoga. His three sons also failed to finish high school, but they did not have the same kind of paternal backing. Their father hired one as a truck driver; the other two left town.

These sketches of Italian immigrants' fortunes after passage to America illustrate an important fact about their careers: their social background strongly influenced both their first job and their subsequent work experience.[3] Italian immigrants came from a variety of social milieux, and a variety of social types filled the migration streams. Some were better prepared than others to enter the industrial world. Those of agricultural origins fared poorly in the skilled and nonmanual occupations in comparison with the sons of artisans and petty merchants. The performance of the artisan group was impressive; nearly half entered skilled callings, and another 40 percent found their first jobs in white-collar occupations. But the most impressive early gains were made by fishermen, more than three-quarters of whom began their American careers as storekeepers.

Why Sicilian fishermen would have made it so quickly as businessmen is not so evident as the fortunes of the others. The explanation lies partly in the fact that fishing in the Mediterranean was a business enterprise, for one crucial job was to distribute the catch. Second, the migration of fishermen was almost always a family movement. And, what is more important, the migration assumed a serial pattern. The first members of eleven of the fourteen fishermen's families arrived in Cleveland in the mid-1890s, before the mass Sicilian movement. Their family firms furnished employment to the newcomers in the early 1900s, and, as several interviews indicate, the more successful uncles were willing to set up their nephews in their own businesses. One should not be too surprised, then, to find that eleven of the fourteen fishermen's sons began their careers in grocery distribution.

A better test of the impact of social origins is over the long run. Among the various village groups, only the artisans experienced important long-term gains. Four of every ten started out in white-collar occupations, and fully a third of those who began as laborers moved into white-collar jobs. Thus twenty years after their arrival in Cleveland almost two-thirds enjoyed middle-class status. The sons of laborers and peasants ended only slightly better off than they had begun, while the tiny group of immigrants from the villages' upper crust remained static. The fishermen's sons, on the other hand, lost their early advantage and ended their careers largely in blue-collar ranks. Moreover, these skidding entrepreneurs turned not to blue-collar jobs that paid as well as or better than clerical or proprietarial positions, but to unskilled and semiskilled jobs. This was not simply a case of the exchange of honorific titles, therefore, but one of a real drop in occupational status. In comparison, day laborers' and peasants' sons made more modest gains; a fourth of this group climbed into white-collar occupations during their careers, and a third ended their careers in middle-class occupations during their careers, and a third ended their careers in middle-class occupations.

Although the tiny sample warrants no generalizations, the discovery of a general advance in status among two social groups within an Italian migration stream suggests what may have been a common pattern in American cities. Sketchy evidence from several studies indicates that the sons of the skilled have commonly maintained their status or have advanced into middle-class occupations. Few of the sons of skilled immigrants in either twentieth-century Boston or Indianapolis were downwardly mobile.[4] Italian immigrants in Cleveland who had been exposed to artisan traditions in the Old World shared this same fortune, for almost all entered the city at an occupational level similar to or higher than that of their fathers.

Most immigrants entered Cleveland as blue-collar workers, however, and twenty years later most remained so. But between 1910 and 1930 a small proportion of manual workers began a slow but steady climb into white-collar jobs. Table 8 presents an overview of the career mobility of the immigrants and their sons. Slightly more than a tenth of the first generation started out in white-collar jobs — as clerks, saloonkeepers, and occasionally as proprietors of some commercial establishment. Over the next twenty years, a third of this favored group skidded into manual employment. But during the same period, 14 percent of the blue-collar starters were able to climb into white-collar positions, so that a fifth of the immigrant generation ended their careers in middle-class occupations.[5]

Table 8. Interclass career mobility rates of the first and second generations (percent).

| | First generation born 1870-90 | | | | Second generation | | | | | | |
| | | | | | born 1900-09 | | | born 1910-19 | | | |
	All	It.	Rum.	Sl.	All	It.	Sl.	All	It.	Rum.[a]	Sl.
Starting white-collar	11	16	14	2	25	29	17	30	27	41	26
Ending white-collar	20	24	24	12	26	28	22	33	28	56	20
Climbing blue-collar starters	14	15	19	12	14	16	11	19	19	36	16
Skidding white-collar starters	33	33	20	—	37	40	25	40	50	18	67
All changing class	16	18	16	12	20	23	13	29	28	28	28
Number	(454)	(230)	(69)	(155)	(124)	(78)	(36)	(187)	(92)	(41)	(54)

[a]Born 1905-1919.

The sons born during the first decade of the century began their careers with a marked advantage over their fathers. A fourth could claim white-collar status for their first jobs. During their careers, more than a third of these found themselves falling to blue-collar jobs — a skid which occurred largely during the depression decade.[6] Like their fathers before them, however, 14 percent of the blue-collar starters escaped their manual status; thus about a fourth of this cohort finished their careers in white-collar occupations.

A similarly slow, steady rise in fortunes characterized the experience of the sons born in the second decade. Thirty percent started out in the mid-1930s and early 1940s in white-collar employment. This status was not permanent, however, for 40 percent of them had dropped into working-class occupations by the early 1950s. Blue-collar starters enjoyed constant gains during the decade of the forties; about a fifth had moved into white-collar positions by 1950. A third of the sons born between 1910 and 1919, then, had made it into the middle class by the early fifties.

The proportions of the groups changing class — from working class to middle class and the reverse — increased from about 16 percent in the immigrant generation to 29 percent in the younger cohort of the second generation. As table 9 indicates, the rates of change between occupational strata — from an unskilled job to a skilled job, for example — grew from 40 percent of the immigrant generation and the older cohort of sons to 56 percent of the younger cohort. The association between the strata of the first and last jobs was moderately strong for both the first generation and the older sons. But for the younger sons, starting out in the late thirties and the early forties, the stratum of the last job was very weakly associated with that of the first job.[7] This means, in short, that the probability of an ordered relationship between the first and last jobs was better than even for both the older groups, while for the younger cohort of sons the chances were only one in three.

The movement between occupational strata was remarkably con-

Table 9. Occupational continuity rates of the first and second generations (percent).

| | First generation born 1870–90 | | | | Second generation | | | | | | |
| | | | | | born 1900–09 | | | born 1910–19 | | | |
	All	It.	Rum.	Sl.	All	It.	Sl.	All	It.	Rum.[a]	Sl.
Continuity rates by stratum of first job											
High white-collar	67	67	80	—	100	100	—	70	60	100	—
Low white-collar	33	40	80	—	47	100	—	21	60	100	—
Skilled	80	89	50	67	78	82	80	86	100	33	88
Semiskilled	53	67	71	20	40	50	33	36	27	50	43
Unskilled	58	60	40	62	53	63	45	36	44	0	50
All	60	60	50	59	60	66	57	44	41	36	56
Association between strata of first and last jobs (gamma)	0.58	0.59	0.46	0.59	0.68	0.69	0.87	0.35	0.33	0.34	0.32
Number	(230)	(122)	(38)	(70)	(81)	(53)	(23)	(92)	(46)	(25)	(25)

[a]Born 1905–1919.

stant in direction over the forty-year span. Among white-collar immigrants and sons, those with an early foothold in a proprietarial or professional job were very likely to stay there throughout their careers, while those with menial white-collar occupations moved out rapidly — almost always down rather than up.

At the bottom of the occupational hierarchy, a long-term move out of unskilled and semiskilled occupations was apparent. For the unskilled, of course, the only way to go was up, largely into semiskilled and skilled jobs. Only a small proportion (never more than a tenth) ever gained even low white-collar jobs. The semi-skilled ended their careers largely in skilled occupations. A remark-able element of stability in the blue-collar group was the small percentage of men in each generation who began their careers as skilled workers.[8] Their tenacity in their occupations probably depressed the proportion of men eventually gaining white-collar status.

Ethnic origins were another important dimension of mobility. In general, as tables 8 and 9 show, differences between Italian and Slovak immigrants tended to disappear during the careers of the second generation. The differences between the Rumanians and the other two groups, however, grew *larger* during the lives of the second generation.

Only a tiny percentage of Slovak immigrants began in white-collar occupations. The first generation made a 10-percent gain in the white-collar category, which they passed on to the second generation. By the end of the careers of the older cohort of sons, the Slovaks had almost caught up to the Italians. The younger cohort of Italians and Slovaks began their careers with nearly the same proportions in white-collar positions, yet a gap opened be-tween the two groups in the early 1950s. A smaller percentage of blue-collar Slovaks managed to climb into white-collar jobs, and a smaller percentage of white-collar Slovaks could hold on to their early status.

The Rumanians, on the other hand, moved much more rapidly than either of the other two groups into the middle class. The immigrants began with no special advantage, although a slightly larger percentage of blue-collar starters climbed into white-collar jobs, and a larger percentage of the white-collar starters kept their positions to the end of their careers. The second generation, however, gained middle-class status at a remarkable rate. The Rumanians began their careers with a decided advantage over the Italians and Slovaks; a larger proportion of the blue-collar starters moved up; and a larger proportion of white-collar starters held on to their jobs. So by 1950 more than half the sons of Rumanian immigrants could claim middle-class status.

The similarity in the patterns of mobility of the Italian and Slovak groups appears even more striking when one examines career continuity rates. Similar high rates of persistence in skilled jobs developed, as well as high rates of movement out of the unskilled and semiskilled strata. Over the forty-year period covered in table 9 the strength of the association between strata of first and last jobs varied from generation to generation in about the same magnitudes for both ethnic groups.

In table 9 the differences between the Rumanians and the other two groups come into clearer focus. Unskilled first-generation Rumanians began climbing into skilled and white-collar occupations in much greater proportions than their peers in the other two ethnic groups — the pattern of the first-generation Rumanians bore a closer resemblance, in fact, to that of their younger sons. This trend continued into the second generation at a remarkable rate — no Rumanian son who had begun as an unskilled laborer in the 1930s or 1940s remained so at the age of thirty. And, as the rates of career mobility show in table 8, more than a third of this movement was into white-collar occupations.

Both generations of the three ethnic groups began their careers largely in manual jobs. During their careers, between 14 and 19 percent of the blue-collar starters were able to climb into white-collar jobs. By 1950 a third of the sons born to immigrant families between 1910 and 1919 could claim white-collar status. The Italians and Slovaks experienced very similar patterns of mobility until the mid-forties, when the second-generation Italians began a slightly more rapid entrance into white-collar occupations. The Rumanians started with no advantage over the other ethnic groups, but the gap that opened between them and the Slovaks and Italians was widened by their sons. By the end of the forties, more than half the second-generation Rumanians prospered in the middle-class situations, while the other two groups could not claim more than a third.

Property as well as occupation confers status. As Max Weber remarks, "Only persons who are completely unskilled, without property and dependent on employment without regular occupation, are in a strictly identical class status."[9] Immigrants who remained unskilled and dependent on casual employment might nevertheless acquire a lot and a modest dwelling and thereby move at least partially into a stable working-class position. Recent studies of the social mobility of nineteenth-century communities suggest that property mobility was particularly characteristic of Roman Catholic groups.[10] The discovery of property-buying habits among the immigrants of both rural Trempeleau County and urban Newburyport has expanded the scope of Oscar Handlin's observation that New York's Irish expended their surplus earnings on higher living standards and comfortable homes.[11]

The crucial problem, however, is to relate acquisition to status, to obtain a rough approximation of the social meaning of property.[12] Table 10 shows that more than half the families of each ethnic community owned some property during their residence in Cleveland. Rumanian and Slovak men who began their careers in white-collar positions consistently held property of higher value

Table 10. Property ownership of immigrants, 1910–1930.

	Owners (% of occupational group)			Median value of property ($)		
	It.	Rum.	Sl.	It.	Rum.	Sl.
Entrance status						
White-collar	55	75	100	5,500	5,000	—
Blue-collar	57	50	63	4,250	2,917	3,143
All	57	55	64	4,546	3,250	3,250
Number	(137)	(42)	(69)			
Interclass career mobility						
Climbing blue-collar starters	69	67	80	3,750	—	4,000
Skidding white-collar starters	33	—	—	—	—	—
Ending white-collar	64	70	88	4,670	7,500	4,250
Ending blue-collar	59	45	65	4,571	2,357	3,143
Number	(120)	(39)	(60)			
Stratum of last job of unskilled starters						
High white-collar	100	33	—	2,625	—	—
Low white-collar	60	—	83	3,750	—	4,500
Skilled	80	20	63	4,000	—	4,500
Semiskilled	—	25	60	—	—	3,000
Static	59	50	60	4,000	2,750	3,000
Number	(71)	(20)	(47)			

than those who began in the working class. The same, however, was not true of the Italians, for the blue-collar starters who gained status owned less valuable property than their peers who remained in blue-collar occupations. The median values of the holdings bore out the social differences in all three ethnic groups: white-collar starters consistently acquired a higher value of property than blue-collar starters.

Over the next twenty years some interesting changes occurred. As table 10 shows, blue-collar Italians climbing into white-collar jobs owned property of somewhat lower value than their peers who remained blue-collar. By 1930 the differences in value of property owned by white-collar and blue-collar Italians had disappeared, while the gaps in value of property owned by blue-collar and white-collar Rumanians and Slovaks widened, as working-class men with relatively valuable holdings climbed into middle-class occupations. Italians who began their careers as unskilled laborers were likely to acquire less valuable property if they were upwardly mobile than if they remained in unskilled jobs. The relationship was exactly the opposite among Slovaks who made their way up the occupational ladder: the higher they climbed, the more valuable their holdings were. Thus patterns of property acquisition reflected no simple enhancement of status. Class and occupational mobility tended to smooth out differences in property holdings among the Italians, while upwardly mobile Rumanians and Slovaks generally held more valuable property than their occupationally static peers. But another relationship limits the force of this contrast. If property ownership indicated status, it also retarded the residential mobility of families. Homeownership reinforced, then, one salient index of immigrant status — residential segregation.

A combination of factors — rising per capita income, installment buying, strict income-grading in housing, and ethnic differences — worked an important transformation in the social meaning of property within each ethnic group.[13] Property acquisition fitted

into a general pattern of upward mobility within the Slovak working class. Property ownership provided one more piece of evidence
that laborers had entered the stable segment of the working class.
But property acquisition was for them, as for the Newburyport
Irish studied by Stephan Thernstrom, "mobility within narrow
limits, mobility which tended to close off future opportunities
rather than open them."[14] On the other hand, property mobility
characterized many working-class Italians, enhancing the opportunities of the second generation to enter the white-collar world.[15]
Property ownership indicated, then, an expenditure of family resources among the Slovaks, while among the Italians the acquisition
of a house and a lot was an index of growing resources. Within the
Rumanian community, however, it was apparently irrelevant to
upward mobility. Property acquisition thus takes on a social meaning only within a trial balance of overall patterns of social mobility.

What was the role of family origins in the careers of the second
generation? The maturation of a new generation born in America
has been a staple theme in historical literature about immigrants.
Yet historians have rarely approached generational transition in
the new communities as a test of the social impact of ethnic origins. Sociologists interested in poverty have sketched a working-
class ethos blocking the upward mobility of the children of
immigrants — a sketch dependent, incidentally, on informants least
exposed to upward mobility opportunities.[16] These students have
focused upon the waning fragment that remained behind in the
shrinking ghetto; their conclusions, then, are based on a skewed
sample of the immigrants who passed through the city. The evidence set forth here, however, suggests that generational transition
brought with it major changes in status. Intergenerational upward
mobility marked an important stage in immigrant assimilation.[17]

The fact that the bulk of the immigrant generation entered the
labor market as blue-collar workers may have accounted for the

rather slow growth in the proportion of the second generation starting out in nonmanual occupations. One expects a larger proportion of the sons of white-collar fathers to have begun their careers in white-collar jobs. Table 11 bears out this expectation to a certain extent. In both birth cohorts, sons of white-collar fathers began their careers in white-collar occupations in larger proportions than those of blue-collar fathers. Yet the advantage did not persist in the older cohort, for nearly three-fourths skidded into blue-collar jobs. The proportion of sons of white-collar fathers in this cohort who ended in white-collar jobs was smaller than that of sons of blue-collar fathers in the same age group. The younger cohort conformed more closely to the expected pattern, since the sons of white-collar fathers both began and ended their careers with higher proportions in nonmanual occupations than the sons of blue-collar fathers.

If one examines the experiences of the two birth cohorts more closely, the pattern of intergenerational mobility emerges more sharply. First, both age groups gained steadily in the proportion leaving their fathers' class during their career. As the upper panel of table 12 indicates, the proportion of sons of blue-collar fathers climbing into white-collar occupations registered a steady increase over the course of their careers. This recruitment into the white-collar class came from all the manual strata — most strikingly, of course, from the unskilled. Another shift, from white-collar origins into the manual strata, replaced many of the climbers. And the downward movement in the younger cohort came primarily from the sons of low white-collar fathers. The sons of proprietors or professionals had a much better chance to hold on to their higher status.

The pattern that developed, then, was quite regular. Sons of both blue-collar and white-collar fathers experienced a good deal of both upward and downward mobility — about one-third of each birth cohort was mobile between classes. The movement between

Table 11. Interclass career mobility rates of the second generation according to class origins (percent).

| | Sons of blue-collar fathers | | | | | | | Sons of white-collar fathers | |
| | born 1900-09 | | | born 1910-19 | | | | born 1900-09 | born 1910-19 |
	All	It	Sl.	All	It.	Rum.[a]	Sl.	All	All
Starting white-collar	23	26	17	27	28	27	27	53	38
Ending white-collar	28	28	27	29	29	43	21	18	46
Climbing blue-collar starters	15	17	11	20	19	30	17	0	13
Skidding white-collar starters	27	36	0	50	50	25	67	71	0
Number	(104)	(69)	(35)	(157)	(79)	(26)	(52)	(15)	(21)

[a]Born 1905-1919.

Table 12. Intergenerational career mobility and occupational continuity rates according to the first and last jobs of the second generation, 1930–1950.

	Sons born 1900-09		Sons born 1910-19	
	First job	Last job	First job	Last job
Interclass career mobility rates (%)				
Climbing sons of blue-collar fathers	22	25	25	30
Skidding sons of white-collar fathers	47	70	58	50
All leaving class origins	25	31	29	33
Occupational continuity rates by stratum of father's job[a] (%)				
High white-collar	20	0	57	75
Low white-collar	30	17	17	10
Skilled	39	40	29	33
Semiskilled	27	0	33	20
Unskilled	44	26	31	21
All	39	26	31	25
Association between strata of father's job[a] and son's last job (gamma)	0.39	0.12	0.14	0.09
Number	(123)	(81)	(137)	(92)

[a]Father's job at time of son's first job.

occupational strata showed a regular increase, so that the association between the fathers' jobs and the sons' jobs steadily weakened in the 1940s and early 1950s. At the end of their careers, sons born in both decades were likely to occupy jobs unrelated to the kind of work their fathers had done.

There were, however, ethnic differences. Sons of blue-collar Italian immigrants began, as table 11 reveals, with an advantage over the Slovaks, but by 1940 it had disappeared. In the younger cohort, sons of blue-collar fathers in all three ethnic groups started in white-collar jobs in approximately the same percentage, but differences appeared in the late forties and early fifties. The Italians consistently ended their careers with about 29 percent in white-collar occupations, while the Slovaks lost some ground at mid-century. The sons of Rumanian blue-collar fathers, on the other hand, surged ahead of both groups in the same decade and ended with 43 percent in white-collar occupations.

As the upper panel of table 13 shows, the ethnic groups had different rates of interclass mobility. A third of the Italians moved either up or down from their fathers' class between 1930 and 1950, while the proportion of Slovaks varied between a fourth and a fifth. More than half the Rumanians changed class during the same period. The continuity rates by stratum of father's job present a varied picture of the sources of interclass mobility. Italians born during the first decade actually moved in larger proportions and further from their origins than their younger brothers. The Slovak experience was the reverse. The amount of movement among the Rumanians was startling; no Rumanian son remained in his father's occupational stratum after twenty years in the labor market.

Thus a large proportion of the second generation born between 1900 and 1919 experienced intergenerational career mobility. One-third of the sons born in the first decade changed class during their careers; the younger cohort sustained the same pattern. Over the course of the forties and fifties, fewer and fewer sons inherited their fathers' jobs. The small sample of Rumanians had striking mobility between occupational strata, but the rates were moderately high among Slovaks and Italians as well. There is little evidence in this study, then, of any ordered relationship between the social origins and the life chances of the second generation.

Table 13. Intergenerational career mobility and occupational continuity rates of the second generation, 1930–1950.

	All sons			Sons born 1900–09		Sons born 1910–19	
	It.	Rum.[a]	Sl.	It.	Sl.	It.	Sl.
Interclass career mobility rates (%)							
Climbing sons of blue-collar fathers	28	50	21	28	22	29	20
Skidding sons of white-collar fathers	55	67	—	71	—	47	—
All leaving class origins	34	53	22	33	25	33	20
Occupational continuity rates by stratum of father's job[b] (%)							
High white-collar	67	0	—	—	—	80	—
Low white-collar	13	0	—	17	—	10	—
Skilled	42	0	40	43	—	38	50
Semiskilled	—	0	18	—	0	—	50
Unskilled	27	0	22	21	33	32	12
All	32	0	22	30	21	34	24
Association between strata of father's job[b] and son's last job (gamma)	0.06	—	0.21	0.03	0.41	0.23	0.05
Number	(107)	(17)	(49)	(54)	(24)	(53)	(25)

[a]Born 1905–19.
[b]Father's job at time of son's first job.

Cleveland was an industrial center; thus immigrants moved largely within the ranks of the working class. No more than one-fifth of the first generation ever climed into white-collar occupations. The newcomers, then, experienced little mobility between classes, and a large proportion spent their lives in the same or related occupational strata. Their sons' careers, however, were significantly different. They had a better chance of gaining middle-class status than their fathers had had; the sons born between 1910 and 1919 moved between occupational strata in larger proportions than their fathers; and few sons inherited their fathers' occupations.

The outlines of the mobility patterns of immigrants and their children become sharper in a comparative perspective. Table 14 juxtaposes the experience of the Cleveland sample with that of a Boston sample. Clearly, an Italian immigrant in Boston had only a slightly better chance than one in Cleveland of ending his career in white-collar employment. But startling differences appear when one compares the immigrants with the native-born. More than half the men born in Boston between 1880 and 1889 began their careers in white-collar occupations, while only 11 percent of the Cleveland sample initiated their careers so fortunately. Neither in Boston nor in Cleveland could the immigrants close the gap between newcomers and natives during their lives. Thus the first generation generally worked at manual jobs; only a trickle ever gained white-collar occupations.

Within the blue-collar world, however, immigrants moved from occupation to occupation in proportions as great as those for the native-born of native parentage. Table 15 shows a remarkable similarity in the rates of interclass mobility and occupational continuity among four samples. In this sense, the careers of immigrants in Boston and Cleveland did not differ significantly from native-born Bostonians of native parentage or from the populations of Norristown and the six other cities. The association between

Table 14. Interclass career mobility rates of the first generation, Boston and Cleveland (percent).

| | Boston, born 1880-90 | | | | | Cleveland, born 1870-90 | | | |
	All	Ir.	It.	W. Eur.	E. Eur.	All	It.	Rum.	Sl.
Starting white-collar	23	33	10	9	34	11	16	14	2
Ending white-collar	39	33	33	26	49	20	24	24	12
Climbing blue-collar starters	28	25	28	19	38	14	15	19	12
Skidding white-collar starters	33	50	20	0	29	33	33	20	—
Number	(206)	(33)	(48)	(35)	(61)	(454)	(230)	(69)	(155)

Source: The Boston data is drawn from Stephan Thernstrom, "Immigrants and WASPs: Ethnic Differences in Occupational Mobility in Boston, 1890–1940," in Thernstrom and Richard Sennett, eds., *Nineteenth-Century Cities: Essays in the New Urban History* (New Haven, 1969), table 8, p. 156.

Table 15. Interclass career mobility and occupational continuity rates of selected samples for ten-year periods, 1880–1950.[a]

	Boston, NBNP, 1880–90	Boston, FB, 1880–90	Cleveland, FB, 1910–19	Norristown, unk., 1910–20	Six Cities, unk., 1940–50
Interclass career mobility rates (%)					
Climbing sons of blue-collar fathers	15	7	9	9	11
Skidding sons of white-collar fathers	8	12	22	8	20
All leaving class origins	10	8	9	8	15
Occupational continuity rates by stratum of first job (%)					
High white-collar	89	90	79	93	62
Low white-collar	72	75	55	66	58
Skilled	81	91	73	86	60
Semiskilled	68	68	72	68	64
Unskilled	57	77	70	70	64
All	75	81	70	76	62
Association between strata of first and last jobs of decade (gamma)	0.87	0.87	0.75	0.78	—
Number	(210)	(211)	(300)	(3,905)	(1,707)

Sources: The Boston sample is from Thernstrom, "Immigrants and WASPs," table 3, p. 138. The Norristown data are reported in Sidney Goldstein, *Patterns of Mobility, 1910–1950: The Norristown Study* (Philadelphia, 1958), table 38, p. 169. Gladys L. Palmer, *Labor Mobility in Six Cities* (New York, 1954), table 48, p. 115, presents the information on Chicago, Los Angeles, New Haven, Philadelphia, St. Paul, and San Francisco. (The tabular arrangement in the Palmer report makes calculation of the gamma measure impossible.)

[a]NBNP = native-born of native parentage; FB = foreign-born; unk. = unspecified parentage.

the strata of the first and last jobs of the decade was moderately strong for all samples. Thus immigrants were not confined to one occupational stratum more than any other group in the population. Rather, the major difference was that they had entered the society at the bottom and could not make up the difference in the course of one generation.

The immigrants did make gains, however, and they passed them on to their sons. The two birth cohorts of the second generation began their careers with an advantage over their fathers, and they steadily built on this beginning. But, as table 16 reveals, Cleveland men of Italian, Rumanian, and Slovak origins required yet another generation to approach their contemporaries of two or more generations in Boston. The major characteristic already discerned about the occupational careers of the immigrants — the relatively low proportions both starting and ending in white-collar occupations — continued into the second generation.

Still, there remains the more important problem: What was the meaning of ethnicity in finding a place in the urban occupational structure? Thernstrom discovered in his recent study of Boston that the second generation was peculiarly restless and mobile and that they moved across occupational lines in greater proportions than either the immigrants or the native-born of native parentage.[18] Table 17 establishes that this was the case in Cleveland as well. The second generation born in the city crossed class lines at rates similar to those for the samples from Norristown and San Jose and to those from a national urban sample. The sons of Cleveland's immigrants, however, experienced a much higher rate of mobility between occupational strata than the other three urban samples. At the age of thirty, no more than a quarter of Cleveland's second generation remained in their fathers' jobs, while between a third and a half of the sons of the other urban samples continued in the same careers as their fathers. The association between the occupa-

Table 16. Interclass career mobility rates of the second generation, Boston and Cleveland (percent).

	Boston		Cleveland	
	born 1880–89	born 1900–09	born 1900–09	born 1910–19
Starting white-collar	51	40	25	30
Ending white-collar	61	47	26	33
Climbing blue-collar starters	32	23	14	19
Skidding white-collar starters	13	17	37	40
Number	(215)	(146)	(124)	(187)

Source: The Boston sample is from Thernstrom, "Immigrants and WASPs," table 8, p. 156.

tional origins of the second generation and the jobs they held at mid-career was notably weaker for the Cleveland sample than for the other three.

Ethnic origins had a different impact upon different generations. The immigrants and their sons remained largely confined to blue-collar occupations. In this sense these three immigrant groups continued in their entrance status for at least two generations. But a radical change occurred in the transition from the first to the second generation. While the fathers' career mobility closely resembled that of the native-born population of native parentage, the sons broke with their origins decisively. The second generation was more highly mobile between occupational strata than urban populations generally.

Ethnic origins, then, continued to be an important factor in the allocation of both fathers and sons within the urban occupational structure. While the fathers experienced important continuities in

Table 17. Intergenerational career mobility and occupational continuity rates of selected samples, 1930–1952.[a]

	San Jose, unk., 1933–34	Cleveland, NBFP, 1930–40	Cleveland, NBFP, 1940–50	USA, unk., 1945	Norristown, unk., 1952
Interclass career mobility rates (%)					
Climbing sons of blue-collar fathers	32	25	30	34	36
Skidding sons of white-collar fathers	39	70	50	14	29
All leaving class origins	36	31	33	25	31
Occupational continuity rates by stratum of father's job (%)					
High white-collar	25	0	75	53	53
Low white-collar	45	17	10	60	15
Skilled	42	40	33	31	33
Semiskilled	29	0	20	43	39
Unskilled	42	26	21	37	14
All	42	26	25	46	35
Association between strata of father's job and son's last job (gamma)	0.35	0.12	0.09	0.49	0.34
Number	(1.547)	(81)	(92)	(637)	(544)

Sources: The San Jose data are from Percy E. Davidson and H. Dewey Anderson, *Occupational Mobility in an American Community* (Stanford, 1937), table 4, p. 20. The two Cleveland columns are separate samples of two birth cohorts and represent jobs held by sons (aged thirty and over) of immigrants within each ten-year period. Richard Centers, "Occupational Mobility of Urban Occupational Strata," *American Sociological Review*, 13 (1948), 197–203, reports the national sample (of urban whites). The Norristown figures are from Sidney Goldstein, ed., *The Norristown Study* (Philadelphia, 1961), p. 109.

[a]NBFP = native-born foreign parentage; unk. = unspecified parentage.

their careers, the sons' careers were characteristically discontinuous with their origins. Thus the major problem is to discover why the intergenerational mobility patterns of second-generation Americans developed so differently from both immigrants and natives.

6 Sources of Mobility: Family and Education

Cleveland's immigrants have thus far been viewed as two discrete generations, the foreign-born fathers and the native-born sons. This perspective was necessary in order to discern occupational distribution at important points in the careers of both generations, and to follow trends in the social mobility of 765 persons over a forty-year period. But this austere approach must now be abandoned in favor of an exploration of some important relationships among social mobility, family patterns, and educational opportunity.

In the following discussion 250 families are divided into three groups according to a broad classification of the fathers' first employment — low-skilled, skilled, and nonmanual. For my purposes here, the distinction between unskilled and semiskilled and between low nonmanual and high nonmanual occupational strata are unimportant, so I have collapsed these groups into two broad categories, low-skilled and nonmanual. Each group of families, in turn, is further divided into social mobility patterns according to the careers of both the fathers and the sons. This approach makes it easier to identify the family's role in social mobility and to discern the sources of generational change.[1]

One hundred seventy-two of the 250 immigrant heads of families

117

who remained in Cleveland for two or more decades began their careers as unskilled laborers. The various destinies of these families are crudely classified here as high-mobility, intermediate-mobility, and static careers. The high-mobility category encompasses families with at least one member who entered a white-collar occupation during the period from 1910 to 1950. Those families whose members all remained confined to unskilled and semiskilled jobs and never accumulated more than $1,000 in real and personal property occupy the static slot. The intermediate classification covers families whose fortunes fell somewhere between these groups.

Forty-two of the 172 families of unskilled starters, or 24 percent, did not advance into either skilled or nonmanual work and did not acquire property. Fathers and sons both spent their lives as common laborers, station porters, and street workers; a few acquired some skill — to operate a drill press, for example. More than a third of the Slovak families starting unskilled fell into this category. The experience of Jozef and Karolina M. was typical.[2] The couple had three children between 1906 and 1909, none of whom attended school past the ninth grade. Juliús, the older of the two sons, acquired some skill as a cutter in an iron foundry, while Jozef, like his father, remained a laborer. The family apparently found it economical to live together, for all three children stayed at home until their early thirties.

A slightly smaller proportion of Rumanians lived out their lives in this impoverished segment of the working class. Andreiu G., for instance, married Ana I. in 1912, and they produced four girls and two boys between 1913 and 1929. The father's lifelong employment was as a riveter in a shipyard near the family's rented house on Tillman Avenue. The older son, George, finished high school in 1925, but he was still working as a riveter in 1950. Nicolae, the youngest of the family, dropped out of school in the ninth grade and became a casual laborer.

Italian families exhibited an important contrast to this depressing picture, for only 14 percent of the families with unskilled heads remained in the propertyless, low-skill universe. Italian families were much more likely than the other two groups to invest in a house and a small lot or to move into white-collar occupations. But those few who remained in the static group had lives as grim as the others. Nicolà C., for example, married Carla C. in 1907, and she bore him six children over the next eleven years. Two of the three boys managed to complete the ninth grade, while Nicolà, the youngest, finished only the eighth. Like their father, all three worked as casual laborers and street sweepers into their early forties. No member of the family, as far as the record shows, ever acquired any property.

Between static families and those who gained middle-class status was the largest group of families, whose stories reflect modest improvement over their origins. The families in this category had at least one member who had gained an occupational skill or had a head of the household holding at least $1,000 in real and personal property. Thirty-seven of the 172 families, or 22 percent, had at least one member who rose into a skilled occupation. In twenty-nine of these cases, it was the father who worked his way through the occupational ranks of shop and factory, while in only eight instances was the son alone responsible for the family's advance.[3] Francesco S. was typical of the immigrant men. He married Anna Di P. in 1901, and six children were born to them between 1904 and 1917. The father served as a plumber's helper for the first fifteen years of his career, then became a master plumber sometime between 1920 and 1930. None of his four boys got past the eighth grade. Nevertheless, Luigi, the oldest, became a skilled machinist after a long apprenticeship, while Urbano, the next oldest, worked most of his life as a bartender. However, the two youngest, Giovanni and Alberto, spent their lives in casual labor. The distinctly qualified success of Francesco S. in passing on his skilled status to his sons was characteristic of the Italian families in this category.

The sons often fell below the occupational grade attained by the father.

Most Slovak families followed the pattern of Ján M.'s family. The father began his career as a furnace worker, then became a grinder, and finally, in 1940, an assembler. Both sons, Michal and Andrej, finished the ninth grade and were apprenticed in their father's foundry. The two young men became assemblers before they were thirty. Like Ján M., other Slovak fathers were able to pass on their skilled status as cement finishers, machinists, or rollers to most of their sons.

The success of the Slovaks in this regard and the relative failure of the Italian requires further comment, for it was in this continuity that the skilled traditions very often recalled by second- and third-generation Slovaks had their origins. The divergence between the two ethnic groups stands out most sharply in the fact that more than half the sons of Italian immigrants gaining skilled status fell back into unskilled jobs, while only 6 percent of second-generation Slovaks found themselves in similar circumstances. Educational patterns cannot account for this striking difference, for in both groups about a fourth of the sons received at least a high school education. Rather, the source of the stability in the Slovak families was the success of the sons in finding semiskilled jobs, from which they quickly moved into skilled and nonmanual occupations. If the careers of the sons between the ages of twenty and twenty-four are examined, the advantages of second-generation Slovaks become readily apparent. More than half the Slovaks in this cohort already held apprenticeships or semiskilled jobs, from which they stepped into skilled or white-collar occupations. Thus between the ages of twenty-five and twenty-nine, three-fourths of the sons of Slovak fathers gaining skilled status had either advanced into a skilled occupation or joined the middle class. In both age cohorts, on the other hand, more than half the Italian sons remained in unskilled jobs.

The sons of Italian laborers who had risen in occupational skill did not generally profit by their fathers' advancement, while the sons of Slovak men with similar careers enjoyed consistent gains. Three possible explanations should be considered. The Slovaks may have had smaller families and thus fewer drains on their resources; they may have held less property and could therefore invest more in their sons; or they may have provided a different kind of help to their sons, aid particularly conducive to mobility within the working class. On the first two counts, the differences between the two groups were too small to account for the wide divergence in occupational inheritance. Both Italian and Slovak laboring fathers gaining occupational skill had relatively large families of about four children. In fact, the Slovaks had slightly larger families than the Italians. Two-thirds of the members of both groups held property of about the same median value of $3,500.

The story of the family of Michal S. suggests that the third possibility offers a partial explanation. Michal and Antonia had seven children between 1900 and 1910, all of whom finished the ninth grade. The father remained a rail hand in a rolling mill all his life but managed to acquire a small lot and tiny house in 1920. All six sons became skilled machinists, while Margaret, the daughter, became a nurse. The significant fact is that three older sons and the daughter continued to live in the parental household into their early thirties while the youngest, Štefan, stayed at home for ten years after his marriage. This residential pattern is chacteristic of eleven of the thirteen Slovak families in this category, while less than 10 percent of the Italian families lived in such households. One can only guess, since the full composition of the households is not known, but the residential patterns suggest that Slovak families furnished some essential support during this prolonged stay in the parental home. As will become clear later, certain Italian families also sponsored their children's mobility, but not in this specific manner.

Within the broad category of intermediate-mobility families, a second group entered the stable working class by acquiring a significant amount of property, even though they remained in the low-skill, low-pay occupational universe.[4] Twenty-four percent of the families of low-skilled starters came into at least $1,000 in property between 1910 and 1930. The tiny group of four families who managed to accumulate $8,000 or more in property represent a triumph of provident habits. A Slovak, Tomaš N., for instance, acquired $8,500 in real property between 1910 and 1930 on the niggardly earnings of a common laborer. His three sons dropped out of school in the ninth grade. Joseph, the oldest, became a clerk after a long career in manual labor, while two of the younger sons worked at the benches of a machine shop. All three sons lived at home into their early thirties, and they may have contributed some of their earnings toward the purchase of property.

A more typical figure among these propertied laborers was the Slovak Johann H., who acquired $1,600 worth of property in the early 1920s. Something is known about the careers of all three of his sons. Štefan, the oldest, worked first as a laborer, then as a press operator in a machine shop. His brother Ján followed exactly the same career, and Jozef, the youngest, finished the ninth grade and became a warehouse clerk. This story is not so spectacular as that of Tomaš N., but a common theme runs through both accounts: at least one of the sons of both families moved into a white-collar occupation.

The career of the Italian Salvatore O. illustrates this relationship between property and occupational mobility in characteristic form. Salvatore worked as a furnace hand for twenty years, but he gained the position of a puddler in a steel plant for the last twenty years of his life. The move brought a modest increase in wages, with which he began to purchase a $5,000 home. The oldest son, Nicola, unluckily finished the ninth grade in 1929 and was forced to get a work permit for casual labor. But the two younger sons graduated from East Technical High School and went on to Ohio State University. In the late 1940s, both were running substantial businesses.

The acquisition of property, then, enhanced the opportunity of at least one son to move into middle-class occupations. The reason is not far to seek, for the same provident habits that enabled these penurious laborers to save enough money to purchase property also implied the ability to sponsor their children's education. In fact, eight of the fifteen sons who were born to men originally low-skilled and who attended college came from this occupationally static but propertied segment of the working class. The acquisition of $3,000 or more of property marked the point at which fathers in this group seemed especially willing to sponsor their sons' education. Several of these families had one or two houses to let, the income from which supplemented the meager earnings of the head of the household. Property thus was an additional resource of families who could claim few discernible gains in the labor market.[5]

Fifty-three of the 172 families who started in an unskilled status, or about one-third, acquired white-collar status. In twenty-four of these cases, it was the father who moved into some business or set up his own; his mobility thus took the form of proprietorship, which required some entrepreneurial ability but no special skills. The story of Nicolae C., a Rumanian immigrant who arrived in Cleveland about 1908, illustrates the rise of an immigrant laborer in classic fashion. Nicolae married Ludovica S. in 1910; they had two children, Nicolae, Jr., in 1913, and Vincent, in 1915. The father began his career on a street gang, and then between 1918 and 1920 he tried bartending in one of the numerous Rumanian saloons along Detroit Avenue. But in 1920 he returned to manual labor, this time as a riveter in a shipyard. Over the next ten years he acquired the skills of a boilermaker, and incidentally, accumulated $5,000 worth of residential property. By that time, his older son had graduated from high school, and Nicolae was able to send

him off to Ohio State. The older son became an accountant, while
the younger son graduated from Ohio State and went on to dental
school at the University of Illinois. In the mid-1940s he returned
to Cleveland to set up his own practice.

The cumulative character of the mobility of Nicolae C.'s family
presents a strong contrast to the fortunes of Italian and Slovak
families whose fathers climbed into the middle class. Jozef and
Juliana H., a Slovak couple, had three children between 1903 and
1910. The father found his first job as a laborer, moved on to
become a machinist, and in the late twenties organized a contracting firm. He purchased a home for about $5,000 in 1929. The
oldest son, Paul, dropped out of school in the ninth grade in 1919
and worked as a janitor. Jozef, Jr., however, was able to finish high
school and to become a teller at the Cleveland Trust Company.
Like the family of Jozef H., those of Ján B. and Karol K. produced
only one successor to the father's white-collar status; the other
sons skidded into the working class.

The process by which the son was likely to follow his father's
career is illustrated in the life of Francesco S., born to Italian immigrant parents in 1918. His father had begun his career as a laborer,
then had established a small butchershop, and had finally bought
a fruit store in the late twenties. Frank's older brother, Anthony,
finished the tenth grade and drove a delivery truck for his father.
But Frank, who also dropped out of school in the tenth grade, got
his first job as a clerk in the neighborhood A & P, and he went on
to become the manager of a large suburban food store in the late
1940s. Even though Frank began his career in a low white-collar
position, he had to repeat his father's rise into the world of business.

Few Italian and Slovak fathers who climbed into the middle
class managed to pass on their higher status to their sons. This
fact emerges most forcefully when one examines the education
which the sons of these mobile men received. Not one son of an

Italian or Slovak climber into white-collar occupations received a college education; more than three-quarters, in fact, did not get past the ninth grade. Significantly, however, every son of a Rumanian climber received a college education, and all the daughters at least finished high school. The consistency of this divergence in educational achievement represents a major difference between the Rumanians and the other two groups. Mobile Rumanian fathers regularly sponsored their sons' education to a fuller extent than either the Italians or the Slovaks.

Twenty-nine of the fifty-three families in the high-mobility category were placed there because one of the sons managed to gain white-collar status. Unlike the immigrants themselves, who usually moved into the middle class through the ownership of a business, the sons frequently advanced their status through the acquisition of clerical, managerial, or professional training. Nicolà and Antonio V., for instance, sons of an Italian laborer, made it through high school and Western Reserve University to become schoolteachers. All three sons of Biagio M., a propertyless laborer, graduated from East Technical High School and went on to manage grocery firms and wholesale houses in the forties and early fifties. In each instance of this kind of mobility among the sons of unskilled laborers, education played a crucial role. This was one of the few forms of sponsorship which a family in this position could extend to its members. It is not surprising to find, then, that the twenty-nine families whose sons became clerks, managers, and professionals were significantly more prosperous than the rest of the unskilled starters. Like the family of Andrej G., whose five sons all became clerks or managers, these families were likely to acquire between $3,000 and $5,000 worth of property. The additional resources commanded by these propertied families meant that their sons could delay their choice of career while extending their education.

Forty-five of the 250 families who spent twenty years or more in Cleveland, or about one-fifth, were headed by an immigrant who had entered a skilled occupation upon his arrival. This segment was most important in the Italian and Rumanian communities, for it comprised more than one-fifth of each group, while less than one-tenth of Slovak families began as fortunately. In the case of the Italians, as I have already shown, the immigrants possessed some skills acquired in the homeland villages. Leonardo P., for instance, had been a mason in the village of Ripalimosano, in the Abruzzi, and he immediately found a bricklaying job when he got to Cleveland in 1904. He married Teresa C. in 1907. Three of their sons also worked in skilled capacities, although the fourth never advanced past casual labor. Two of Leonardo's three daughters finished high school, a good record compared with most Italian families. The striking feature of all these families' careers was the effectiveness with which their children either acquired occupational skills or advanced into the middle class. As one examines the few documents of these families which remain, one encounters their remarkable solidarity and resilience. The family of the Slovak Ján D., a skilled machinist who managed to acquire $10,000 in property during his forty active years, serves as another example of this prosperous segment of the working class. Both his sons entered apprenticeships in their seventeenth year, and by the age of thirty they were experienced coremakers.

As the comparison made earlier between Slovak and Italian laborers who had moved into skilled positions showed, the important element in this continuity was not a technical education but rather an early training in the shop. Between the ages of twenty and twenty-four more than half the sons of skilled starters occupied semiskilled and skilled jobs; before they reached the age of thirty, more than three-fifths had gained skilled positions.

An even more striking characteristic of the families of skilled starters was that two-fifths moved into the middle class. In five of these nineteen cases, the father made the transition. Four of these upwardly mobile men were Italian carpenters and masons who set up their own contracting businesses. Angelo Michele I., for instance, exercised his old craft of masonry for twenty years before he organized a contracting firm in 1927. One of his three sons, Giovanni, finished East Technical High School in 1926 and went on to a design school. He got a job with the monument firm of Giuseppe Carabelli, for whom the father had worked when he first arrived in Cleveland. The lone member of the other two ethnic groups to shift from his skilled origins to an entrepreneurial occupation was the Rumanian Ioan M., who bought a saloon.

In the remainder of the nineteen cases, the families of skilled starters moved into the middle class because of a son's gain. The fascinating family of Biagio L. illuminates some of the processes at work in these family transitions. Biagio married Rosa A. in 1905, and they had five boys and two girls between 1906 and 1917. The father remained a mechanic all his life, but the four sons who survived to age twenty all acquired superior educations. Francesco, the oldest, graduated from the city's old elite high school, Central, in 1925, then entered Ohio State and went on to dental school. Giuseppe graduated from East Technical High School in 1929 and pursued a successful career as a technical illustrator. James followed his older brother through Central High School and graduated from Cleveland College in 1934. The youngest boy, Anthony, studied in the School of Social Work at Western Reserve and became a case worker at Hiram House, a social settlement in the midst of the old Sicilian colony.

In the careers of Biagio L.'s sons, then, education again appears as a central theme. The Italian families in this group, in fact, produced a disproportionate number of college graduates, for nearly half of the total graduates in the sample derived from these households. Thus most of the sons moving into middle-class occupations were professionals — social workers, teachers, physicians. The higher wages of their skilled fathers provided much greater resources for sponsoring the children's educations. If Sabino F., for example, could acquire over $30,000 in property on a bricklayer's earnings and still pay the way of two of his sons through medical school, then the advantages of these families were substantial. These families were, on the whole, remarkably prosperous, for the median property holding was $8,000.

Only thirty-three of the 250 families, or 13 percent, had heads who had started as white-collar workers. All of these families were Italians or Rumanians. (As mentioned earlier, no Slovaks entered Cleveland in nonmanual capacities.) The typical Italian immigrant businessman opened a small fruit stand, worked his way up to a small grocery store, and acquired about $5,000 in property. The families in this category, however, lacked some strength, some willingness to see their sons through the critical early years of their careers, for only about 5 percent of the sons earned even a high school diploma. This left more than half the sons in unskilled and semiskilled jobs, while the few who managed to remain in the middle class had to undertake the same laborious routes taken by their fathers. Thus the third of the second-generation Italians who persisted in white-collar situations did so by virtue of entrepreneurial ability and proprietorship.

The Rumanian families, on the other hand, followed a conspicuously different course. More than 90 percent of the sons finished high school, and 70 percent of those went on to a college or professional education. The middle-class positions which they found were professional or managerial. The story of the family of Ioan C. is typical of the Rumanians. The father established a poolroom and coffee house about 1915; four years later he bought out the neighboring dance hall as well. The oldest son, Iosif, graduated from West Technical High School in 1927 and received an appointment to the Naval Academy in 1930, but he chose to attend Wittenberg College instead. He subsequently served as an executive in a Rumanian national mutual benefit association. His brother John graduated from West Tech in 1930 and attended Cleveland College of Embalming. He established a funeral house which still serves a predominantly Greek Orthodox clientele from an impressive building on Detroit Avenue. The stories of these remarkable families should make one doubt the pessimism with which many sons and grandsons view the past — and yet, of course, they were a very small part of the community.

If one source of mobility was the sponsorship of the family, then an important index of the family's capacity to facilitate social mobility should have been family size. An immigrant man and wife, starting out with few resources in a new urban setting, might be expected to restrict family commitments in order to compete in the city's labor market. One would expect upwardly mobile families, then, to control the number of children born so as to limit long-term expenditures.[6]

The information from my Cleveland study, however, does not lend consistent support to this hypothesis, for no clear relationship develops between fathers' entrance status and the size of completed families. Italian and Slovak marriages resulted in relatively large families no matter what the origins of the husband, while the variations in the size of Rumanian families were tiny. As table 18 shows, the father's first job in Cleveland had little relation to the size of his family.

If one looks at the families in terms of mobility, on the other hand, one does see a consistent effort to limit family size among upwardly mobile Rumanians. Rumanian fathers who climbed into the middle class were heads of significantly smaller families than those who remained in manual occupations, while Italian families who gained middle-class status were only slightly smaller than their working-class counterparts and similarly mobile Slovak families were larger than all other families. Thus the Rumanian families who achieved white-collar status had fewer children than any

Table 18. Mean number of children ever born to immigrant families.

	It.	Rum.	Sl.
Father's first job			
White-collar	3.71	2.57	—
Skilled	4.88	2.67	3.67
Low-skilled	4.23	2.66	4.22
All	4.29	2.65	4.16
Number of families	(164)	(48)	(69)
Father's interclass career mobility			
Climbing blue-collar starters	3.93	2.25	5.00
Skidding white-collar starters	3.83	—	—
Ending white-collar	3.79	2.40	4.63
Ending blue-collar	4.32	3.15	4.04
Number of families	(126)	(37)	(54)
Highest job of fathers starting unskilled			
White-collar	4.45	2.20	5.00
Skilled	3.69	2.00	4.00
Static	4.22	2.67	4.31
Number of families	(73)	(25)	(41)

other occupational group, while the differences within the Italian group actually shrank because of the mobility of relatively large families. And among the Slovaks the relationship between mobility and family size is contrary to one's expectations.

These gross patterns of fertility, however, call for a finer analysis, for family limitation should have been most useful to the families beginning at the bottom of the occupational hierarchy. The meager wages of laborers and operatives meant that families had to husband their resources carefully if they were to support their sons' start in life. The third panel of table 18 confirms the general relationship discovered earlier: Rumanians climbing from unskilled into skilled and nonmanual occupations consistently limited the size of their families. The relationship here is the classic one appearing in most studies of differential fertility.[7] Both Italians and Slovaks, on the other hand, had larger families as they moved up into white-collar jobs.

The Rumanians present a fascinating picture of rural immigrants adopting urban norms of small families and restricted commitments. Italians and Slovaks, however, did not sacrifice traditional family values through the limitation of births.[8] Rather, upwardly mobile parents in these ethnic groups seem to have had enough confidence to rear larger families than those who remained in the same class.

But my major concern here is to discern how these different fertility patterns may have affected the mobility of the sons. It is in this regard that the potentially greater resources of small families may have had an important impact, if indeed family size mattered at all. Again, the analysis concentrates on immigrants who began their careers as unskilled laborers, since they represent the group in which prosperity and limited families are most likely to be linked.

The first place one might expect to find a significant association between small family size and upward mobility is in the education of the sons. Presumably, families with fewer children — especially those with fathers starting out in low-paying jobs — could afford to sponsor their sons' education to a fuller extent than large families. Table 19 indicates that this relationship was very weak, however. Children from small Italian families (those with fewer than four children) had a small advantage over children from larger families, an advantage that grew somewhat as sons reached the age of college entrance. Rumanian and Slovak children, on the other hand, derived mixed benefits from their membership in smaller

Table 19. Highest educational achievement of sons of unskilled immigrants (percent).[a]

| | Number of children ever born to family | | | | | | | |
| | 1-3 | | | 4-6 | | | 7 or more | |
	It.	Rum.	Sl.	It.	Rum.	Sl.	It.	Sl.
Junior high school	64	57	82	72	64	77	92	69
Senior high school	27	0	12	20	21	23	8	25
College or professional school	9	43	6	8	99	0	0	6
Number	(11)	(7)	(17)	(64)	(14)	(39)	(12)	(16)

[a]Percentages sometimes do not add to 100 because of rounding.

households. Children from the larger Slovak families, in fact, had a slightly better chance of earning at least a high school diploma. Thus the table shows that family size had little to do with the opportunities of second-generation immigrants to pursue an education.

Hard on this conclusion, however, follows the surprising discovery that family size had an important impact on the occupational mobility of the sons of unskilled Italian laborers, for 44 percent of the sons born to small families began their careers in white-collar jobs, as table 20 shows. Over the course of their careers, members of small Italian families enjoyed increasing advantages in competing for high-status positions. At age thirty, when the careers of these men seem to have been set for life, 83 percent of the sons from small Italian families occupied middle-class positions, while only 47 percent of the sons from large households enjoyed similar status, and no members of the largest families. Neither the Rumanians nor the Slovaks, on the other hand, exhibited a strong association between family size and occupational mobility.

Family size thus impinged on social mobility only in specific instances. Italian sons from small families clearly had a better opportunity to enter white-collar positions than those from large families. Yet the factor of family size accounts for little of the mobility of second-generation Italians, since so few families limited births. On the other hand, Rumanians probably enjoyed the greatest advantage, because their families were consistently smaller than those of either the Italians or the Slovaks. The Rumanians' rapid adaptation to the pattern of characteristically small urban families may have given the whole group an important edge over the Italians and the Slovaks in the sponsorship of their children's mobility. The generally higher educational achievement of second-generation Rumanians probably stems in part, then, from the immigrant generation's effort to limit family size.

Table 20. Intergenerational career mobility rates of sons of unskilled immigrants (percent).[a]

| | Number of children ever born to family | | | | | | | |
| | 1-3 | | | 4-6 | | | 7 or more | |
	It.	Rum.	Sl.	It.	Rum.	Sl.	It.	Sl.
Son's first occupation								
Unskilled	56	63	83	56	60	43	71	60
Skilled	0	0	8	18	30	26	29	10
White-collar	44	38	8	27	10	31	0	30
Number	(9)	(8)	(12)	(57)	(10)	(39)	(14)	(10)
Son's last occupation								
Unskilled	17	34	77	27	25	24	72	58
Skilled	0	0	11	26	50	35	27	0
White-collar	83	67	11	47	25	41	0	42
Number	(6)	(6)	(9)	(34)	(4)	(17)	(11)	(7)

[a]Percentages sometimes do not add to 100 because of rounding.

The son's transition from the status of his parents to that of his adult occupational role was mediated by schooling; hence education was a second important source of mobility. The acquisition of an occupational role involved two stages: the transition from the status of the family to a certain level of educational achievement, and the step from a given educational category to an occupational status. The assertion, then, that education is an important means of mobility implies at least three things: first, that there is a strong connection between education and subsequent occupational status (that is, education determines occupation to a large extent); second, that there is a high rate of educational mobility, so that children coming from different social strata have about the same chance of reaching various educational levels; and third, that there are no appreciable delayed effects of the father's status on the son's career, in the sense that the father's status exerts little impact on the son's choice of occupation beyond its influence on education.[9] The isolation of these three processes allows one to examine in some detail the actual pattern of education and mobility in immigrant families.

The statement that there is a strong association between education and social mobility describes, of course, a general relationship. The great majority of men holding university degrees pursue professional careers, while those with ninth-grade educations customarily work at manual jobs. Cleveland's immigrants were no exception to this general rule. Three-fourths of the college-educated sons held professional positions, while the proportion of sons occupying white-collar jobs shrank relentlessly as the educational level dropped. More refined tabulations taking account of ethnic origins exhibit the same consistent relationship. Education did then provide one avenue of mobility for second-generation immigrants.

The impact of schooling on a community depends, however, on whether educational opportunities are open to all, regardless of the status of their parents. The Cleveland data indicate that paren-

tal status did not exert important influence on the second generation's access to education. Thus, as table 21 shows, the sons of
laboring men had about the same chance for a high school education as the sons of skilled machinists, clerks, or businessmen. Had
there been a consistent relationship between the father's career
and the son's educational achievement, the measures of association
would depart much further from zero than they do. The consistently low scores indicate that access to education was open to all
the sons, whatever their father's career.

Neither the close relationship between educational and occupational status nor the relatively open access to educational
opportunities establishes education as the major source of intergenerational mobility. Even though there was a close association
between educational achievement and entrance into nonmanual
occupations,[10] still about a third of the second-generation immigrants who climbed into white-collar positions got there without
the benefit of even a high school education. Education does
little to help explain the source of this movement. And if the
father's status had little effect on the educational career of the son,
as mentioned above, still the impact of the son's origin may have
extended beyond the termination of schooling into his active life.
Hence the fortunate third of the second generation who enjoyed
middle-class status without benefit of education may have profited instead from the gains of their upwardly mobile fathers. Here
the family of Salvatore G., who figured in the discussion of career
mobility in chapter 5, may serve as an example. None of Salvatore's three sons finished high school, yet each became an officer
in the father's wholesale distribution business.

Of the continuing impact of the father's status on the son's
career there can be little doubt. Table 22 illustrates the relationship
in a simple manner. Sons with little schooling, as a comparison of
the proportion of junior high school graduates in columns 1 and
2 shows, began their careers similarly distributed in nonmanual

Table 21. Highest educational achievement of sons of immigrants according to father's highest occupation (percent).[a]

| | Father's highest occupation | | | | | | | | |
| | Unskilled | | | Skilled | | | White-collar | | |
	It.	Rum.	Sl.	It.	Rum.	Sl.	It.	Rum.	Sl.
Junior high school	71	57	81	60	64	71	78	31	71
Senior high school	23	21	16	22	36	21	17	13	29
College or professional school	6	21	3	17	0	7	4	56	0
Number	(48)	(14)	(37)	(43)	(11)	(28)	(46)	(16)	(17)

[a]Percentages sometimes do not add to 100 because of rounding.

Table 22. Entrance of the second generation into white-collar occupations.

Son's highest educational achievement	(1) Sons of white-collar origins persisting in white-collar occupations (%)	(2) Sons of blue-collar origins moving into white-collar occupations (%)	Index of inequality: (1)/(2) $\times 100^a$	Number White-collar	Blue-collar
First job					
Junior high school	21	18	117	(39)	(110)
Senior high school	64	33	194	(11)	(30)
College or professional school	100	79	127	(11)	(14)
Last job					
Junior high school	36	19	189	(22)	(59)
Senior high school	100	44	227	(6)	(16)
College or professional school	100	86	116	(7)	(7)

[a]100 = perfect equality. Thus, the further the number in this column departs from that figure, the more disproportionate is the representation of sons of the same educational achievement but different social origins in white-collar occupations.

occupations. The index of inequality departs very little from a score of perfect equality. The same was true at the other extreme, among those sons who earned a college degree. Among those with a high school diploma, however, the sons of fathers who spent most of their careers in nonmanual occupations had a significant head start over the sons of working-class fathers. As the second panel of the table shows, this gap between men of similar educational background but different social origins widened as the sons matured in their careers. Thus the index of inequality increases from 194 for the first jobs of those with a high school education to 227 for their last jobs. The fathers' status also significantly affected the careers of sons who acquired little education, for despite this shortcoming, sons of white-collar fathers made important gains during their lifetimes, advances not shared in any sense by working-class sons. The college-educated, as one might expect, experienced little such disparity in their careers.

One sees, then, that education had a close relationship to the social mobility of the sons of immigrants; that education was generally available to the second generation, regardless of social origins; but that education did not function independently of parental status. Rather, the status of the parents limited the impact of education on the careers of the sons, especially within the group that graduated from high school. The gap between sons of middle-class and those of working-class fathers appeared as sons got their first jobs, and it continued to widen as they reached the age of thirty. Thus while education facilitated the entry of the second generation into white-collar positions, the more important fact in their careers was the fortunes of their fathers.

The discovery of the impact of the father's status on the son's occupational career raises a critical issue in this study of the social mobility of Cleveland's immigrant families. Was social mobility typically a cumulative process? Did mobile fathers generally pass along their own gains to their sons, or did each generation repeat the story of the last?

Table 23 tabulates gross patterns of the second generation's career mobility according to the father's highest occupational status. Sons of fathers who remained in the working class for the

Table 23. Cumulative career mobility rates of the second generation (percent).

| | Highest occupational status of father | | | | | | | |
| | Blue-collar | | | | White-collar | | | |
	All	It.	Rum.	Sl.	All	It.	Rum.	Sl.
All sons								
Starting white-collar	23	25	21	18	49	35	71	40
Ending white-collar	25	25	43	19	60	43	93	40
Climbing blue-collar starters	15	15	20	14	30	23	75	0
Skidding white-collar starters	43	44	0	63	14	30	0	0
Number	(226)	(126)	(24)	(76)	(67)	(37)	(15)	(15)
Sons of fathers whose first job								
was unskilled								
Starting white-collar	19	23	15	16	48	—	—	—
Ending white-collar	21	22	43	16	69	—	—	—
Climbing blue-collar starters	16	18	20	13	40	—	—	—
Skidding white-collar starters	59	63	0	71	13	—	—	—
Number	(151)	(70)	(13)	(68)	(27)	—	—	—

whole of their lives did not, on the whole, make impressive gains during their careers; 23 percent began their careers in white-collar jobs, and 25 percent occupied nonmanual positions a decade later. A similar experience characterized the large group of sons whose fathers started unskilled and never escaped manual occupations; a fifth of the sons started out in white-collar occupations, and the group gained very little over the next ten years. Moreover, the experience of these men was a mixed one, for more than half of the white-collar starters ended up in manual labor, while only 16 percent of blue-collar starters managed to gain a toehold in nonmanual positions. The casualty rate was somewhat lower for all sons of nonmanual origins; still, 43 percent had lost their initial advantage by the age of thirty. Thus sons of working-class origins barely held their own.

Sons of immigrants who attained middle-class status, on the other hand, had a very different experience. Half began their careers in white-collar jobs, and ten years later 60 percent enjoyed middle-class status. The gains of white-collar starters of nonmanual fathers from laboring origins were even more impressive, for 69 percent eventually reached middle-class status. Hence more than half the sons of middle-class immigrants experienced mobility as a cumulative process.

Ethnicity, as I have shown earlier, was a differentiating factor in the process of career mobility. The role of ethnic group membership appears even more striking in patterns of cumulative mobility. Second-generation Rumanians moved quickly into white-collar jobs; only one-fourth of the Italians, and fewer than one-fifth of the Slovaks, enjoyed comparable status. Rumanian sons of middle-class fathers achieved a remarkable level of continuity with their origins, for 93 percent ended their careers in professional or managerial occupations. Only about 40 percent of second-generation Italians and Slovaks, however, managed to remain in white-collar positions.

Social mobility thus was a cumulative experience for sons of white-collar fathers. Second-generation men of working-class origins, while experiencing some initial gains, remained largely confined to manual jobs. Young Rumanian men enjoyed striking mobility into white-collar jobs; the movement of Italians and Slovaks into the middle class evokes a mixed judgment at best. Steady progress from generation to generation thus characterized only those families in which the fathers managed to move up to a white-collar occupation, and one ethnic group, the Rumanians, accounted for most of this movement.

Count Lájos Ambrozy, an acute Hungarian observer of American immigrant life, reports a conversation he had in 1908 with a German-speaking Slovak in a Passaic saloon. The man had complained of low wages and little work and had told Ambrozy of his difficulties in supporting his family. The count — rather officiously, I think — exhorted the Slovak to think of the opportunities in America that he would have missed in Slovakia. To this, the Slovak retorted: "A poor man stays a poor man, and the rest is nonsense."[11]

If poor immigrants remained poor, it should be abundantly evident by now that they and their sons grew a good deal less poor during the course of their lives. The transformation of agricultural laborers, peasant proprietors, and craftsmen into industrial laborers, owners of city lots, and skilled machinists took half a lifetime.[12] When the immigrants looked back on their lives, what they saw were modest gains of skill, property, and income. And as they gathered their thoughts about their sons, they saw them becoming foremen of plants, owners of small businesses, and sometimes professionals. But they recalled as well that most of their sons had not got past the ninth grade, that many of them still were casual laborers, and that most could not hope to move out of the working class. In what perspective, then, should one place the findings of this study?

The fact that the bulk of the immigrants -- more than two-thirds — began their lives in Cleveland as unskilled laborers is a decisive one in interpreting their subsequent careers, for their beginning at the bottom of the occupational hierarchy meant that most of these men would not escape manual labor. But the newcomers did not remain in an identical class position. Even though mobility was largely within the working class, the movement of unskilled laborers into skilled jobs or their purchase of property represented significant gains over their origins.

This chapter has shown that family mobility falls into three crude patterns. First, slightly less than a fourth of the unskilled starters and their sons remained laborers for their whole lives. A static work experience characterized fully a third of the Slovak families, while a slightly larger proportion of both Italians and Rumanians rose out of their laboring origins. Both the immigrants and the second generation took menial jobs as sweepers or diggers, or, in the case of the Slovaks, stoked the foundry furnaces along the Cuyahoga River. Their wages left them little margin to invest in property, and their employment provided few opportunities to acquire skill.

Nevertheless, many men who had begun in similar positions managed to gain skills and accumulate property. A little less than 50 percent of the families of unskilled starters moved into the skilled and propertied segment of the working class. In about half of this group, family members acquired skills, while in the other half the families advanced their position through the purchase of property. This kind of mobility was especially important in the Slovak community, for it established skilled traditions in about a third of the families whose fathers had started out as laborers. The sons of Italian laborers who gained skilled occupations, on the other hand, frequently had to take unskilled jobs. Despite the ethnic differences, the acquisition of skill and property made this group a stable segment of the working class.

A step above the working class was the lower middle class, into which about a third of the families of unskilled starters gained entry. The immigrant communities produced no David Levinskys; rather, the newcomers most often attained white-collar status through proprietorship or the acquisition of clerical skills. The rapidity with which Rumanian immigrants and their sons entered the middle class is impressive. Rumanian fathers consistently formed more successful businesses than the other two groups, and they were able to pass on their higher status to more than nine out of ten of their sons. Neither the Italian nor the Slovak second generation could claim that kind of continuity with their fathers' status. What strikes one about the Rumanian families is the coherent patterns of mobility: they had fewer children, they sent their children through more years of schooling, and they were substantially more prosperous than either Italian or Slovak families. The highly mobile Rumanian families represent a model of the movement of rural immigrants into the middle class.[13]

It would be a mistake, however, to regard the careers of unskilled laborers as characteristic of the whole immigrant community, for one-fifth of the new arrivals found their first employment in skilled occupations. This remarkably stable and prosperous group provided most of the movement of second-generation Italians into the white-collar strata. The sons of Italian masons and carpenters enjoyed the benefits of their families' extended sponsorship of their education. This group of families was also the source of more than half of the second generation's skilled workers. Thus a comparatively small segment of the Italian immigrant community produced a disproportionately large number of skilled workers, businessmen, and professionals.

Finally, a tiny group of Italians and Rumanians — about one-tenth of the two communities — entered Cleveland in nonmanual occupations. Here again the Rumanian families conformed closely to the norms of middle-class mobility, since they consistently provided their children with at least a high school education. The Italians, on the other hand, failed conspicuously to sponsor their children's mobility, and most of their sons ended their careers in the working class.

What were the sources of these various patterns of social mobility? The character of family life provides one important clue to the differing fortunes of these families. Clearly, the lack of information on the full composition of the household handicaps the exploration of the relationship between family structure and mobility.[14] Nonetheless, small family size evidently facilitated the movement of working-class Italians into white-collar occupations. Moreover, the consistently smaller size of all Rumanian families gave the whole group an advantage in competition for middle-class status, for these small families could more easily sponsor their children's mobility than the larger Slovak and Italian families. Hence the limitation of family commitments was an important source of working-class mobility into the middle class.

A second important source of mobility was schooling. I have argued here, however, that the impact of education was not independent of the second generation's social origins; rather, the sons of mobile immigrants were likely to gain higher status than the sons of static men, even when educational achievement was similar. Thus it does no good simply to assert that education was the high road to social mobility, for the urban classroom was set in a definite family and community context.[15] Education consistently had a greater impact on the sons of mobile men than on young men from static households. Moreover, the character of local communities probably shaped the use to which the second generation put its education. Slovak immigrants sent about 80 percent of their sons to Roman Catholic parochial schools until the eighth

grade. Here they associated largely with other working-class Slovaks, to the exclusion of significant contact with middle-class
children. In this sense, then, Catholic parochial education may
have confined the aspirations of Slovak children to working-class
mobility.[16] Both Italians and Rumanians, on the other hand, were
educated overwhelmingly in public schools. Hence from the first
grade on these sons had contact with a variety of occupational
groups, especially as families began to move toward the residential
ring of the city.[17] This integration of social types and ethnic groups
provided, I suggest, a powerful motive for young men to complete
their schooling and to move into middle-class pursuits.

Despite the important relationship of education to social mobility, the overriding fact in the careers of the second generation was
the fortunes of the immigrant fathers.[18] The remarkable tenacity
with which Rumanian immigrants held on to clerical jobs and
small businesses gave their sons a solid lead in competition for
entrepreneurial and professional occupations. Second generation
Rumanians were more sharply upwardly mobile than the other two
groups because they possessed the cumulative advantages of small
families of origin, extended schooling, and mobile fathers. Both
first- and second-generation Italians and Slovaks, on the other
hand, experienced characteristically Roman Catholic forms of
social mobility.[19] They moved largely into the skilled and propertied working class and into low white-collar occupations.

7   The Emergence of the Second Generation

The 1890 charter of the Slovak Catholic Union exhorted every member to teach his son Slovak and to rear him in the national tradition, "so that the next generation will remain faithful and thus become worthy of their forebears and at the same time deserving of American citizenship."[1] Most organizations assumed that immigrants would declare their American civic loyalty, but to "become worthy of their forebears" was a controversial task, a problem which required several decisions. The union's bylaws specified, for instance, that every member should send his children to a Catholic school. "Slovak children must attend a Slovak school daily," wrote Štefan Furdek in an 1891 manifesto, "— and where else but in a Catholic school can they learn the religion of their fathers and their native tongue?"[2] The cultural program of Catholic Slovaks was, a parish committee declared in 1896, "our own church, our own school, and worship in our own language."[3]

The earliest Catholic Slovak parishes in Cleveland — St. Ladislaus (1888) and St. Martin (1893) — established schools soon after their founding. Ursuline nuns at St. Ladislaus and the Sisters of St. Joseph at St. Martin taught catechetical and Biblical history classes in Slovak and the other elementary subjects in English. Fragmentary reports suggest that instruction in English rather than Slovak, except in religious subjects, was widespread by 1900. In 1904, for instance, in Passaic, six nuns — one Slovak-, one Hungarian-, and four English-speaking — had charge of 360 children. They taught all subjects in English (from necessity, one suspects) and devoted one hour daily to Slovak lessons. Matuš Jankola worked very hard between 1903 and 1910 to place Slovak-speaking sisters in the parochial schools, with mixed results. Elementary subjects contin-ued to be taught in English, and only religious instruction was given in Slovak. The growth of the Slovak-speaking teaching order of SS. Cyril and Methodius after 1907 seems to have altered this language pattern very little.[4]

The third Plenary Council of 1884 insisted for the first time upon the establishment of parochial schools: "No parish is com-plete till it has schools adequate to the needs of its children, and the pastors and people of such a parish should feel that they have not accomplished their entire duty until the want is supplied." As Robert Cross has suggested, the parochial school was part of American Catholicism by 1890, and the increasing reliance of the Catholic church on national parishes to accommodate the influx of immigrants made new ethnic groups potential recruits for the "German" parochial school system.[5] Both German and Czech parishes had established parochial schools in Cleveland before 1885. By the time Furdek established St. Ladislaus, German and Czech parishes undoubtedly served as convenient models. J. M. Koudelka, for example, a Czech priest who later became auxiliary bishop of Cleveland, was instrumental in recruiting both clergy and teaching sisters from Moravia when St. Wendelin, the fourth Slovak parish in the city, was founded in 1905.[6] The connection between design and result was not often so clear, but some continuity between older groups' designs and newcomers' formative efforts was usually evident.

As the second generation's numbers increased, the scope of parochial education expanded. St. Martin's school packed 140 students into three rooms as early as 1900. Four new parishes were established between 1903 and 1907, at the height of the mass migration; all organized schools within a few years of their founding. Most of the early schools had four grades, but after 1905 all had either six or eight. During the first years of Nativity parish (1903), the school had only five grades, but, as the parish priest wrote in a remarkable report, the parish committee decided in 1909 "to make the school as good as any public school." So they expanded the school to eight grades and enrolled 135 students in 1909; by 1912 the enrollment had grown to 265 children. Each room had slightly over fifty pupils, a figure that compared favorably with the average number of students per room in the city's public schools. The school added evening classes in 1911 as well as commercial courses and preparation for civil service examinations. Occasional newspaper accounts of graduation exercises suggest, however, that the growth of parochial school enrollment may have been confined largely to the first four grades. The largest graduating class between 1908 and 1912 was seven, that being at the city's largest Slovak school, St. Martin's; the average graduating class may have had no more than four or five students.[7]

Attendance dropped in the upper grades, a priest explained in 1913, because young men "had to leave the school for the shop." Every parish in the city suffered from this premature exodus of the young; but why, asked the priest, did it happen? As he watched the annual departure of young men from his school, he blamed their leaving upon the community's lack of an educated class to serve as a model for the young: "There is not one educated Slovak priest, doctor, lawyer, banker, or clerk, nor even one educated merchant."[8] As chapter 6 has shown his observations of the rapid turnover of students and the lack of occupational success of the second generation were not far from correct. Table 24 indicates that more than three-fourths of a sample of Slovak children attended parochial schools for their elementary schooling. Even so, about a fifth of the males attended public elementary schools. The radical

Table 24. Parochial and public school attendance of the second generation (percent).

	Males			Females		
	It.	Rum.	Sl.	It.	Rum.	Sl.
Elementary school						
Public	96	92	22	94	92	11
Parochial	4	8	78	6	8	89
Number	(270)	(52)	(116)	(199)	(49)	(111)
Middle school						
Public	98	91	88	97	91	73
Parochial	2	9	12	3	9	27
Number	(177)	(42)	(81)	(106)	(44)	(56)
High school						
Public	96	97	94	96	93	88
Parochial	4	3	6	4	7	12
Number	(76)	(30)	(33)	(47)	(30)	(25)

Sources: The sample consists of children of the immigrants in the sample described in the Appendix. Attendance information is from Cleveland school censuses, 1922–1935, in the Bureau of Census, Cleveland Public Schools, and from elementary school, middle school, and high school records.

transition came between the elementary and secondary levels, when the proportions were almost exactly reversed; the table indicates that over 75 percent entered public junior high and high schools. In part, of course, this change was due to the fact that the first Slovak high school was not established until 1928. Still, a significant proportion of the girls — 27 percent — attended parochial high schools. For children born of Slovak immigrant parents between 1900 and 1920, then, education took place in dissonant contexts; probably three-fourths of the sample studied here experienced both parochial and public schooling.

Youth organizations underwent a development similar to that of parochial schools. The Catholic Slovak Union authorized the formation of a youth section at its ninth convention in 1900; the section's statutes specified that young men between the ages of thirteen and eighteen could join. The new organization made little headway until 1906, when the St. Aloysius Society was founded in Cleveland. The leaders appealed first to adolescents between the ages of ten and sixteen, and after 1908 to boys six to sixteen. The period of greatest national growth came between 1910 and 1912, when 191 new youth auxiliaries were organized. By 1912 at least ten Catholic Slovak Union lodges in Cleveland had formed youth sections, and the movement continued to grow during the twenties.[9] But to observers of the city's local societies, it appeared that, even while youth organizations were expanding, more and more young men remained outside the circle of Catholic associations.[10]

The first decade of the twentieth century saw, then, the completion of the organization of the Slovak Catholic community. Parishes, parochial schools, youth societies — not only did these agencies order the life of the community, but they also institutionalized norms which by 1910 came to define the perimeters of the ethnic group. Membership in a Slovak parish, elementary education in a Slovak parochial school, and adherence to some local branch of a national benefit union — these facts constituted the norm of Slovak ethnicity.

As the formal aspects of Slovak ethnicity became more secure, however, the community's cultural life experienced an important transition. Parochial schools, as noted earlier, usually taught elementary subjects in English; Slovak was customarily used in religious instruction and was itself a subject of instruction. Language, then, although a symbol of group membership, emerged as the most contested aspect of Slovak Catholic ethnicity. A man who had once boasted about the Slovaks' organizational progress might suddenly confront a problem: "What if our sons were no longer to remember Slovak, and we fathers to know no English?" Newspapers discussed in column after column the remorseless decline of the second generation's language ability and nostrums for its cure. But when commentators looked more closely, they found that not only children but parents also were responsible for the gains of English over Slovak. Correspondents often pointed out during the early part of the century that parents sent their children to public, not parochial schools, and that children's language ability suffered accordingly.

Jakub Molitoris and others discovered that newspapers played an important role in maintaining parents' and children's reading knowledge of Slovak. After a year's travel in the United States in 1908, Count Lájos Ambrozy, the perceptive Hungarian observer of immigrant communities mentioned in chapter 6, concluded that the family's use of Slovak was the key to the language's persistence. Everywhere he found working-class Slovak children learning English very quickly, and he noted that they continued to read Slovak but preferred to speak English, even in the home.[11]

During the period of generational transition, language tended to become less the possession of an inherited culture and more a cultural goal. Slovak grew less a customary fixture of immigrant life, more a measure of subjective feelings of group identity.

Immigrant groups of Roman or Byzantine Rite Catholic and Greek Orthodox religious traditions characteristically carried from their homeland village an important lay religious figure — the Catholic organist-teacher, the Byzantine Rite cantor-teacher, and the Orthodox cantor. These men stood in a peculiar relationship to the early development of immigrant religious institutions: they held a traditional place in religious structures, much like that of the Talmudist from the Galician *shtetl*, but they acquired a new role in the American context, that of preserving the children's knowledge of the language.[12]

Sketches of the lives of a Slovak organist-teacher and his sons suggest the role played by these lay teachers in Catholic parishes and the transition that occurred between 1905 and 1910. Juraj Ďumbier was born in the county of Šariš in 1863 and began his career as a teacher before the age of twenty. In 1887 he came to the United States with his wife and children. Between the year of his arrival and 1910, Ďumbier taught Slovak classes and formed choirs in six Pennsylvania and Ohio mining towns. In each community he was also instrumental in organizing mutual benefit societies and religious associations. He taught four of his five sons to play the organ and gave all of them good educations. In 1919 three of the sons were organist-teachers in widely scattered American towns, while one became a school teacher in Slovakia.[13]

In 1905, when Ďumbier's sons were coming into their maturity, a Brotherhood of Slovak Roman Catholic Organist-Teachers was formed. The proceedings of the brotherhood's first meeting indicate that at the midpoint of the mass migration the organist-teacher's role was already in transition. The delegates could not agree on a description of their place in the parish or in the community, except to declare that they must preserve the Slovak language — which every other organization claimed as well. As the growing teaching orders assumed tasks that were once the responsibility of the male lay teacher, the organist-teacher became the director of children's choirs and theater groups. Choirs and theater had been part of the immigrant community from the mid-1890s, but usually as branches of adult societies or family organizations. Between 1908 and 1912, however, children's choirs and theater groups increased remarkably; all Slovak parishes in Cleveland had such organizations by 1910. They always performed in Slovak, and they were active at parochial school graduation exercises, at anniversary celebrations of mutual benefit societies, and during religious holidays. A kind of choir system developed in which emphasis fell on the formally correct use of Slovak.[14]

Thus while Juraj Ďumbier was a formative member of the ethnic community, his sons occupied a restricted role in communal life.

The fathers were lay teachers in an ambiguous setting; the sons became language teachers, music instructors, and, in some cases, parochial school principals. So as the organist-teacher's role was institutionalized, the lay teacher adopted a more formal means of consolidating children's relationship to the ethnic past. By 1914 organist-teachers had virtually disappeared as an identifiable group. Advertisements sometimes came from small mining towns in Pennsylvania or West Virginia in which a lay teacher announced his qualifications, but few urban parishes needed him any longer.[15] A Slovak ethnic community had appeared in which functions were specific; the lay teacher fitted no role in this institutional subsociety.

A new cultural leadership was developing at the same time. In 1902 Matuš Jankola, a Slovak priest long active in Catholic education, had called for the cultivation of a literary Slovak among the young, rather than simple preservation of a native tongue. Later he advised young men to attend St. Procopius College, a Czech Catholic school in Lisle, Illinois, where contact with Slovak scholars might deepen their literary culture. Jozef Kratky and Julian Badjik, both sons of immigrant laborers, studied there and returned to Cleveland in 1910 to become part of a new generation's leadership. This new group, educated largely in Catholic institutions, worked a change in the immigrant community's approach to language after 1910. One Cleveland youth society, for instance, set out to develop a knowledge of literary Slovak among its members. Another, the National Slovak Club of Cleveland, established a library, a choir, and an amateur theatrical company. Other youth groups conducted Slovak classes and used the new grammars and dictionaries appearing at Cleveland and Pittsburgh presses as well as the serial grammar which *Jednota* began to run in 1910. And 1910 saw the Literary Society of Slovak Student Youth publish the first number of its journal *Mladež* [Youth] in Pittsburgh.[16]

Yet it is difficult to judge the extent of this change. A contem-

poraneous current in the immigrant generation flowed counter to
the new emphasis on Slovak. English classes had been as much a
fixture of the Slovak community's early years as of the Italian.
But after 1910 English language instruction may have grown far
more general than before. St. Ladislaus, the Slovak parish founded
by Štefan Furdek in 1888, sponsored one of the city's largest
English evening schools in 1909 for immigrants aged sixteen to
forty-five. Correspondence schools began to advertise in the same
year that they could teach "correct business English" in six months
— painlessly. And Albert Mamatey, an official of the National
Slovak Society, added a final irony in 1910 when he brought out
the first number of the *English Language School*, a little journal
for self-taught laborers.[17]

While the identification of ethnicity and Roman Catholicism
continued into the second generation in the Slovak community,
a new era soon arrived in the Italian community. The secretary of
the San Biagio Society observed this maturation of new leaders in
1910: "Certain of the older men want to take part only to govern,
not recognizing the splendid young men now among them who
could organize any enterprise." Humberto Rocchi saw the same
process of generational succession at work in his parish and began
to hold English missions at St. Anthony's as early as 1905 and
organized several sodalities for young men and women in 1913.
Societies too experienced a transition of membership. Often new
members were simply younger immigrants who had recently arrived. But others, like Charles Oddo, came to Cleveland in their
adolescence, learned English well in public school, then succeeded
their fathers as leaders. A continuous membership cycle characterized the lives of organizations after 1900, but between 1908
and 1914 the second generation's coming-of-age affected a larger
segment of the community than ever before.[18]

It was during these years that priests and laymen tried to establish a parochial school. Holy Rosary, the largest parish in the city, purchased land and borrowed money in early 1908 to build a school. But nothing came of the affair; the property was sold at auction in midsummer of the same year. In 1917 the National Catholic Church of St. James Mariano organized a parish school. This was not a recognized parish, however, and the project soon foundered. Not until 1924 was a parochial school established in any Italian parish in Cleveland. The relationship between parish and community was apparently the most important factor. In Pittsburgh, for instance, local priests were able to gain the support of mutual benefit associations in their campaign for a school. Parishioners and societies alike joined together to erect a school in Utica. In San Francisco, on the other hand, early settlers and entrepreneurs endowed an Italian school.[19] Neither priest nor philanthropist took similar steps in Cleveland.

This left the education of Italian children to the public schools. Table 24 shows that almost all of the second-generation Italians attended the city's schools. The few who attended Cathedral Latin or Loyola were all of relatively prosperous families — children of barbers, foremen, and merchants. Parochial education began to have some impact on the attendance of children starting school in the thirties. Yet the city's largest Italian parish did not build a school until 1955.

The graduates of public schools often announced their adulthood in no uncertain terms. Vincenzo Marcogiuseppe, the son of Michele, who was mentioned earlier, impatiently demanded the formation of a society to "Americanize" Italians. He had learned, he wrote in 1910, soon after his return from the University of Michigan Law School, that "the only way to achieve success is to adopt American manners and to speak English with ease."[20] The volumes of the *Central High School Annual* indicate the rapidity with which the children of the immigrants who had arrived around the turn of the century followed the young lawyer's prescription. Josephine Lipa, a member of an early family from Alcara Li Fusi, was one of the first to graduate, in 1906, but she belonged to no social or literary clubs. Her brother Charles graduated in 1910, a member of Le Lycée Français and captain of the football team. The editor of *La voce del popolo italiano*, Olindo Melaragno, announced his daughter's graduation from high school in 1909 as the second generation's coming out.[21]

Francesco Aidala's response to the transition from generation to generation points to a pattern in the immigrant community's attitudes. Aidala had left his native village of Bronte, Catania, in 1900 as a young man, but he returned to Italy for his legal education. "America offers," he wrote a year after his return to Cleveland in 1908, "the chance to enjoy the educational benefits of universal schooling. But the country obviously cannot instruct each group in its own language and culture." This is a task for each community's associations and leaders, he continued. The urban colonies "need above all schools, hospitals, and civic institutions, not festivals and impossible church edifices in which immigrants sink hundreds of dollars." He advised priests to establish schools rather than churches.[22]

The response to the second generation sometimes took the form of private agencies. Raffaele Raineri and Salvatore Ciricillo opened schools of art and music, each with emphasis on the institution's conservative role. When Ciricillo organized his music school in 1909, he declared that his "spontaneous philanthropic work" would provide "a dignified and correct profession which will assure success to the children of Italians." Vincenzo Marcogiuseppe, Giuseppe Nucio, and Calogero Longo, all lawyers, taught both English and Italian classes. Their private visions of education's role in the community were often sponsored by settlement houses.[23] It was the new leadership that had emerged with mass migration and the proliferation of societies that responded to Aidala's appeal for "schools, hospitals, and civic associations." And in their expectations of educational agencies one can discern the transition to a new Italian immigrant community.

The new leaders' response involved a mixture of private efforts with public institutions. Petitions flowed to the city's school board from heavily Italian districts asking for the creation of night schools. These schools offered courses in both Italian language and the basic elements of English, as well as shop courses, commercial education, and preparation for civil service examinations. One of the most active men in this effort to combine Italian culture and vocational education in the public schools was Silvestro Tamburella, a lawyer and labor organizer. He succeeded in getting himself installed as an Italian teacher in the public schools in 1911, and he also supervised the organization of private language classes. The Social Studies Circle sponsored the most interesting of the private schools. Ludovico Caminita, a lawyer, taught Italian while two other men tutored students in math and geography. Michele Trivisonno, another professional, opened English and Italian classes in 1913.[24]

The Rumanians also tried to preserve the ethnic community beyond the immigrant generation. "There are no Rumanian schools, nor can there be," lamented a Cleveland official of a mutual benefit society in 1906, "because the families cannot support them. One generation, at most two, and there will be no more Rumanians." Middle-aged immigrants organized the Rumanians, wrote another observer, but now that they are getting old, the community faces extinction. "The local societies need to inscribe all our youth, so they will support our newspaper and our cultural efforts," wrote a newspaper editor from Cleveland in 1909. Yet a third Cleveland correspondent observed that the first generation had founded societies not simply for mutual benefit, but also as "means of popular enlightenment."[25] Without a firm organizational base, all of these observers feared, the people would slip away from the community.

This crisis of transition was to be expected. A tiny elite — an engineer, two doctors, a journalist, a lawyer, and three pharmacists — had originally formed the city's insurance societies. This group had succeeded in organizing the immigrant generation, but the second generation, which had passed through different experiences, was looking for a different identity. Their cultural interests were very different from those of their fathers; the organizations thus had to undergo profound changes. By 1916 the local Cleveland societies felt the discontinuity so keenly that they began to gather materials to write their own histories to remind their children of the passing of a once flourishing community.[26]

The first response to the children's disaffection was an effort to recruit them for membership in the old societies. In Cleveland several mutual benefit societies organized auxiliary singing groups, theatrical companies, libraries of popular Rumanian literature, and debating clubs. But these efforts were largely formal, aiming at no more than assuring a minimal command of the Rumanian language. "We must teach one another our language," the young president of a choir told his friends in 1912, "or we will lose our national spirit." These local measures eventually led to increased enrollment of the second generation in mutual benefit associations, and by 1925 the national societies could report healthy balances in reserve funds.[27]

A diffuse educational response to the second generation accompanied the formal organizational effort. The leaders of immigrant organizations noted in their own careers the changing meaning of education. What had been a means of personal mobility in the homeland became in the American context a way to enhance the status of the whole immigrant group. Education amounted to a way of advancing "the interests of the people as a whole." As a newspaper editor wrote after a two weeks' tour of immigrant communities, if ethnic sentiment was to be maintained, education had to be extended not only to the intelligentsia but also to the mass of working-class Rumanians.[28]

The determination to preserve the ethnic group was most evident as Cleveland's immigrants organized religious and language schools as soon as the first children reached five or six years of age. In 1911 alone, the Rumanian Orthodox parish of St. Mary's established four separate schools. By 1915 a variety of weekend and evening schools held classes in Rumanian literature and culture.[29] What had begun as an effort to maintain a local community soon took on the character of a campaign to conserve an inherited culture. Both Orthodox and Byzantine Rite parishes and benefit societies sponsored students, while several national student associations organized conferences and supported newspapers and journals. These formal organizations seemed to assure the survival of Rumanian culture in the second generation.[30]

Yet the reality of the children's education eroded their commitment to the traditional culture. English-language schools cropped up as fast as Rumanian schools, and they enjoyed widespread support in the immigrant community. The pervasive interest in learning English is shown in the circulation of short texts and in the growth of a variety of correspondence schools.[31] And the overwhelming reality, as table 24 shows, was that more than 90 percent of the Rumanian children attended public schools. The small proportion of children who went to parochial schools were largely members of upwardly mobile families. For the bulk of the second-generation Rumanians, then, English had become the everyday language.

But schools, after all, were set within the local urban community. What mattered more, as a Cleveland priest wrote in 1907, was the life of the household, where the "weaving of social life" colored the second generation's future.[32] Unfortunately, here one can follow only the barest threads of evidence. Nevertheless, what scraps remain indicate that the Rumanians, like the Italians and Slovaks, grew increasingly perturbed at the felt dissolution of family life. So, beginning in 1912, they formed a number of family societies in which parents and children participated in common activities. These societies exphasized their concern to link family life closer to parish activities. In the Byzantine Rite parish of the Most Holy Trinity, for instance, the formation of the St. Mary's Society in 1916 led to such a proliferation of family societies that by 1922 every household belonged to one or another group. As the children began to form their own families in the late 1920s, they assumed leadership in these societies, and in the 1930s they were still quite active.[33]

The emergence of the second generation, then, threatened the continuity of the ethnic groups. The communities' typical reaction was to form educational agencies to make possible the transference of particular values. But even with the provision of parochial and weekend schools, choirs, and youth societies, the customary experience was cultural discontinuity between parents and children. When children left the immigrant households, their departure portended broad changes in the ethnic groups.

The age at school entry marked the first important transition in the immigrant households. The pattern, as table 25 shows, was quite regular. The mean age, about six, shows little variation by either ethnic identity or sex. The immigrant households were thus following the general norm of urban school attendance in the 1920s and 1930s.

Major differences emerge, however, in the next important measure, the age at leaving school. Among both Italians and Slovaks, half or more of the children left school at age sixteen, all of them to begin jobs.[34] A small proportion of young Italian and Slovak men, and a somewhat larger proportion of young women, persisted

Table 25. Age of children of immigrants entering and leaving school (percent).

	Males			Females		
	It.	*Rum.*	*Sl.*	*It.*	*Rum.*	*Sl.*
Age at entering school						
6	62	57	58	51	63	43
7	30	28	29	36	31	42
8	7	12	15	10	6	14
9	1	4	0	3	0	1
Mean age	(6.42)	(6.63)	(6.55)	(6.72)	(6.44)	(6.64)
Number	(262)	(51)	(112)	(190)	(48)	(109)
Age at leaving school						
15	6	0	2	3	2	0
16	50	21	59	51	33	65
17	14	14	11	6	15	10
18	19	26	18	30	37	26
19	10	19	9	10	12	0
20+	1	19	1	1	2	0
Mean age	(16.7)	(18.1)	(16.7)	(16.9)	(17.3)	(16.6)
Number	(172)	(42)	(82)	(95)	(41)	(51)

Sources: See note to table 24.

in school until their eighteenth birthday. But for both Italian and Slovaks, the mean age at school leaving was between sixteen and seventeen — they finished the ninth grade, as the law required, and went immediately to work.

Rumanian children persisted longer in school than either of the other two ethnic groups, the males to a mean age of eighteen, the females to seventeen. The longer period in high school led, in the case of a third of the Rumanian men, to college and professional training. (Less than 10 percent of the Italians and only 4 percent of the Slovaks had similar training.) Rumanian girls finished high school in much larger proportion than Italian or Slovak girls. Rumanian children had a more prolonged period of childhood and schooling than the Italian and Slovak children, who had to make decisions about their futures at the age of sixteen, which made them adults at an early age.

The most important transition in the generational sequence was marriage, when the children broke off from the immigrant households to form their own homes. As table 26 indicates, the mean age of bridegrooms was between twenty-five and twenty-six, with a few marrying before twenty or after thirty. The mean age of marriage was somewhat lower for women, being about twenty-one for Rumanians and slightly above twenty-three for Italians and Slovaks. Clearly, then, these young people were not leaving school to get married. The Italians and Slovaks were working for several years before marriage. The Rumanians were pursuing technical and professional training beyond the high school level. Marriage was not a step taken lightly in these communities. It was a decision made some time after the second generation had left the world of childhood and entered the world of work.

It is marriage that provides the best measure of the assimilation of the second generation. As pointed out earlier, intergenerational social mobility was notably high, so the sons often had work experiences divergent from those of their fathers. Thus pathways for assimilation were established through mobility within the job hierarchy and movement about the city. These opportunities began to alienate a large part of the second generation from the traditional ethnic culture. In this context, a growing number of the immigrants' children married outside the ethnic group.[35]

Intermarriage, however, has a number of aspects, each of which must be explored before any conclusions can be made about it. The first important dimension is the generation of the partners. Most of the immigrants' children in the sample married someone

Table 26. Characteristics of second-generation marriages (percent).

	Males			Females		
	It.	*Rum.*	*Sl.*	*It.*	*Rum.*	*Sl.*
Age at first marriage						
15–19	4	0	0	22	46	18
20–24	46	40	32	45	33	41
25–29	31	55	50	26	21	36
30–34	14	0	11	3	0	5
35–39	4	5	7	2	0	0
40+	2	0	0	2	0	0
Mean age	(25.8)	(25.5)	(26.7)	(23.4)	(20.8)	(23.4)
Number	(126)	(20)	(54)	(94)	(24)	(22)
Generation of spouse						
Adult immigrant	4	5	0	28	17	0
Child immigrant	2	5	6	7	21	5
2d generation	76	65	80	48	42	46
3d generation or more	18	25	15	17	21	50
Number	(126)	(20)	(54)	(94)	(24)	(22)
Ethnic identity of spouse						
Ingroup	61	40	59	72	67	41
Other immigrant	29	35	35	14	20	27
Anglo-American	10	25	6	14	13	32
Number	(126)	(20)	(54)	(94)	(24)	(22)
Religious affiliation of spouse						
Roman Catholic	89	35	89	85	21	77
Greek Catholic and Orthodox	2	40	2	1	63	0
Protestant	10	25	9	14	17	23
Number	(121)	(20)	(54)	(93)	(24)	(22)

Sources: The sample consists of children of the immigrants in the sample described in the Appendix. Marriage information is from Cuyahoga County marriage records, parochial records, and interviews.

who belonged to their own generation or who had arrived in the United States before the age of twelve. As table 26 shows, about 60 percent of the second generation chose spouses who shared similar childhoods and adolescences.

But the picture is complex. As is evident in the table, the young women followed a somewhat different course from that of the men. More than a fourth of the Italian women married adult immigrants. Most of these young women were born between 1900 and 1909, and about 80 percent married between the ages of fifteen and twenty-four. They were typically the oldest girls of the family, three-fourths of them having been born first or second in the family; three-fifths married before 1929. The young Rumanian women who married adult immigrants shared these characteristics. The first- and second-born girls were marrying in the 1920s, when the immigrant groups still maintained a coherent culture. Both the Rumanian and the Italian families made some effort to match their eldest daughters with the least assimilated men available, the last adult immigrants to arrive before immigration was shut off in 1924. In this connection, it is important that most of these families were working-class; very few upwardly mobile families made matches of this sort.

On the other hand, a significant proportion of the immigrants' children married husbands and wives who were born in America of native parents. Except in the case of Italian men, at least three-quarters of the members of this category were born after 1910 and were married in the 1940s. These marriages were not closely related to social mobility except in the case of Italian men. And here the sample is large enough to admit some conclusions. Eighty percent of the Italian men who married young women of at least three generations' residence were born before 1909 and were married (in their thirties) during the late 1930s and early 1940s, when all the groups had begun to wed third-generation spouses. And 80 percent belonged to upwardly mobile families, whose members were moving into white-collar and professional occupations. It was the Italians who had completed advanced education and gained technical and professional status, then, who preferred wives who could claim three generations of American residence.

Yet not all of these spouses of three or more American generations were Anglo-American. In the case of Slovak marriages, about half of the native-born partners of native parentage were Anglo-Americans; the other half were third-generation Germans and Irish. In the Italian marriages, about two-thirds were Anglo-American, and in the Rumanian marriages, four-fifths. As table 26 shows, the proportion of the second generation marrying Anglo-American spouses was a quarter or less in every case except for Slovak women, where the sample is too small to permit any conclusions. When the second generation searched for husbands and wives, they most often sought men and women from their own or other ethnic groups, rather than from the old Anglo-American stock of the city. Only in the 1940s, the decade of the Second World War, did they begin to marry persons of English or Scottish backgrounds in any significant numbers, and then it was the youngest children, those born fourth, fifth, and sixth into the immigrant families.

The analysis must be taken one step further before the distinctive character of ethnic intermarriage emerges. Even Slovak women, who married into the older ethnic stocks in larger proportions than any other group, were reluctant to marry Protestants; thus fully a third of their Anglo-American husbands were English Catholics. As table 26 illustrates, between 80 and 90 percent of the second-generation Roman Catholics chose Roman Catholic mates. Only among the Rumanians did marriage outside the religious group bulk large. The largest proportion of Rumanian religious intermarriages, however, involved Roman Catholic partners of immigrant backgrounds, rather than oldline Protestants.

Intermarriage statistics, then, do not reveal a simple pattern of second-generation assimilation. What they do indicate is that the sons and daughters born fourth, fifth, and sixth chose husbands and wives outside the ethnic group much more readily than their older brothers and sisters. Yet for the bulk of both Italians and Slovaks, marriage outside the ethnic group was confined largely within the boundaries of the Roman Catholic Church. Thus marital relationships were selective, and these choices precipatated a remorseless decline in the second generation's participation in the ethnic community but also allowed a continuing pattern of association within a larger religious community.

This conclusion is supported by two careful studies of intermarriage during the same period. Ruby Kennedy's study of New Haven and Milton Barron's account of a small Connecticut city both show a similar loosening of ethnic ties.[36] The comparisons offered in table 27 indicate that there was a long-term decline in the proportion of ingroup marriages. There are two weaknesses in this information, however, which need to be pointed out. First, neither of the two studies separates the second generation from the immigrants, and thus each inflates the percentage of ingroup marriage. Second, both studies were conducted in communities where one ethnic group accounted for a large majority of possible marriage partners. Hence in New Haven the great predominance of Italians meant that most of the second-generation Italians had to marry other Italians. Despite these weaknesses, however, the comparisons indicate that the experience of the Cleveland communities was not an isolated phenomenon but was part of a broader trend.

A second comparison, set forth in table 28, also confirms the findings of the Cleveland study. The trend during the late 1930s and the 1940s toward marriage across ethnic lines was accompanied by a continued emphasis upon shared religious identification. The Italians, Irish, and Poles of New Haven, like the Italians and Slovaks of Cleveland, most often found husbands and wives among their Roman Catholic coreligionists. And since a large proportion

Table 27. Ingroup marriages.

Year of marriage	Cleveland[a]				Derby, Conn.[b]				New Haven[b]			
	It.		Sl.		It.		Pol.		It.		Pol.	
	%	N	%	N	%	N	%	N	%	N	%	N
1920	68	(59)	86	(7)	—	—	—	—	—	—	—	—
1930	72	(105)	62	(29)	88	(114)	71	(30)	87	—[c]	68	—
1940	52	(56)	43	(40)	83	(116)	77	(48)	82	—	53	—
1950	—		—		—		—		77	—	41	—

Sources: For Derby, Conn., Milton L. Barron, *People Who Intermarry: Intermarriage in a New England Industrial Community* (Syracuse, 1946), pp. 124, 127; for New Haven, Ruby Jo Reeves Kennedy, "Single or Triple Melting Pot? Intermarriage in New Haven, 1870–1950," *American Journal of Sociology*, 58 (1952–53), table 1, p. 56.

[a]Second generation. The data are for marriages during the entire decade.

[b]Generation unspecified.

[c]Not given.

Table 28. Roman Catholic marriages.

Year of marriage	Cleveland[a]				New Haven[b]	
	It.		Sl.		It., Ir., Pol.	
	%	N	%	N	%	N
1920	85	(59)	86	(7)	—	—
1930	93	(104)	96	(29)	82	—
1940	79	(56)	78	(40)	84	—
1950	—	—	—	—	73	—

Source: For New Haven, Kennedy, "Single or Triple Melting Pot?" table 2, p. 57.

[a]Second generation. The data are for marriages during the entire decade.

[b]Generation unspecified.

of the marriages between Roman Catholics and Protestants in both Cleveland and New Haven were sanctioned by Catholic nuptials, many of the Protestant spouses may have converted to Catholicism.[37]

Both of these comparisons show, then, that the second generation's move toward assimilation was not a random process, nor a mere mixing of peoples in a great city. Rather, the ethnic groups sorted themselves into new groupings that served to transform the rapport between ethnicity and social status. Hence while the strength of ethnic ties waned, the loyalties bound up in ethnic relationships were articulated anew within the broader context of religious communities.[38]

Conclusion

In J. C. Hronský's great Slovak novel, *Chlieb* [Bread], Rozála
hopes because she has a son in America.[1] The hopes of villagers
in Podhrabníc (Rozála's village), in Fontamara (the scene of Ignazio
Silone's famous novel), or in Poiana (the birthplace of an old Rumanian immigrant with whom I shared a room in Cleveland) were
limited by the realities of a grudging soil and a niggardly allocation
of land. Still the peasants hoped. "After several generations,"
Silone remembers, "the mudsills, the laborers, the workers, the
poor artisans hoped, through privation and unheard-of sacrifice, to
climb a rung on the social scale; but they rarely succeeded."[2] So
they left, or at least some of them did, first the artisans, then the
peasants and the day laborers; first the solitary, then whole families, finally whole villages. *Calabria desolata*, a novelist called his
land in 1905; the same could have been said about parts of eastern
Slovakia or about the Carpathian foothills of Rumania.

What were the origins of these hopes and of the mass migration
that emptied the villages? The relatively broad distribution of land
in areas of peasant agriculture held out the chance of property
ownership to the children; many forms of tenure, from sharecropping to sharefarming, allowed the agriculturist a share in the land's
produce and provided an avenue to ownership. But the miserable
income of the mass of southern Italians, Rumanians, and Slovaks

threatened always to reduce the peasant to the despised status of the laborer. Moreover, the formation of households depended upon access to land, at least to a piece large enough for a few potatoes and onions. Emigration was a way of conserving a small inheritance, of avoiding a loss of status in the village. And the small savings brought back by the emigrant would assure his son's inheritance and the continuity of the family.[3]

Many stayed in Cleveland; most went back home, but pioneer immigrants settled into the tiny houses of Slovak steelworkers or the subdivided houses of Italian laborers, they persuaded others to come, from their own or neighboring villages. So distinctive patterns of migration developed, and they influenced the destination of individuals and families who took leave of their villages. The migration streams that grew because of communication between early emigrants and villagers shaped the new immigrant communities in important ways. At least three-fourths of the newcomers found familiar dialects and social usages and, in the case of the Italians, old neighbors and friends. The localism of the Italian community had its origins in the pattern of migration from particular villages. Both the Rumanian and Slovak communities, because they drew their population from larger geographical areas, developed a broad cultural identity. The development of distinctive immigrant settlements was partly an outcome of different patterns of migration.

But the tangible communal reality to which the newcomers clung also represented a continuity of traditional models of social order. The Old World villages were not simply agglomerations of discrete families — they were laced with the strands of many organizations, which gave an indirect expression to the social structure of the rural community. In the new urban settlements, voluntary associations became the characteristic social unit and "provided a matrix within which the group organized its policing devices, family life, marriage, churches, educational systems, and associations for cultural and social ends."[4] The ethnic community, then, was partly

a reconstitution of a village and partly an accommodation to the
fragmented social order of the metropolis. It was in this accommodation that immigrants developed distinctive orientations toward the prospects of upward mobility and assimilation.

The realities of family life reflected striking differences in values.
The Slovaks, for whom the ethnic community provided a pattern
of stability and continuity, remained largely in the working class.
Although the fathers gained skills and property which they were
able to pass on to their sons, their social mobility and education
served not as avenues to the middle class but rather as a means of
gaining a stable working-class life. The Slovak community created
social institutions emphasizing the value of order and maintaining
the continuity of the ethnic group.

The Italian settlement shared the Slovak emphasis on continuity, but the basis lay in particularistic cultural values rather than in
an amalgam of religious and associational loyalties. Despite this
stong localism, the community developed a large group of young
and ambitious leaders who cultivated the memories of the village
but also encouraged expectations of upward mobility and success.
The expectations were fulfilled to a certain extent at least. Again,
however, the working-class families developed a stable work orientation, a coherent pattern of family structure, education, and
mobility, which gave the sons a decided edge in the urban labor
market. Italian fathers who gained middle-class status, on the other
hand, consistently failed to pass on their status to their children.
As a result, the second generation started out in the thirties with
no better chances than those with which the immigrants had begun.

It is the Rumanians who present the classic rise of an immigrant
group. The secular orientation of their ethnic culture, the alacrity
with which they adopted an urban small family life, and their consistent use of education as a means of upward mobility facilitated
their rapid gain of middle-class status. The cumulative advantages
of small families, extended schooling, and upwardly mobile fathers

provided a middle-class competence for most of the second generation.

Despite varying value orientations and strikingly different patterns of social mobility, the stories of these three communities have the same ending. The sons and daughters began to lose meaningful contacts with their parents' origins in the 1920s; during the late 1930s and the 1940s an increasing proportion married outside the group. Thus the melting pot absorbed them into the larger community of Cleveland and widened that community's limits. But even as the old ethnic mosaic of the city began to disappear, a new system of religious groupings emerged as the characteristic social order of the metropolis. Memories of place, cultural loyalties, and social relations were now articulated within the boundaries of religious groupings of Protestants, Catholics, and Jews, rather than within the ethnic community and the neighborhood. It is in this widening of the Anglo-American community that this story takes on its larger meaning.[5]

"Grant us a safe lodging, and peace at the last." So reads a prayer of St. John Chrysostom above the portal of an Eastern Orthodox church in Cleveland. Whether absorption into the larger urban community fulfilled the hopes of the peoples from Alcara Li Fusi, Sibiel, and Hermanovce remains to be seen. But one thing is sure: the lives of the immigrants and their children traced the patterns that define our own urban inheritance. And it is only as we begin to sort out the different meanings of the legacy of ethnicity that our involvements with each other will begin to make sense.[6]

Appendix   Notes   Index

Appendix

The samples that form the basis of chapters 3, 5, 6, and 7 are composed of reconstituted families. The Italian and Rumanian families were reconstituted from extant registers of Italian Roman Catholic and Rumanian Orthodox and Byzantine Rite Catholic parishes. The baptisms listed in the parish records were checked against Cleveland birth and death certificates. The Slovak families were reconstituted from the insurance records of the First Catholic Slovak Union and the city's vital records. All three samples consist, then, of families living within the confines of parishes or mutual benefit lodges. In short, the samples are made up of the affiliated, and it is the affiliated, after all, who constitute the ethnic community.

The only comparison which offered itself was with the information collected by the U.S. Immigration Commission on Italians and Slovaks living in certain areas of downtown Cleveland in 1908. The commission's report included detailed occupational classifications, which made a comparison possible between the occupational distributions in its sample and those in the Italian and Slovak samples used here. As table A shows, the percentages are reasonably close and indicate that the samples used in this book reflect in some measure the experiences of the larger immigrant communities. The commission's samples show a substantially lower pro-

Table A. Distribution of parish and immigration commission samples according to occupational strata (percent).

	Italians		Slovaks	
Occupational strata	Parish samples, 1910	Immigration commission sample, 1908	Parish samples, 1910	Immigration commission sample, 1908
High white-collar	4.1	1.5	0.6	0.5
Low white-collar	10.3	9.1	1.3	5.3
Skilled	20.5	13.6	10.3	8.1
Semiskilled	1.5	0.8	7.1	2.4
Unskilled	63.6	74.5	80.7	81.9
Number	(230)	(132)	(155)	(210)

Source: U.S. Congress, Senate, *Reports of the Immigration Commission: Immigrants in Cities*, 61st Cong., 2d sess., 1911, S. Doc. 338, vol. 2, pp. 190–192.

portion of Italians in high white-collar and skilled jobs and a somewhat higher proportion in unskilled jobs. The commission's samples, however, were collected in a very restricted area of downtown Cleveland and thus missed many of the skilled and white-collar immigrants.

Tables B–F illustrate the occupational ranking which has been used throughout this study. The tabular presentation of these selected measures of occupational rankings does not prove conclusively the validity of the ranking used here. Rather, the tables serve as a tentative effort to rank occupational groups in four years — 1900, 1910, 1930, and 1935 — in Cleveland.

Table B. Unemployment rates according to occupation and length of time unemployed, 1900.

Occupations	Number	Months unemployed (% of group)		
		1–3	*4–6*	*7–12*
High white-collar				
Teachers	331	26.0	2.1	5.4
Lawyers	610	0.2	0.7	0.7
Physicians and surgeons	764	0.1	0.9	0.4
Merchants and dealers (retail)	4,963	1.2	1.1	0.6
Low white-collar				
Bookkeepers and accountants	2,261	3.1	2.3	2.3
Clerks and copyists	5,238	3.5	2.7	1.7
Hucksters and peddlers	1,142	10.5	5.2	2.2
Salesmen	4,356	3.4	2.2	1.6
Skilled				
Blacksmiths	1,456	9.7	3.8	2.5
Carpenters and joiners	4,208	13.3	16.8	4.7
Machinists	5,810	16.9	4.8	2.4
Stonecutters	441	17.2	27.4	5.9
Boilermakers	567	14.6	7.2	3.2
Semiskilled				
Iron- and steelworkers	8,769	18.2	8.6	3.3
Textile mill operatives	136	5.1	6.6	1.5
Wiremakers	1,876	26.1	14.2	2.3
Unskilled				
Laborers	17,946	18.6	18.7	6.7

Source: U.S. Bureau of the Census, *Twelfth Census, 1900: Special Reports, Occupations*, pp. 526–530.

Table C. Mean days worked and mean annual wages according to occupation, 1910.

Occupations	Number	Mean days worked	Mean annual wages ($)
Skilled			
Rollers (steel)	35	256	2,470.40
Boilermakers (boiler, engine, and tank)	56	302	957.34
Stonecutters (marble and granite)	58	295	949.90
Carpenters (foundry and machine-shop products)	82	288	829.44
Machinists (foundry and machine-shop products)	1,686	291	823.53
Coremakers (foundry and machine-shop products)	474	289	760.07
Semiskilled			
Machine hands (tin, sheet iron, and galvanized iron)	32	304	711.36
Blast furnace workers (steel, iron, and tin)	197	306	658.44
Machinist's helpers (foundry and machine-shop products)	349	301	614.04
Boilermakers' helpers (boiler, engine, and tank)	55	301	592.97
Unskilled			
Laborers (roofing)	50	291	529.62
Laborers (foundry and machine-shop products)	5,715	287	493.64
Laborers (machinery)	645	282	465.30
Laborers (steel, iron, and tin)	877	241	426.57

Source: Ohio Bureau of Labor Statistics, *Thirty-fifth Annual Report*, 1910, pp. 161–210.

Table D. Unemployment rates according to industrial categories, 1930.

Industrial categories	Number	Persons out of a job, able to work, and looking for a job (%)	Persons with jobs but laid off without pay, excluding those sick or voluntarily idle (%)
Professional service, except recreation and amusement	9,120	2.8	0.4
Trade			
Banking and brokerage	3,176	3.6	0.31
Wholesale and retail, except automobiles	38,535	7.5	1.1
Manufacturing and mechanical industries			
Building	27,092	23.8	4.8
Automobiles	14,558	15.7	2.9
Blast furnaces and steel rolling mills	18,556	12.6	4.3
Other iron and steel	39,426	13.4	3.7
Metalworking except iron and steel	5,655	12.3	3.8
Independent hand trades	1,279	6.9	0.9
Transportation			
Construction and maintenance of streets, roads, and sewers	4,277	28.8	5.5
Steam railroads	14,375	9.1	2.2
Street railroads	3,286	5.7	2.5
Domestic and personal service			
Hotels, restaurants, boarding houses, etc.	7,592	10.9	0.7
Laundries, and cleaning, dyeing, and pressing shops	2,301	7.0	0.7

Source: U.S. Bureau of the Census, *Fifteenth Census, 1930: Unemployment*, I, 790.

Table E. Comparison of 1935 unemployment and 1930 employment according to occupational strata.

Occupational strata	(1) Number employed, 1930	(2) Number unemployed 1935	(2)/(1) × 100
High white-collar	33,291	1,651	5.0
Low white-collar	75,594	5,257	6.7
Skilled	84,435	10,995	13.0
Semiskilled	51,321	18,668	36.4
Unskilled	50,143	17,308	34.5

Sources: for 1930 employment, U.S. Bureau of the Census, *Fifteenth Census, 1930: Population, Occupations, by States*, pp. 1240–1248; for 1935 unemployment, Works Progress Administration, Division of Social Research, *Workers on Relief in the United States in March 1935*, I, *A Census of Usual Occupations*, by Philip M. Hauser, pp. 980–981.

Table F. Some elements of the work structure, 1910–1950.

	1910	1930	1950
Occupations			
Laborers, all industrial categories	17.6	12.7	7.2
Operatives, all industrial categories	12.2	13.0	21.8
Skilled workers, all industrial categories	25.7	21.4	13.9
Clerks of all kinds (office and sales)	16.1	19.1	22.2
All other occupations	28.4	33.9	34.9
Industrial categories			
Manufacturing and mechanical industries	51.4	44.3	45.7
Building	9.1	6.1	5.1
Clothing	6.3	1.5	2.1
Misc. textiles	0.9	1.8	0.7
Bakeries	0.4	0.6	0.5
Iron, steel, shipbuilding, and automobiles	18.5	14.9	9.5
Metalworking, except iron and steel	1.1	1.4	1.3
Paper and printing	1.2	1.4	2.9
All other manufacturing	13.9	16.6	23.6
Nonmanufacturing industries	48.6	55.7	54.3
Wholesale and retail	13.3	13.8	19.3
Transport and communication	9.1	9.5	7.0
Professional and semiprofessional, except entertainment	4.7	5.9	8.2
Hotels, laundries, domestic service	10.5	11.5	5.2
Other nonmanufacturing employment	11.0	15.0	14.6
Number	(248,886)	(394,842)	(390,424)

Sources: for 1910, U.S. Bureau of the Census, *Thirteenth Census, 1910: Population, Occupational Statistics*, pp. 152–165; for 1930, *Fifteenth Census, 1930: Population, Occupation, by States*, pp. 1240–1248; for 1950, *Seventeenth Census, 1950: Population, Characteristics, Ohio*, pp. 461–462.

Notes

ABBREVIATIONS

AdS   Archivio di Stato
AS   Arhivele Statului
IA   Immigrant Archives, University of Minnesota Library
IKSJ   First Slovak Catholic Union
Jednota kalendár   Jednota katolícky kalendár
MOL   Magyar Orszagos Levéltár, Budapest (microfilm, IA)
Národný kalendár   Národný kalendár pre rimsko- a grécko-katolíkov a
              evangelikov
Noviny   Amerikánsko slovenské noviny
USRA   Union of Rumanian Societies in America
La voce   La voce del popolo italiano

The immigrant newspapers and periodicals used in this study are listed below. The dates are those of the issues used in my research and do not indicate the history of publication. Unless otherwise specified, they are from the University of Minnesota Library's Immigrant Archives.

America (Cleveland), 1906–1930
Amerikánsko slovenské noviny (Pittsburgh), 1893–1904
L'avvenire (Utica), 1900–1905
Calendarul America (Cleveland), 1906–1950
Catholic Universe (Cleveland), 1900–1910, Diocese of Cleveland Archives
Catolicul american (Aurora, Ill.), 1908, author's possession
Il corriere del popolo (San Francisco), 1916–1925
La fiaccola (Buffalo), 1909–1912
Hlas (Cleveland), 1920–1927
Jednota (Cleveland), 1893–1930
Jednota katolícky kalendár (Cleveland and Middleton, Pa.), 1893–1950
Kalendár Bratstvo pre rimsko- a grécko-katolíkov (Wilkes-Barre, Pa.),
   1914–1915

Kalendár pre slovenských kalvinov (Pittsburgh), 1927, author's possession
La luce (Utica), 1901-1916
Il messaggiero dell'ordine (Utica), 1936-1940
Národný kalendár pre rimsko- a grécko-katolíkov a evangelikov (Pittsburgh), 1899, 1901, 1903-1906, 1908-1913, 1917-1920, 1925-1928
Národné noviny (Pittsburgh), 1910-1930
Il pensiero italiano (Utica), 1917-1918
Poşta română (Pittsburgh), 1908, author's possession
Românul (Cleveland), 1906-1930
Slovák v Amerike (New York), 1894-1904
Solia (Detroit), 1936-1950
Steaua noastră (New York), 1912-1921
La Trinacria (Pittsburgh), 1917-1925, Center for Research Libraries, Chicago
La voce del popolo italiano (Cleveland), 1909-1922, 1937

INTRODUCTION

1. Interview with Mrs. Ilie Martin, August 15, 1968, Sibiu; *Calendarul America*, 1912, pp. 103-104.

2. Ilie Martin, *Istoria Americei*, 2 vols. (Cleveland, 1906), I, v.

3. John Higham, "Immigration," in C. Vann Woodward, ed., *The Comparative Approach to American History* (New York, 1968), p. 92. Cf. the critique of this tradition in Sam Bass Warner, Jr., and Colin B. Burke, "Cultural Change and the Ghetto," *Journal of Contemporary History*, 4 (1969), 173-187.

4. Oscar Handlin, *Boston's Immigrants: A Study in Acculturation*, rev. ed. (Cambridge, Mass., 1959); Handlin, *The Uprooted*, 2d ed. (Boston, 1973).

5. Oscar Handlin, "The Social System," in Lloyd Rodwin, ed., *The Future Metropolis* (New York, 1961), p. 22.

6. Oscar Handlin, "The Modern City as a Field of Historical Study," in Handlin and John Burchard, eds., *The Historian and the City* (Cambridge, Mass., 1963), pp. 15-17.

7. Marcus Lee Hansen, *The Immigrant in American History* (Cambridge, Mass., 1940), pp. 13, 82.

8. Cf. John Higham, "Another Look at Nativism," *Catholic Historical Review*, 44 (1958), 151-152.

9. Higham, "Immigration," pp. 95-96.

10. Cf. Oscar Handlin and Mary F. Handlin, "The New History and the Ethnic Factor in American Life," *Perspectives in American History*, 4 (1970), 15-21.

11. Argentina: I. Ferenczi and W. F. Willcox, eds., *International Migration*, 2 vols. (New York, 1929-1931), I, 543. Australia: Charles A. Price, *The Methods and Statistics of 'Southern Europeans in Australia'* (Canberra, 1963). Brazil: Ferenczi and Willcox, *International Migration*, I, 548-552; *Anuário*

estatístico do Brasil, 1954, p. 59. Canada: M. C. Urquhart and K. A. K. Buckley, eds., *Historical Statistics of Canada* (Toronto, 1965), series A252, 318, 327-328, 330-331. USA: U.S. Bureau of the Census, *Historical Statistics of the United States, Colonial Times to 1957* (Washington, D.C., 1960), series C88, 97, 99. On the 1965 immigration bill, see Charles B. Keely, "Effects of the Immigration Act of 1965 on Selected Population Characteristics of Immigrants to the United States," *Demography*, 8 (1971), 157-169.

12. Cf. Charles A. Price, *Southern Europeans in Australia* (Melbourne, 1963), pp. 254-274, and Price, *Methods and Statistics*, pp. 39-46.

13. John Porter, *The Vertical Mosaic: An Analysis of Social Class and Power in Canada* (Toronto, 1965), pp. 63-64; Brinley Thomas, *Migration and Economic Growth: A Study of Great Britain and the Atlantic Economy* (Cambridge, 1954), pp. 24-25, 59-62, 153-154; E. P. Hutchinson, *Immigrants and Their Children, 1850-1950* (New York, 1956), pp. 114, 139-142, 171-180, 203-214; Peter M. Blau and Otis Dudley Duncan, *The American Occupational Structure* (New York, 1967), pp. 227-238, 240-241.

14. *Protestant, Catholic, Jew*, 2d ed. (Garden City, N.Y., 1960).

15. *Beyond the Melting Pot*, 2d ed. (Cambridge, Mass., 1970).

16. John Higham, review of *Beyond the Melting Pot, Labor History*, 6 (1965), 171-173.

17. I owe much here to Charles A. Price, "The Study of Assimilation," in J. A. Jackson, ed., *Migration* (Cambridge, 1969), pp. 181-237.

18. Everett S. Lee, "A Theory of Migration," *Demography*, 3 (1966), 47-57; William S. Petersen, "A General Typology of Migration," *American Sociological Review*, 23 (1958), 256-266; Price, *Southern Europeans in Australia*, pp. 169-199.

19. Milton M. Gordon, *Assimilation in American Life: The Role of Race, Religion, and National Origins* (New York, 1964), pp. 60-75.

20. Ibid., pp. 71, 76-77, 81.

21. U.S. Bureau of the Census, *Historical Statistics*, series C236, 239, 245-246, 250, 252, 261.

22. The method of reconstitution is a modified version of the one sketched in E. A. Wrigley, ed., *An Introduction to English Historical Demography* (New York, 1966).

23. Timothy L. Smith offers convincing arguments for this method in "New Approaches to the History of Immigration in Twentieth-Century America," *American Historical Review*, 71 (1966), 1265-1279.

24. Cf. Norman B. Ryder, "The Cohort as a Concept in the Study of Social Change," *American Sociological Review*, 30 (1965), 843-861.

25. Cf. Maurice Stein, *The Eclipse of Community: An Interpretation of American Studies* (Princeton, 1960), p. 94.

CHAPTER 1   THE GROWTH OF A CITY

1. Walter Isard, "Some Locational Factors in the Iron and Steel Industry since the Early Nineteenth Century," *Journal of Political Economy*, 56 (1948), 203-217.

2. Willard Glazier, *Peculiarities of American Cities* (Philadelphia, 1886), pp. 148-149.

3. *A Visit to the States: A Report of Letters from the Special Correspondent of The Times*, 1st ser. (London, 1887), pp. 403-404.

4. This approach is adopted from Sam Bass Warner, Jr., "If All the World Were Philadelphia: A Scaffolding for Urban History, 1774-1930," *American Historical Review*, 73 (1968), 26-43.

5. Donald J. Bogue, *Population Growth in Standard Metropolitan Areas, 1900-1950* (Washington, D.C., 1953), pp. 10-15, appendix table I.

6. The 1890-1920 data were estimated by means of census survival rates; for a full explanation, see Everett S. Lee et al., *Population Redistribution and Economic Growth: United States, 1870-1950*, 3 vols. (Philadelphia, 1957-64), I, 15-56. The 1920-1950 data are from *Sheet-a-Week*, 19, no. 22 (February 7, 1952).

7. Colin Clark, *The Conditions of Economic Progress*, 2d ed. (London, 1951), chap. 12.

8. Sam Bass Warner, Jr., *Streetcar Suburbs: The Process of Growth in Boston, 1870-1900* (Cambridge, Mass., 1962); Warner, *The Private City: Philadelphia in Three Periods of Its Growth* (Philadelphia, 1968).

9. *Proceedings of the City Council of Cleveland Relative to the Cleveland Railway Company from February 21, 1910, to January 1, 1914* (Cleveland, 1914), pp. 124-125, 134-135, 261-262; Cleveland Chamber of Commerce, Committee on Housing and Sanitation, *An Investigation of Housing Conditions of War Workers in Cleveland* (Cleveland, 1918), pp. 29-30; Barclay, Parsons and Klapp, *Report on a Rapid Transit System for the City of Cleveland* (Cleveland, 1919), pp. 22-46.

10. Greater Cleveland Transportation Committee, *Report of Passenger Transportation in the Cleveland Metropolitan Area* (Cleveland, 1925), p. 24; *Bulletin of the Cleveland Association of Building Owners and Managers*, 1 (July 23, 1923), 1, and 5 (June 4, 1927), 2; *Sheet-a-Week*, 2, no. 15 (January 10, 1935), 3, no. 23 (March 5, 1936); DeLeuw, Cather and Company, *Report of Cleveland Transit Modernization* (Cleveland, 1945), exhibits 2-11; Robinson Newcomb, "Home Financing in Cleveland with Special Reference to Junior Mortgages," mimeographed (Washington, D.C., October 1931), pp. 76-78.

11. Cleveland Chamber of Commerce, Housing Committee, *Housing Conditions in Cleveland: Report of Progress* (Cleveland, 1904), pp. 15-27, 57-61; Cleveland Chamber of Commerce, Committee on Housing and Sanitation, *An Investigation of Housing Conditions; Fourth Annual Report of the Charity Nurse Association of Cleveland*, 1905, pp. 26-27; *Cleveland Press*, February 10, 1910; *Sheet-a-Week*, 7, no. 24 (March 7, 1940).

12. Thomas A. Knight, *Picturesque South Brooklyn Village* (Cleveland, 1903), n. pag.

13. Newcomb, "Home Financing," pp. 18, 24-26, 66; Cleveland, City Plan Commission, *Reports Received on the Tentative Zoning Ordinance for Cleveland* (Cleveland, 1928), pp. 40-41; *Real Property*, no. 86 (December 28, 1939); Cleveland, Department of Public Safety, Division of Buildings, "Annual Report, 1939," mimeographed (Cleveland, Municipal Reference Library), chart 3; *Real Property Inventory of Metropolitan Cleveland*, no. 28 (1951), pp. 12-13.

14. Cf. Leo F. Schnore, *The Urban Scene: Human Ecology and Demography* (New York, 1965), pp. 222-241, 255-272; for location of Cleveland's population, see *Sheet-a-Week*, 18, no. 39 (June 7, 1951).

15. A value of 25 in table 2 furnishes a convenient boundary between strong and weak residential clustering; see Karl E. Taeuber and Alma F. Taeuber, *Negroes in Cities: Residential Segregation and Neighborhood Change* (Chicago, 1965), pp. 43-62.

16. Stanley Lieberson, *Ethnic Patterns in American Cities* (New York, 1963), shows similar patterns in ten American cities between 1930 and 1960.

17. Cuyahoga County, Recorder's Office, "Societies: Religious, Fraternal, Etc.," I, 8.

18. Ibid., I, 122, 197, 206-207, 424, II, 30, 82; *Deutsche Verein- und Logenkalendar, für Cleveland*, 1900, pp. 9-93; *Cleveland und sein Deutschtum* (Cleveland, 1897-98), pp. 105-116; Jakob Mueller, *Aus den Erinnerungen einer Achundvierzigen* (Cleveland, 1896), pp. 200-204; *Památník padesátiletého trvání Sokolske Jednoty Čech-Havliček, Cleveland, O., 1879-1929* (Cleveland, 1929), pp. 13-24; Frank L. Viček, *Povidka mého života* (Cleveland, 1928), pp. 173-180.

19. For good examples of the broad impact of immigrant cultural activities, see the following: *Gedenkbuch der Goethes-Schiller-Denkmalweihe in Cleveland . . . 9. Juni 1907*, pp. 44-48, 52-54, 74-76; *Festschrift für den Deutschen Tag in Cleveland . . . 21. 22. und 23. August 1909*, pp. 14-22; *Egyesült Magyar Egyletek, 1902-1937* (Cleveland, 1937), n. pag.; *Golden Jubilee Celebration Program Honoring Rt. Rev. Msgr. Oldrich Slaval* (Cleveland, 1954), n. pag.; *Lakewood Independent*, February 10, 1910; Vlček, *Povidka mého života*, pp. 341-346.

20. W. Scott Robinson, ed., *Cleveland, 1888* (Cleveland, 1888), p. 402.

21. See *Historical Sketch and Financial Report of the Cleveland Association of the Home for Aged Colored People . . . 1893-1908*, pp. 4-6; *Nineteenth Annual Report of the Cleveland Home for Aged Colored People . . . 1914 . . . 1915*; J. C. Anderson to Mayor's Advisory War Board, January 17, 1919, Mayor's Advisory War Committee Papers; George Bellamy to Bruno Lasker, March 1, 1924, Hiram House Records, box 3. (Both in Western Reserve Historical Society.)

22. *Annual Report of the Public Health Department of Cleveland*, 1902, pp. 937-938, 1903, pp. 4-9, 1906, pp. 6-8; Howard Whipple Green, "Death

Rates from Important Causes of Death, Cleveland, Ohio, 1900–1930," mimeographed (Cleveland Health Council, 1931).

23. Marvin Lazerson, *Origins of the Urban School: Public Education in Massachusetts, 1870–1915* (Cambridge, Mass., 1970), pp. xi–xvi, 241–257; Warner, *Private City*, pp. 111–123.

24. Mary B. Ingham, *Women of Cleveland* (Cleveland, 1893), pp. 114–117; *Annual Report of the Superintendent of the Cleveland Industrial School,* 1858, pp. 6–7; Cleveland Young Men's Christian Association, *Report of the City Missionary Society,* 1861–62, pp. 6–8; Samuel P. Orth, *A History of Cleveland,* 3 vols. (Chicago, 1910), I, 397, 405.

25. *Report of the Industrial School and Home,* 1893, p. 14; *An Account of the Goodrich Social Settlement* (Cleveland, 1900), pp. 28–29; *Hiram House Life,* 4 (May 1902), 9; *Annual Report of Hiram House,* 1907, p. 3; T. W. Garvin, "Annual Report of Boys' Work at Hiram House, 1910," Hiram House Records, box 8.

26. *Report of the Educational Commission Appointed by the Board of Education* (Cleveland, 1906), p. 56.

27. *Annual Report of the Board of Education,* 1868, pp. 8–9, 36–41, 50–51, 1892, pp. 78–79, 85, 1903, pp. 29–30; *Annual Report of the Board of Health,* 1875, p. 110; *Report of the Educational Commission,* p. 38; *Report of the Citizens' School Committee* (Cleveland, 1923), pp. 3–8; Akers, *Cleveland Schools,* pp. 294–295; *Proceedings of the School Council of the Board of Education,* 1902–03, p. 6; Cleveland Chamber of Commerce, Committee on Education, *Second Report on Organized Americanization Work* (Cleveland, 1918); *The Cleveland Teachers' Federation: Historical Review, 1916–1923* (Cleveland, 1923), pp. 23–29.

28. Edward Bushnell to Harry L. Davis, April 19, 1917; minutes of Women's Americanization Committee, August 21, 1917; minutes of Executive Committee of Americanization Committee, October 11, 1917; Bushnell to T. C. Wellsted, May 10, 1917; "Report of the Work of the Community Centers, January 1919." (All in Mayor's Advisory War Committee Papers.)

29. *Proceedings of the Board of Education,* 1917, pp. 353, 357–359, 1919, p. 102; Cleveland *Plain Dealer,* May 6, 18, 1919; *Cleveland Americanization Bulletin,* January 15, 1920; *Cleveland Night School Messenger,* 1 (December 17, 1923), 3.

30. *Cleveland Teachers' Federation Bulletin,* June 12, 1924. Charles A. Nicola to Cleveland R. Cross, July 24, 1926, box 11; Katherine A. McCarthy to P. D. Graham, April 24, 1933, box 1; "Review of the Past Year's Work of Cooperation between the Schools and Hiram House (1934)," box 1. (All in Hiram House Records.)

31. See Sharon C. Kingsley, Amelia Sears, and Allen T. Burns, *Survey of Cleveland Agencies Which are Giving Relief to Families in Their Homes* (Cleveland, 1914), p. 62 and map; Welfare Federation of Cleveland, "Preliminary Statistical Analysis of Data Relative to the Five Hundred Thirty-three Deserted Families Known to Cleveland Social Agencies, October 15,

1928, to April 15, 1929," mimeographed (Cleveland Public Library), pp. 1-2, 5, 10.

CHAPTER 2   ORIGINS

1. Francesco Coletti, "Dell'emigrazione italiana," in Reale Accademia dei Lincei, *Cinquant'anni di storia italiana*, 3 vols. (Milan, 1911), III; Gusztáv A. Thirring, *A magyarországi kivandorlás és a külföldi magyarság* (Budapest, 1904). The same theme runs through the earliest (and still best) American accounts of these movements: Robert F. Foerster, *The Italian Emigration of Our Times* (Cambridge, Mass., 1919); Emily Green Balch, *Our Slavic Fellow Citizens* (New York, 1910); and Harry Jerome, *Migration and Business Cycles* (New York, 1926).

2. On the structure of peasant agriculture, see A. V. Chayanov, *The Theory of Peasant Economy* (Homewood, Ill., 1966), pp. 90-117. I have adapted this hypothesis from John S. MacDonald, "Some Socio-Economic Emigration Differentials in Rural Italy, 1902-1913," *Economic Development and Cultural Change*, 7 (1958), 55-72, and "Agricultural Organization, Migration, and Labour Militancy in Rural Italy," *Economic History Review*, 2d ser., 16 (1963-64), 61-75.

3. Karol Rebro, "Agrárne reformy v Habsburskej Monarchii od začiatku 18. storočia do r. 1848 s osobitným zrtetl'om na Slovensko," *Historické štúdie*, 13 (1968), 5-28; Vincenzo Ricchioni, "Le legge eversive della feudalità e la storia delle quotizzazioni demaniali nel Mezzogiorno," in Cassa per il Mezzogiorno, *Problemi dell'agricoltura meridionale* (Naples, 1953), pp. 223-242.

4. Imre Wellmann, "Esquisse d'une histoire rurale de la Hongrie depuis la première moitié du XVIIIe siècle jusqu'au milieu du XIXe siècle," *Annales: ESC*, 23 (1968), 1189-1190, 1193-1196, 1202-1210; Tibor Kolossa, "Statistische Untersuchung der sozialen Struktur der Agrarbevölkerung in den Landern der österreichisch-ungarischen Monarchie (um 1900)," in *Die Agrarfrage in der österreichisch-ungarischen Monarchie* (Bucharest, 1965), pp. 94-95, 104, 123-130, 150-151; Scott M. Eddie, "The Changing Patterns of Landownership in Hungary, 1867-1914," *Economic History Review*, 2d ser., 20 (1967), 297-298; A. N. J. Hollander, "The Great Hungarian Plain: A European Frontier Area (II)," *Comparative Studies in Society and History*, 3 (1960-61), 157-165.

5. Antonio di Rudinì, "Terre incolte e latifondi," *Giornale degli economisti*, 2d ser., 10 (1895), 171. Cf. Vincenzo Ricchioni, *Studi storici di economia dell'agricoltura meridionale* (Florence, 1952), pp. 172-194; Renzo Paci, *Agricoltura e vita urbana nelle Marche: Senigallia fra Settecento e Ottocento* (Milan, 1962), pp. 60, 64-66, 72, 75; Alberto Caracciolo, *L'Inchiesta agraria Jacini* (Turin, 1958), pp. 143-151; Sidney Sonnino, *I contadini di Sicilia*, II, Leopoldo Franchetti and Sonnino, *La Sicilia nel 1876*, 2 vols. (Florence, 1877), pp. 27-33, 35-48; *Inchiesta parlamentare sulle condizioni*

dei contadini nelle provincie meridionali e nella Sicilia, 15 vols. (Rome, 1909-11), IV, fasc. 2, pp. 216-240.

6. MacDonald, "Agricultural Organization," p. 68; Sydel F. Silverman, "'Exploitation' in Rural Central Italy: Structure and Ideology in Stratification Study," *Comparative Studies in Society and History*, 12 (1970), 335-336.

7. MacDonald, "Agricultural Organization," pp. 65-68.

8. Nino Savarese, *Rossomano, storia di una terra* (Milan, 1935), p. 177. Cf. Napoleone Colajanni, *Gli avvenimenti di Sicilia e le loro cause*, 2d ed. (Palermo, 1896); Salvatore F. Romano, *Storia dei Fasci siciliani* (Bari, 1959); Renée Rochefort, "Un Pays du latifondo siciliene: Corleone," *Annales: ESC*, 14 (1959), 448-451; Renato Zangheri, ed., *Lotte agrarie in Italia: La Federazione nazionale dei lavoratori della terra, 1901-1926* (Milan, 1960), pp. xiv-xvii, xxviii-xxxi, xlii-xlv, lxxx-lxxxiii.

9. Kolossa, "Statistische Untersuchung der sozialen Struktur," pp. 113-114; Stefan Pascu et al., "Einige Fragen der landwirtschaftlichen Entwicklung in der österreichisch-ungarischen Monarchie," in *Die Agrarfrage in der österreichisch-ungarischen Monarchie* (Bucharest, 1965), pp. 16-18; Damian Hurezeanu, "Privire critică asupra studierii problemei agrare în România la începutul secolului al XX-lea," in Academia Republicii Populare Romîne, Institutul de Cercetări Economice, *Studii privind istoria economică a Romîniei*, I (Bucharest, 1961), 47-137; Zoltán Sárközi, "Príspevok k dejinám slovenských pol'nohospodárskych sezónnych robotníkov," *Historický časopis*, 12 (1964), 75-103; Geoffrey Drage, *Austria-Hungary* (London, 1908), pp. 308-317. For my characterization of landless laborers, I have depended on Gyula Illyés's novel *People of the Puszta* (1936; Eng. tr., Budapest, 1967).

10. Franca Assante, *La Puglia demografica nel secolo XIX* (Naples, 1967), pp. 96-97, 105; Luigi Izzo, *La popolazione calabrese nel secolo XIX: Demografia ed economia* (Naples, 1965), pp. 171-188.

11. Domenico Demarco, *La Calabria: Economia e società* (Naples, 1966), pp. 78-79.

12. Giuseppe Medici, *La distribuzione della proprietà fondiaria in Italia: Relazione generale*, 2 vols. (Rome, 1948), I, 22-39.

13. Thirring, *A magyarországi kivándorlás*, pp. 103-105.

14. *Magyar statisztikai közlemények*, n.s., 27 (1906), 3-5.

15. This pattern was first pointed out to me in the village of Fîntînelle (formerly Cacova), a noncollectivized community southwest of Sibiu.

16. Pascu et al., "Einige Fragen," pp. 25-27.

17. H. J. Habakkuk, "Family Structure and Economic Change in Nineteenth Century Europe," *Journal of Economic History*, 15 (1955), 1-12; cf. Antonio Gramsci, "Alcuni tema della questione meridionale," in Giansiro Ferrata and Niccolò Gallo, eds., *2000 pagine di Gramsci*, 2 vols. (Milan, 1964), I, 810-811.

18. Salvatore Carbone and Renato Grispo, eds., *L'inchiesta sulle condizioni sociali ed economiche della Sicilia (1875-1876)*, 2 vols. (Bologna, 1968-1969), I, 351, II, 715-717, 1064-1066.

19. Sonnino, *I contadini*, pp. 192-193; cf. pp. 63-81, 114-121, 133-160.

20. *Inchiesta parlamentare*, VI, fasc. 1, p. 261; cf. fasc. 2, p. 231.

21. *Atti della Giunta per l'Inchiesta agraria e sulle condizioni della classe agricola*, 13 vols. (Rome, 1881–86), XIII, fasc. 2, pp. 200–232, 250–251, 261–264; *Inchiesta parlamentare*, VI, fasc. 1, pp. 319–340, fasc. 3, pp. 341–379.

22. *Inchiesta parlamentare*, VI, fasc. 3, p. 343.

23. *Inchiesta agraria*, IX, fasc. 1, pp. 49–51, 57–61, XII, fasc. 1, pp. 363–385, 443–449; *Inchiesta parlamentare*, II, fasc. 1, pp. 9–33, 43–51, 152–153, V, fasc. 1, pp. 20–31, 49–52. Sydel Silverman develops a similar theme in "Stratification in Italian Communities: A Regional Contrast," in Leonard Plotnicov and Arthur Tuden, eds., *Essays in Comparative Social Stratification* (Pittsburgh, 1970), pp. 215–216, 219–220. See the local studies of Adriano Pizzutti, *Le affitanze agrarie nel Fucino prima della riforma fondiaria* (Avezanno, 1953), pp. 23–55, and Franca Assante, *Calopezzati: Proprietà fondiaria e classi rurali in un comune della Calabria, 1740–1886* (Naples, 1964), pp. 60–74, 83–87, for confirmations of this view in particular settings.

24. Georg Bariţ, "Locuitorii cultivatori de pămînt în Ungaria și Transilvania," in Victor Cherestesiu et al., eds., *Scriere social-politice* (Bucharest, 1962), pp. 387–390.

25. David Mitrany, *The Land and the Peasant in Rumania* (London, 1930), pp. 208–209; Henry L. Roberts, *Rumania: Political Problems of an Agrarian State* (New Haven, 1951), p. 366. On the Banat, see Constantin Corbu and Augustin Deac, *Mișcari și frămîntări țărănești în România la începtul secolului al XX-lea (1904–1906)* (Bucharest, 1961), pp. 98–102, 105–107, 114–116.

26. Juliús Mésáros̆, "Die Expropriation des Bauerntums und die Überreste der feudalen Unterdrückung in der Slowakei in der zweiten Hälfte des 19. Jahrhunderts," in *Studia Historica: Studien zur Geschichte der österreich-isch-ungarischen Monarchie* (Budapest, 1961), pp. 62, 66–68; Mésáros̆, *K problematike prezitkov feudalizmu na Slovensku v druhej polovici XIX storocia* (Bratislava, 1955), pp. 98–101; Ladislav Tajták, "Presov v období rokov, 1900–1918," in Imrich Sedlák, ed., *Dejiny Presova*, 2 vols. (Kosice, 1965), II, 60–62.

27. Juliús Mésáros̆, "Rol'nicka otázka na východnom Slovenska v 19. storoci," in L'udovít Holotík, ed., *Prispevky k dejinám východného Slovenska* (Bratislava, 1964), pp. 177–193; Ladislav Tajták, "Vychodoslovenské vyst'ahovalectvo do prvej svetovej voyny," *Nové obzory*, 3 (1961), 223–232.

28. Ministero di Agricoltura, Industria e Commercio, Direzione Generale dell'Agricoltura, *Notizie intorno alle condizioni dell'agricoltura: Variazioni del fitto dei terreni* (Rome, 1886), pp. 129–137, 192–215.

29. Giuseppe Salvioli, "Contadini e gabellotti in Sicilia nella zona del latifondo," *La riforma sociale*, 1 (1894), 76.

30. Sonnino, *I contadini*, pp. 40–43, 87, 128–130, 132–133, 230–236; cf. *Inchiesta agraria*, XIII, fasc. 2, pp. 227–228, 250–251; *Inchiesta parlamentare*, V, fasc. 1, pp. 95–108, VI, fasc. 1, pp. 144–234.

31. Mésáros̆, "Die Expropriation des Bauerntums," pp. 70–79; B. V. Cerny, "Emfyteutické smlouvy v Trenc. Teplicich v pocatku XIX. stor.," *Vsehrd*, 17 (1935–36), 382–387.

32. Ludovic Vajda, "Despre situația economică și social-politică a Transilvaniei în primii ani ai secolului al XX-lea," in Academia Republicii Populare Romîne, Institutul de Istorie, *Studii și materiale de istoria modernă*, I (Bucharest, 1957), 331-333; Imre Kovacs, "Despre nivelul dezvoltării agriculturii din Transilvania la sfîrșitul sec. al XIX-lea și începutul celui urmator și formele de exploatare a țăranilor," *Anuarul Institutului de Istorie din Cluj*, 9 (1966), 143-165; Constantin Garoflid, *Chestia agrară în România* (Bucharest, 1920), pp. 100-118; Drage, *Austria-Hungary*, pp. 311-313, 315, 323.

33. On Italy, see Dino Taruffi, Leonello De Nobili, and Cesare Lori, *La questione agraria e l'emigrazione in Calabria* (Florence, 1908), pp. 333, 348-350; *Inchiesta parlamentare*, VI, fasc. 4, pp. 463-464. On Slovakia and Rumania, see Emil Simonffy, "A parasztföld és a tagosítás," in István Szabó, ed., *A parasztság Magyarországon a kapitalizmus korában, 1848-1914*, 2 vols. (Budapest, 1965), I, 207-264.

34. Carbone and Grispo, *L'inchiesta sulle condizioni sociali*, II, 1077-1079; *Inchiesta agraria*, XII, fasc. 3, p. 112; *Inchiesta parlamentare*, VI, fasc. 2, pp. 708-736; Raffaele Giura Longo, *Clero e borghesia nella campagna meridionale* (Matera, 1967), pp. 201-209; Giuseppe Lo Giudice, *Agricoltura e credito nell'esperienza del Banco di Sicilia tra l'800 ed il 900*, Catania, Università degli Studi, *Studi e ricerche della Facoltà di Economia*, 3 (Catania, 1966), pp. 30-34, 43-56, 167-174.

35. Georg Eichmann, *Entwicklung und Stand der Kredit- und Genossenschaftswesens der Siebenburger Sachsen* (Berlin, 1903), pp. 174-187; C. Daicovich, ed., *Enciclopedia română*, 3 vols. (Sibiu, 1898-1902), s.v. "Gurarîului," "Orlat," "Poiana"; Zoltan I. Toth, *Magyarok és románok* (Budapest, 1966), pp. 397-401.

36. On Sicily, *Statuto della Società Figli di Lavoro di Mutuo Soccorso . . . Valguanera* (Catania, 1893), p. 1, and the report on the same society dated 1893 in AdS (Caltanissetta), Pubblica Sicurezza, busta 8; *Giornale imparziale* (Messina), September 26, 1895; Subprefect of Patti to Prefect of Messina, October 29, 1910, AdS (Messina), Prefettura, fasc. 49; *Giornale di Sicilia* (Palermo), February 7, 1899; *Il sole del Mezzogiorno* (Palermo), February 7, 1901. On Rumania, Ioan Lupaș, *Monografia Casei de Pastrare din Saliste* (Sibiu, 1909); Situația (c. 1929), fol. II, p. 3, Sibiel, Parish Archives; Statutele Societății Cooperative de Aprovizionare și Defacere in Comun din comuna Tilișca, Tilișca, Parish Archives.

37. Emilio Sereni, *Il capitalismo nelle campagne (1860-1900)*, 2d ed. (Turin, 1968), pp. 38-39, 351-369; Vasile Liveanu et al., *Relații agrare și miscări țărănești în România, 1908-1921* (Bucharest, 1967); Ján Hanzlík, "Začiatky vyst'ahovalectva zo Slovenska do USA a jeho priebeh aš do roku 1918, jeho príčiny a následky," in Josef Polišenský, ed., *Začiatky českej a slovenskej emigrácie do USA* (Bratislava, 1970), pp. 49-96.

38. Cf. the typology of pesantries in Eric R. Wolf, "Types of Latin American Peasantry: A Preliminary Discussion," *American Anthropologist*, 57 (1955), 452-471, and "Cultural Dissonance in the Italian Alps," *Comparative Studies in Society and History*, 5 (1962-63), 1-14.

39. On Italy, see Giotto Dainelli et al., *Atlante fisico-economico d'Italia*

(Milan, 1940), map 26; British Naval Intelligence Division, *Geographical Handbook Series, Italy,* II (August 1944), 504-510; on Rumania, Romulus Vuia, "Le Village roumaine de Transylvanie et du Banat," in *La Transylvanie,* Academia Română, *Connaissance de la terre et de la pensée roumaines,* II (Bucharest, 1938), pp. 709-791; on Slovakia, Jaroslav Prokeš, "Überkommene Siedlungsformen," in Václav Brdlik, ed., *Die sozialökonomische Struktur der Landwirtschaft in der Tschechoslowakei* (Berlin, 1938), pp. 53-86.

40. *Almanacco del contadino per l'anno 1898* (Palermo, 1897); Sonnino, *I contadini,* pp. 84-86, 133; *Inchiesta agraria,* XII, fasc. 3, p. 101.

41. Sonnino, *I contadini,* pp. 82-83.

42. A. de Gerando, *La Transylvanie et ses habitants,* 2d ed., 2 vols. (Paris, 1850), II, 18-21; A. A. Paton, *The Goth and the Hun; or, Transylvania, Debreczin, Pesth, and Vienna in 1850* (London, 1851), pp. 127-129, 133; Ján Koma, "Drotárstvo na Spiši," *Nové obzory,* 3 (1961), 271; Rudolf Pokorný, *Z potulek po Slovensku,* 2 vols. (Prague, 1883-85), I, 163-171.

43. See Edward C. Banfield, *The Moral Basis of a Backward Society* (Glencoe, Ill., 1958), pp. 7-12.

44. Parish marriage records, Alcara Li Fusi; "Elenco di individui nati in altri comuni . . . 1913," Alcara Li Fusi, Archivio Comunale; census schedules (1901), Villavallelonga, Archivio Comunale.

45. Antonio Bussaca, *Dizionario geografico, statistico, e biografico della Sicilia,* 2d ed. (Messina, 1860), pp. 5, 80, 97; census schedules (1871), Sant'Agata di Militello, Archivio Comunale; parish marriage records, Militello Rosmarino, Church of Maria SS. Assunta.

46. Personal communication from Mark Stolarik, November 29, 1969; Pavel Horvath, *Poddaný l'ud na Slovensku v prvej polovici 18. storočia* (Bratislava, 1963), pp. 212-253; Ján Sirácky, *St'ahovanie slovákov na Dolnú zem 18. a 19. storoči* (Bratislava, 1966), pp. 102-192, 210-218.

47. These eleven villages were not selected at random but were chosen because they all had a regional trading center in Sibiu and also different district trading towns.

48. Cf. Joseph Lopreato, *Peasants No More: Social Class and Social Change in an Underdeveloped Society* (San Francisco, 1967), pp. 152-154.

49. Nicolae Dragomir, "Din trecutul oierilor Marginei din Săliște și comunele din jur," *Lucrările Institutului de Geografie al Universității din Cluj,* 2 (1924-25), 193-251.

50. Parish marriage and death records of Galeș, Sacel, and Talmacel, in AS (Sibiu), Colecția Starea Civilă, and Sibiel, Parish Archives; interviews in Sibiel, Tilișca, and Chîrpar, July-August 1968.

51. Census schedules, Sant'Agata and Villavallelonga; cf. Guido Vincelli's similar analysis of a village in Campobasso in *Una comunità meridionale* (Turin, 1958), p. 90.

52. N = 28.

53. Cf. Francesco Coletti, *La popolzione rurale in Italia* (Piacenza, 1925), pp. 33-34; and Manning Nash, "Kinship and Voluntary Association," in

Wilbert E. Moore and Arnold S. Feldman, eds., *Labor Commitment and Social Change in Developing Areas* (New York, 1960), pp. 314-315.

54. "Iscrizione degli aluni della scuola serale del 1881-1882," October 16, 1881, Alcara Li Fusi, Archivio Comunale; minutes of Società Agricola di Mutuo Soccorso, September 18, 1892, January 15, 1893, in the society's archives, Alcara Li Fusi.

55. Report of school expenditures (1891), AdS (Caltanissetta), Prefettura, busta 3805; "Statuto della Società Anonima Cooperativa 'La Coltura' fra falegnami e muratori . . . Chiusa Scalfano, 1908," AdS (Palermo), Prefettura, busta 396; *Giornale di Sicilia* (Palermo), February 26, 1899; P. Barjo to Prefect of Basilicata, May 4, 1883, AdS (Potenza), Prefettura, cat. XXIV, busta 440, fasc. 80; *Statuto . . . Società operaia di mutuo soccorso di Castelgrande* (Melfi, 1888), p. 11.

56. School records, 1887-1890, Alcara Li Fusi, Archivio Comunale; school records, 1898-1899, Villapriolo, in Villarosa, Archivio Comunale.

57. "Relazione finale della scuola mista posta in Ferretta, 1910-1911," Militello Rosmarino, Archivio Comunale; school records, 1891-1904, Villarosa, Archivio Comunale; school records, 1893-1900, Valledalmo, Archivio Comunale. Cf. Giovanni Scarninaci, *Note ed osservazioni sulla scuola primaria di Castelvetrano* (Palermo, 1893), pp. 5-8; *La nuova imera* (Termini Imerese), June 8, 1906.

58. *Organul pedagogic* (Sibiu), 1 (1863), 6-16, 45; P. Pipoș, "O privire în istoria școalei," *Biserica și școala* (Arad), 11 (1877), 13, 19; A. Bîrseanu, "Casa parintească și școala," *Școala și familia* (Brașov), 1 (1886), 26-27; "Legatura întima dintre școala și familie ca un mijloc puternic de educație," *Școala și familia*, 2 (1888), 551-558.

59. "Registrul pruncilor obligația frecuenta școla," 1869-1918, Sibiel, Parish Archives; interviews in Sibiel and Sibiu, August 1968.

60. N = 107.

CHAPTER 3   MIGRATION AND SETTLEMENT

1. *La Sicilia cattolica* (Palermo), June 21, 1894; *Bollettino dell'emigrazione* (Rome), 1905, no. 14, pp. 34-38; *Società S. Raffaele per la protezione degli emigrati siciliani, statuto* (Palermo, 1907).

2. See the excellent report by Johann Lichtenstadt, a Viennese editor, who traveled to the United States aboard a ship of the Austro-American Line in 1910: Vienna, Allgemeines Verwaltungsarchiv, October 4, 1910, 38054/1910 (microfilm, IA).

3. AdS (Trieste), Marittimo, fasc. 876.

4. John S. MacDonald and Leatrice D. MacDonald summarize these observations in "Chain Migration, Ethnic Neighborhood Formation, and Social Networks," *Milbank Memorial Fund Quarterly*, 42 (1964), 82-97; see also Rudolph J. Vecoli, "Chicago Italians prior to World War I: A Study of Their Social and Economic Adjustments" (Ph.D. thesis, University of Wisconsin, 1963), pp. 71-234.

5. *Annual Report of the Commissioner-General for Immigration*, 1907, pp. 60–61.

6. The argument follows Charles A. Price, *Southern Europeans in Australia* (Melbourne, 1963), pp. 107–139, and Price, *The Methods and Statistics of 'Southern Europeans in Australia'* (Canberra, 1963), pp. 14–16.

7. Emily Green Balch, *Our Slavic Fellow Citizens* (New York, 1910), pp. 100–101; cf. František Bielik and Elo Rákoš, eds., *Slovenské vyst'ahovalectvo: Dokumenty*, 1 vol. to date (Bratislava, 1969–), I, 62–63, 68–72, 77–79.

8. Interviews in Cleveland, April 1968 and July 1970, and in Rumania, August 1968; Lájos Ambrozy to Ladislaus von Hengelmüller, November 9, 1908, MOL, K-26/1909/XXII/1953/ad1954; Ambrozy to von Hengelmüller, December 2, 1908, ibid., K-26/1909/XXII/1950; minutes of Erster Deutsch ungarischen unterstützungs Verein von Cleveland, December 26, 1907, IA.

9. These early emigrants appear in "Liste di estrazione della leva . . . 1875," AdS (Enna), Circondario di Piazza Armerina, no. 36. Cf. Sidney Sonnino, *I contadini di Sicilia*, II, Leopoldo Franchetti and Sonnino, *La Sicilia nel 1876*, 2 vols. (Florence, 1877), pp. 59–61, 451–457.

10. Guglielmo Josa, 'L'emigrazione nel Molise," *Bollettino dell'emigrazione* (Rome), 1907, no. 10, pp. 52–53.

11. *Società operaia di mutuo soccorso . . . in Brindisi di Montagna* (Potenza, 1889), p. 6; Mayor of Episcopia to Prefect of Basilicata, May 24, 1889, AdS (Potenza), Prefettura, fasc. 441. Cf. Renée Rochefort, "Un Pays du latifondo sicilien: Corleone, "*Annales: ESC*, 14 (1959), 449; Mayor of Valguanera to Prefect of Caltanissetta, April 4, 17, 1896, AdS (Caltanissetta), Prefettura, busta 3811.

12. Two problems seem evident here and in the following account of chain migration. First, the differing migration patterns may simply reflect the unequal sizes of the Cleveland settlements. A crude preliminary analysis of the migration of some 8,000 members of the Union of Rumanian Societies before 1920 and of a random sample of some 40,000 membership applications to the First Slovak Catholic Union, however, yield figures not very much different from these (both collections in IA). Second, the more numerous Italian chains may simply derive from the large southern agrotowns, while the smaller Rumanian and Slovak villages could not support heavy chain migration. This objection arises largely from a stereotype of Italian agricultural settlement. The districts that furnished the largest chains to Cleveland — Benevento and Campobasso (Abruzzi) and Patti (Sicily) — are in areas where the median population of agricultural villages in 1901 was between 800 and 1,200. The median size of Transylvanian agricultural villages in 1900 was 1,000, of Slovak villages 600. Price shows in *Southern Europeans in Australia* and in *Methods and Statistics* (pp. 62–125) that areas such as the central Dalmatian coast, where the median size of agricultural villages in 1920 was a mere 200, were capable of supporting village chains.

13. These and the following persistence rates were calculated from a variety of sources: city directories, parish censuses, manuscript censuses of

the school-age population, school records of individuals, membership lists and beneficiary designations of mutual benefit societies, and tax assessment records. The city directories are the most comprehensive source, and their usefulness has been clearly demonstrated: see Peter R. Knights, "City Directories as Aids to Ante-Bellum Urban Studies: A Research Note," *Historical Studies Newsletter*, 2 (September 1969), 1-10; and Stephan Thernstrom and Peter R. Knights, "Men in Motion: Some Data and Speculations about Urban Population Mobility in Nineteenth-Century America," *Journal of Interdisciplinary History*, 1 (1970), 7-35. In order to assess the reliability of the Cleveland directories, I compared their inclusiveness against the parish censuses of 1912 (Archives of the Diocese of Cleveland), against the 1923 manuscript census of Cleveland's school-age population, and against the listings of Slovak and Rumanian benevolent societies for 1909 and 1915. In each of the tests, I found that the directories excluded no more than 5 percent of the names appearing in the other listings. The directories erred most in the area of Cleveland between East Ninth and East Twenty-fifth streets, where subdivided housing prevailed. The highest rate of inclusion was between West Fifty-ninth and Sixty-fifth, where the directories included 96 percent of the Rumanian members of the Carpaţina lodge in 1909, 97 percent in 1915. As Knights points out, the chief problem in the use of directories is not their exclusion of low-status residents but their bias against recent arrivals. Before 1920 the rule seems to have been to include individuals after two years' residence; after 1920 the period stretched to three years. I have tried to overcome this bias by searching through a variety of listings.

14. *Kalendár pre slovenských kalvínov*, 1927, pp. 113-139; membership records of Lodge 33, Slovak Calvinist Presbyterian Union, Lakewood, Ohio.

15. Evidenţa membrilor Uniunei, 1916-1917; Petru Veza to Adam Prie, December 29, 1921, folder marked "Aradană, 1921"; USRA, *Rapoartele . . . şi darea de seama . . . 1920* (Cleveland, 1920), pp. 9-10; USRA, *Rapoartele . . . şi darea de seama . . . 1922* (Cleveland, 1922), pp. 10-11; USRA, *Proces verbal . . . 24 şi 25 aprilie 1921* (Cleveland, 1921), pp. 1-2. (All in USRA Collection.)

16. Cf. John S. MacDonald, "Migration from Italy to Australia" (Ph.D. thesis, Australian National University, 1958), pp. 226-278.

17. Cf. Price, *Southern Europeans in Australia*, pp. 226-237, 251-252; Price, *Methods and Statistics*, p. 19.

18. The basis of this paragraph is a series of maps on which I plotted the moves of individual settlers and of village, district, and regional groups between 1910 and 1930. The sample of settlers is composed of those persons who persisted in Cleveland for at least ten years after marriage. The number of moves, plotted at five-year intervals, is as follows: Italians, 485; Rumanians, 219; Slovaks, 166.

19. There are three principal difficulties with the traditional intermarriage ratio, X_b/S_b, where X_b = intermarriage between members of a given birthplace group in a given country of settlement, and S_b = the total marriages by members of that group in that country: (1) The typical inconsistency

between ethnic grouping and birthplace or nationality. Birthplace and nationality categories, which are the usual designations found in official records such as censuses, marriage records, and certificates of naturalization, are sometimes helpful in identifying ethnic origins, but often they furnish misleading information. Both Rumanians and Slovaks, for instance, were of Hungarian nationality, but their ethnic affiliations were based on village origins, church membership, and language — information proved by no official records, but consistently provided by church and lodge records. (2) The difference between sociological generation and birthplace categories. The historian is interested not merely in the birthplace of an immigrant but also in the age at which he arrived in his new country. As Chapter 7 shows, immigrants who arrived before age twelve behaved quite differently from adult immigrants. (3) The problem of identifying the population at risk of intermarriage. The marriage statistics of a country or area of settlement understate the number of grooms exposed to risk of intermarriage because they ignore the men who came to a new country, returned to their homeland to find a bride, and then came back; these marriages were registered only in the place of marriage. The marriage records used here avoid the first two problems but not the third. The third difficulty, however, is least likely to create a large margin of error. See the excellent discussion of these problems in Charles A. Price and Jerzy Zubrzycki, "The Use of Inter-Marriage Statistics as an Index of Assimilation," *Population Studies*, 16 (1962), 58-69, and in Price, *Methods and Statistics*, pp. 39-43.

20. Office of the Ohio Secretary of State, *Acts of Incorporation*, vol. 73, pp. 229, 238, vol. 85, pp. 114, 257.

21. Ibid., passim; *La voce*, 1909-1937; interviews in Cleveland, April 1968, June 1969, July 1970, in Alcara Li Fusi and Militello Rosmarino, September 1968, and in Ripalimosano, June 1971.

22. *La voce*, May 1, 15, July 24, August 7, October 23, December 4, 1909; minutes of Società Agricola di Mutuo Soccorso, January 16, 1914, and Luigi Angiani to "Illmo. Sig. Presidente," June 15, 1919 (both in the society's archives, Alcara Li Fusi).

23. *La Voce*, May 15, 1915.

24. Konstantín Čulen, *Dejiny Slovákov v Amerike*, 2 vols. (Bratislava, 1942), I, 197, 206; *Národný kalendár*, 1926, p. 70; *Acts of Incorporation*, vol. 37, pp. 173, 505; *Jednota kalendár*, 1940, p. 122.

25. This conclusion is based on a study of the membership of eighteen lodges of the First Catholic Slovak Union in Cleveland (*N* = 266).

26. L'udovit Štur (1815-1856) was the author of a decisive treatise on the Slovak language, *Narečja slovenskuo alebo potreba pisanja v tomto nárečí [The Slovak Speech, or the Necessity of Writing in this Dialect]* (Bratislava, 1846). The Matica Slovenská was the national cultural academy of the Slovaks, founded in 1862 at Turčiansky Sv. Martin.

27. Ján Pankuch, *Dejiny clevelandských a lakewoodských Slovákov* (Cleveland, 1930), pp. 24-27, 271-272; *Slovák v Amerike*, August 31, 1901,

January 22, April 11, 1902; Balch, *Our Slavic Fellow Citizens*, p. 380n.; *Noviny*, March 1, 1894, June 8, 1904; *Acts of Incorporation*, vol. 92, p. 148; *Jednota*, May 11, 1904, June 29, 1910; *Národné noviny*, November 24, 1910.

28. Konsul Wein to Karl von Giskra, June 9, 1903, MOL, K-26/1903/XVI/263; *America*, December 15, 1907.

29. *Programul serbarii jubilare . . . parohia ortodoxă română Sfta. Maria din Cleveland, Ohio* (Cleveland, 1929), pp. 5-6; *America*, October 19, 1906; Moise Balea to "Onorate Domnule Parinte," November 1, 1906, Letterbook, USRA Collection; *Calendarul America*, 1925, pp. 107-109, 127. Cf. Karl von Giskra to Graf Goluchowski, June 18, 1903, MOL, K-26/1903/XXI/1792; *Catholic Universe*, December 1, 1905, July 6, 1906.

30. "Evidenţa membrilor, 1915," I, 66-70. The membership of societies in Chicago, Detroit, and Indianapolis, which were organized contemporaneously, indicate that the same process was at work everywhere: ibid., I, 76-83, 130-132, II, 31-32, 64-65, 70-72, 101; "Evidenţa membrilor Uniunei după societăţi, 1913," pp. 39-41. (All in USRA Collection.)

31. See Geza Sztaja, "Die rumänische Einwanderung und deren nationale Bestrebungen in Amerika," May 30, 1909, and "Rumänische Propaganda in Amerika," November 21, 1909, MOL, K-26/1910/XIV/715/3533, 4856. *Istoria Uniunei şi Legei Societaţilor Române de Ajutor şi Cultura . . . 1906-1931* (Cleveland, 1931), is a useful general account. For Greek Catholics, see minutes of Asociaţia Română Americană Liga şi Ajutorul, December 25, 1913, USRA Collection.

32. *Românul*, February 6, 1909; *America*, March 11, 1909; *Istoria Uniunei şi Legei*, p. 32.

33. *Românul*, June 12, 1910, February 19, 1911; minutes of USRA, December 17, 1912, USRA Collection; USRA, *Proces verbal . . . 5-6 maiu 1917* (Cleveland, 1917), p. 4; M. G. Croitori to Adam Prie, December 10, 1928, folder marked "Banaţiană, 1928," USRA Collection. Bishop Policarp complains about regionalism in *Solia*, May 17, 1936.

CHAPTER 4   ETHNIC COMMUNITIES IN THE MAKING

1. Robert T. Anderson and Gallatin Anderson, "The Indirect Social Structure of European Village Communities," *American Anthropologist*, 64 (1962), 1025; Anderson and Anderson, "The Replicate Social Structure," *Southwestern Journal of Anthropology*, 18 (1962), 368-369.

2. Philip Gleason, *The Conservative Reformers: German-American Catholics and the Social Order* (Notre Dame, 1968), p. 10.

3. On adaptive functions of associations, see E. J. Hobsbawm, *Social Bandits and Primitive Rebels* (Glencoe, Ill., 1959), p. 108; Kenneth Little, *West African Urbanization: A Study of Voluntary Associations in Social Change* (Cambridge, 1965), pp. 164-166; Michael Anderson, "The Study of

Family Structure," in E. A. Wrigley, ed., *Nineteenth-Century Society: Essays: on the Use of Quantitative Methods for the Study of Social Data* (Cambridge, 1972), pp. 51-52.

4. Sidney Sonnino, *I contadini di Sicilia*, II, Leopoldo Franchetti and Sonnino, *La Sicilia nel 1876*, 2 vols. (Florence, 1877), pp. 427-442, 457-459.

5. Ministero di Agricoltura, Industria e Commercio, Direzione Generale della Statistica, *Elenco delle società di mutuo soccorso, 1898*, pp. 188-198.

6. "Elenco delle società operaie, 1890," AdS (Palermo), Prefettura, busta 115; "Società della provincia, 2° trimestre, 1873," AdS (Potenza), Prefettura, cat. XXIV, busta 283, fasc. 5.

7. *Organizarea provizorie a învăţămîntului naţional confesional în mitropolia gr. or. a românilor din Ungaria şi Transilvania* (Lugoj, 1872), p. 18.

8. Ion Codru Drăgăşanu, *Peregrinul transilvan* (Bucharest, 1942), pp. 67-72; Pavel Hapák, "Prešov v rokoch 1848-1900," in Imrich Sedlák, ed., *Dejiny Prešova*, 2 vols. (Košice, 1965), II, 53-56; Eléonora Kisslingová, "O politicke l'udnej a liberálnej strany v zaklade nitrianskej spoločnosti na prelome storočia," in Alexandru Csandu, ed., *Kapitoly z dejín Nitry* (Bratislava, 1963), pp. 106-118.

9. "Jurnalul de cassa, fondul de şcola, 1883-1922," Sibiel, Parish Archives.

10. "Bericht-Obershulrichter, Tilişca," November 13, 1898, AS (Sibiu), fond Comitaţ (Vicecomitele), fasc. 306; Petru Juga to "Onorată Representanţa Comunală," March 14, 1898, ibid.; Minutes of Representanţa Comunală, Boiţa, October 30, 1898, ibid.; Greek Catholic Parish, Reşinari, to Representanţa Comunală, September 17, 1899, ibid., fasc. 330; Gustáv Valkonič, "K vývinu nitrianskeho školstva," in Csandu, *Kapitoly z dejín Nitry*, pp. 182-201; Karol Golán, ed., *Ako sa kedysi na slovensku učilo* (Bratislava, 1958), pp. 177-199.

11. *Statuto fondamentale della società operaia di mutuo soccorso "La Fratellanza" in Lauria Superiore* (Potenza, 1880), pp. 3-4.

12. Giuseppe Cristalli to Prefect of Basilicata, August 5, 1883, AdS (Potenza), Prefettura, cat. XXIV, busta 440, fasc. 80; Prefect of Caltinessetta to Direzione dei Servizi di Pubblica Sicurezza, June 5, 1887, AdS (Caltanissetta), Pubblica Sicurezza, busta 9; *L'amico del popolo* (Palermo), February 13, March 7, 1891; *Giornale di Sicilia* (Palermo), February 9, March 3, April 8, 1899; minutes of Consiglio Comunale, March 6, 1906, Valguanera, Archivio Comunale; *La difesa* (Termini Imerese), June 1, 1906; *La vita nuova* (Castelvetrano), January 16, 1913.

13. *Statuto della società di mutuo soccorso fra gli artigiani ennesi* (Castrogiovanni, 1876), art. 17; *Statuto fondamentale della società di mutuo soccorso di Montescaglione* (Matera, 1872), art. 1; *Statuto per l'associazione operaia G. Mazzini in Miglionici* (Matera, 1886), pp. 17-18; *Statuto della società operaia e cooperativa di mutuo soccorso di Castrogiovanni* (Castrogiovanni, 1889), art. 2; *Statuto della società operaia di mutuo soccorso Domenico Minolfi Scovazzo . . . Valguanera* (Valguanera, 1895), p. 1; report on same society, c. 1894, in AdS (Caltanissetta), Pubblica Sicurezza, busta 8.

14. *Inchiesta parlamentare sulle condizioni dei contadini nelle provincie meridionali e nella Sicilia*, 15 vols. (Rome, 1909-11), VI, fasc. 1, p. 336; cf. *Germinal* (Nicosia), February 24, 1910.

15. Minutes of Società Agricola di Mutuo Soccorso, February 1, 1914, in the society's archives, Alcara Li Fusi; Subprefect of Patti to Prefect of Messina, February 29, 1909, AdS (Messina), Prefettura, fasc. 1; summaries of societies in AdS (Potenza), Prefettura, cat. XXIV, buste 440-441, and in AdS (Messina), Prefettura, fasc. 193.

16. "Statutele Reuniunei de Casina Românească in Reşinari," February 6, 1891, AS (Sibiu), fond Comitat (Vicecomitele), fasc. 34; "Statutele Reuniunei Femeilor Greco-orientale din Avrig," February 18, 1904, ibid.; "Poiána Román Kasinó," December 12, 1896, ibid., fasc. 227; "Statutele Reuniunei gr. or. Române de Cântări din Mercurea," c. 1911, ibid., f. Comitat (Comitele), fasc. 634; "A Péterfalvai Polgári és Munkás Olvasókäi," September 23, 1907, ibid.; "Statutele Societăţii Meriaşilor din Reşinari," December 13, 1910, ibid.; Primaria Comunală, Selişte, to "Onorabile Domnule Prinpretor," January 20, 22, 1896, ibid., f. Comitat (Vicecomitele), fasc. 234. On banking, see Nicolae N. Petru, *Bancile româneşti din Ardeal şi Banat* (Sibiu, 1936), and *Pätdesiat rokov slovenskej banky, 1879-1930* (Bratislava, 1930).

17. "Situaţia" (c. 1929), fol. II, p. 3, Sibiel, Parish Archives; "Statutele Societăţii Cooperative de Aprovizionare şi Defacere în comun di Comuna Tilişca" (c. 1914), Tilişca, Parish Archives; interviews in Alcara Li Fusi and Militello Rosmarino, September 1968; minutes of Società Agricola di Mutuo Soccorso, in the society's archives, Alcara Li Fusi, January 15, 1893, March 8, 1914; "Elenco dei sodalizi esistenti nel Circondario di Patti al 27 Aprile 1917," AdS (Messina), Prefettura, fasc. 193.

18. *Almanach, suvenire de la primul jubileu ale societăţii de lectura Andreiu Şaguna* (Sibiu, 1894); memorandum, December 3, 1891, AS (Sibiu), fond Comitat (Vicecomitele), fasc. 326; Greek Catholic Parish, Reşinari, to Representanţa Comunală, December 3, 1899, ibid., fasc. 330; *Almanahul învăţătorului român, 1899-1900* (Reşita Montană, 1900); *Reuniunea învăţătorilor arhidiecezani* (Blaj, 1913); cf. Erich Prokopowitsch, *Die rumänische National-bewegung in der Bukowina und der Dako-Romanismus*, III, *Studien zur Geschichte der österreichisch-ungarischen Monarchie* (Graz, 1965), pp. 86-88.

19. *Tovarysstvo* (Ruzomberok), 1-3 (1893-1900), chronicles the development of various organizations. Cf. František Bokeš, "Kultúrne pomery vychodného Slovenska v obdobi kapitalizmu," in L'udovit Holotík, ed., *Prispevky k dejinam vychodného Slovenska* (Bratislava, 1964), pp. 233-244; Július Mésároš and Miroslav Kropilák, eds., *Matica Slovenská v nasich dejinách* (Bratislava, 1963); Peter Sugar, "The Nature of the Non-Germanic Societies under Habsburg Rule," *Slavic Review*, 22 (1963), 25-28; Zoltan I. Toth, *Magyarok és románok* (Budapest, 1966), pp. 386-392.

20. Cf. S. de Lorenzo, *Coltura popolare religiosa in Calabria* (Reggio Calabria, 1913), reprinted in Pietro Borzomati, *Aspetti religiosi e storia del movimento cattolico in Calabria (1860-1919)* (Rome, 1967), pp. 443-458;

report of Questore of Palermo, 1886, AdS (Palermo), Prefettura, busta 120; *Prima lettera pastorale di Monsignor Mariano Paleno* (Palermo, 1887), pp. 20-21; *Statuto della Società siciliana primaria per gl'interessi cattolici* (Palermo, 1891), arts. IV-V; *Bollettino ecclesiastico della diocesi di Nicosia*, 5 (1911), 96-98.

21. *Il sole del Mezzogiorno* (Palermo), February 1, 1901.

22. Štefan Furdek, "Z Ameriky," *Tovaryšstvo* (Ružomberok), 1 (1893), 235; Richard Osvald, "Štefan Furdek," ibid., 3 (1900), 289-292.

23. Samuel P. Orth, *A History of Cleveland*, 3 vols. (Chicago, 1910), I, 410-411; Office of the Ohio Secretary of State, *Acts of Incorporation*, vol. 37, p. 644; *La voce*, January 8, 1910, January 1, 1937; Charles W. Coulter, *The Italians of Cleveland* (Cleveland, 1919), p. 17.

24. Lájos Ambrozy to Ladislaus von Hengelmüller, November 26, 1908, MOL, K-26/1910/XIV/715/1947; *Românul*, March 9, 1907; *Acts of Incorporation*, vol. 102, p. 156; *Calendarul America*, 1912, pp. 103-104.

25. Recorder's Office, Cuyahoga County, "Societies: Religious, Fraternal, Etc.," I, 117, II, 40-41; Konštantin Čulen, *Dejiny Slovákov v Amerike*, 2 vols. (Bratislava, 1942), I, 98; *Jednota kalendár*, 1902, p. 78; *Hlas*, April 15, 1925, March 11, 1937.

26. A study of the membership of eighteen mutual benefit societies in Cleveland suggested this generalization about regional origins (N = 266); information compiled from membership applications in IKSJ Papers, 1A. Cf. Ján Pankuch, *Dejiny clevelandských a lakewoodských Slovákov* (Cleveland, 1930), pp. 21-22; *Noviny*, January 14, 1897; *Jednota kalendár*, 1902, p. 207, 1903, p. 208.

27. Štefan Furdek, "Všeličo z Ameriky," *Tovaryšstvo* (Ružomberok), 3 (1900), 294; *Noviny*, March 14, 1895, September 28, 1899; *Jednota kalendár*, 1902, p. 76; *Slovák v Amerike*, August 20, 1896; *Národný kalendár*, 1899, pp. 166-174; *Jednota*, April 8, 1908, April 17, 1912, May 14, 1913, November 19, 1919.

28. *Hlas*, February 27, 1925; *Acts of Incorporation*, vol. 58, p. 627; *Noviny*, January 18, 1896; Jozef Paučo, *75 rokov Prvej Katolickej Slovenskej Jednoty* (Cleveland, 1965), p. 24; *Národný kalendár*, 1899, pp. 166-174, 1906, p. 220, 1912, pp. 58-62.

29. *La voce*, April 10, September 11, 1909, December 30, 1916, September 1, 1917, March 8, 1919, February 4, 1937; *Acts of Incorporation*, vol. 124, p. 131, vol. 138, p. 271; *Catholic Universe*, May 5, 1905.

30. *Acts of Incorporation*, vol. 73, pp. 229, 238, vol. 85, pp. 114, 257; *Bollettino dell'emigrazione* (Rome), 1908, no. 24, p. 98; cf. *Venticinque anni di missioni fra gl'immigrati italiani di Boston, Mass., 1888-1913* (Milan, 1913), pp. 197-198.

31. Orth, *History of Cleveland*, III, 1078-1079; *La voce*, April 3, November 13, 1909, May 14, June 25, 1910, March 16, 1913; cf. *La Trinacria*, July 1, 1921, December 22, 1922, and *Il corriere del popolo*, July 16, 1916.

32. *L'emigrato italiano in America* (Piacenza), 5 (1907), 155-156; Pacifico Capitani, *La questione italiana negli Stati Uniti d'America* (Cleve-

land, 1891), pp. 5-6, 23; Pred. Luke, C. P., to Ignaz Horstmann, October 14, 1896, Diocese of Cleveland Archives, Parish Files, folder marked "Holy Rosary"; Vittorio Gregori, *La vita e l'opera d'un grande vescovo* (Piacenza, 1926), p. 476; *La voce*, June 11, 1910; *Venticinque anni di missioni*, pp. 84-88, 354-356. I have depended heavily here on the suggestions of Rudolph J. Vecoli, "Prelates and Peasants: Italian Immigrants and the Catholic Church," *Journal of Social History*, 2 (1969), 217-268.

33. *Calendarul America*, 1927, pp. 133-136; *Calendarul Solia* (Detroit), 1940, p. 90; *Istoria Uniunei şi Legei Societăţilor Române de Ajutor şi Cultura . . . 1906-1931* (Cleveland, 1931), pp. 26-28; *Românul*, May 20, 1906; *America*, November 30, 1906, December 15, 26, 1907; minutes of Reuniunea de Cântări Traianâ, June 25, September 15, 1909, USRA Collection.

34. Anda Hodobay to Karl von Giskra, March 20, 1903, March 9, 1904, MOL, K-26/1903/XVI/263; Moise Balea to Ioan Ganca, October 12, 1906, and Ioan Simtion to Ioan Ionus, November 21, 1906, Letterbook, USRA Collection; *Poşta românã*, July 4, 1908; *America*, February 25, March 11, 1909; *Jubileul de aur al bisericii ortodoxe române "Sfânta Maria"* (Cleveland, 1954), pp. 30, 40-59; *Calendarul America*, 1922, pp. 22-27.

35. *Catholic Universe*, July 6, 1906; Alexandru Nicolescu, "Cuvinte din înima," *Catolicul american* (Aurora, Ill.), 2 (April 1909), 5-6; undated minute of Geza Sztaja, MOL, K-26/1913/XXIIIB/1665/6359a; minutes of Asociaţia Liga şi Ajutorul, July 4, 1913, July 3, 1917, USRA Collection; Aureliu Haţiegan to John P. Farelly, June 25, 1916, Diocese of Cleveland Archives, Parish Files, folder marked "Most Holy Trinity."

36. *Istoria Uniunei şi Legei*, pp. 29, 31-32; *Românul*, February 18, 1906, March 9, 1907, May 2, 1908, January 23, 1910, February 19, 1911, August 8, 30, October 13, 1912; *America*, June 14, 1907; Geza Sztaja, "Rumänische Propaganda in Amerika," November 21, 1909, MOL, K-26/1910/XIV/715/4856; Dionisie Moldovan, *Advocatul poporal* (Cleveland, 1910); USRA, *Proces verbal . . . 9-11 novembrie 1918* (Cleveland, 1918), p. 6; *Serbările unirii, 1929* (Bucharest, 1929), p. 40; *Solia*, October 25, 1936

37. Čulen, *Dejiny Slovákov*, I, 197; *Národný kalendár*, 1926, pp. 43-44, 70; *Acts of Incorporation*, vol. 37, p. 505.

38. Čulen, *Dejiny Slovákov*, I, 206; *Acts of Incorporation*, vol. 58, p. 173. "Dejiny spolku sv. Jozefa," *Jednota kalendár*, 1940, p. 122, contains the minutes of the first meeting, May 5, 1889; cf. *Jednota*, September 20, 1905, April 11, 1906. The characterization of leadership is based on a sample of thirty founding members of these societies.

39. *Jednota kalendár*, 1898, pp. 132-133, 135; Čulen, *Dejiny Slovákov*, I, 207-208; Paučo, *75 rokov Prvej Katolickej Slovenskej Jednoty*, p. 11; *Katolické noviny*, September 18, 1890, quoted in *Jednota*, September 9, 1908.

40. Pankuch, *Dejiny Slovákov*, pp. 24-27, 271-272; *Slovák v Amerike*, August 31, 1901, January 21, April 11, 1902; Emily Green Balch, *Our Slavic Fellow Citizens* (New York, 1910), p. 380n.

41. *Slovák v Amerike*, July 17, 1900.

42. *Noviny*, January 27, May 12, 19, August 12, 1898, February 20, October 29, 1902, December 16, 1903, May 4, 1904.

43. Ibid., February 20, 1902.

44. Čulen, *Dejiny Slovákov*, II, 69-70; *Jednota kalendár*, 1912, pp. 173-177; *Jednota*, December 29, 31, 1919.

45. See the brilliant discussion of Catholic festivals in Octavio Paz, *El laberinto de la soledad*, rev. ed. (Mexico City, 1963), pp. 37-42.

46. *La voce*, September 25, 1909, March 19, July 30, August 13, 1910, October 28, 1916, August 23, 1919; *Acts of Incorporation*, vol. 138, p. 271; cf. Gerald Suttles, *The Social Order of the Slum: Ethnicity and Territory in the Inner City* (Chicago, 1968), pp. 105-107.

47. Eric R. Wolf, "Aspects of Group Relations in a Complex Society: Mexico," *American Anthropologist*, 58 (1956), 1075-1076, develops the image of a broker. For what follows, I have to thank John W. Briggs for his stimulating suggestions.

48. Orth, *History of Cleveland*, III, 99-100; *La voce*, May 22, 1909, January 29, February 12, July 30, 1921, February 18, April 15, 1937; *Acts of Incorporation*, vol. 102, p. 500; Elroy McKendree Avery, *A History of Cleveland and Its Environs*, 3 vols. (Chicago, 1918), II, 318-319.

49. *La voce*, August 7, September 18, 1909, September 24, 1910. The paragraph rests on an analysis of the leadership of twenty-eight societies appearing in *La voce*, 1909-10 ($N = 364$).

50. *La voce*, February 5, July 30, August 6, 20, 1910, August 26, 1911.

51. Amy A. Bernardy, *Italia randagia attraverso gli Stati Uniti* (Turin, 1913), pp. 238-239.

52. Giovanni Preziosi, *Gl'italiani negli Stati Uniti del Nord* (Milan, 1909), p. 192; Preziosi, *La "Dante Alighieri" e l'emigrazione italiana negli Stati Uniti* (Rome, 1911), pp. 38-43; Luigi Carnovale, *Il giornalismo degli emigrati italiani nel Nord America* (Chicago, 1909), pp. 66-68; *La fiaccola*, August 5, 1911; *Il corriere del popolo*, August 1, December 12, 15, 1916; cf. Aurelio Palmieri, *Il grave problema religioso italiano negli Stati Uniti* (Florence, 1921), pp. 46-67.

53. *La voce*, April 27, 1912, May 10, 1913, March 14, 1914, May 15, 1915; Baldo Aquilano, *L'Ordine Figli d'Italia in America* (New York, 1925), p. 42.

54. *La voce*, May 15, July 31, 1915, February 8, 1919, October 2, 9, 1920; cf. *Il corriere del popolo*, March 21, 1919, *La Trinacria*, August 16, 1919, and *La luce*, February 13, 1915.

55. *La voce*, May 27, 1916, February 8, March 1, April 22, 26, May 17, August 23, 1919, March 20, May 1, October 30, 1920; George Bellamy to Samuel Mather, July 31, 1918, Western Reserve Historical Society, Hiram House Records, box 1.

56. Quotes from *Românul*, March 25, 1906, and *America*, December 28, 1906. See *Românul*, May 6, 27, June 3, November 11, 1906, February 2, April 13, May 11, 1907, *America*, January 14, 20, 1907; *Istoria Uniunei și Legei*, pp. 29-30.

57. *Românul*, February 25, 1906; *America*, March 4, September 22, November 12, 1909, April 17, 1910.

58. See *America*, January 28, June 10, 1909, April 10, 1910; minutes of Reuniunea de Cântări Traianǎ, October 6, 1912, USRA Collection; *Steaua noastrǎ*, August 20, 1913; Lájos Ambrozy to Ladislaus von Hengelmüller, January 16, 1909, MOL, K-26/1910/XXII/2720/ad59796.

59. *America*, March 3, 1910; Aureliu Hatiegan to Diomedie Falconio, June 8, 1911, Diocese of Cleveland Archives, Parish Files, folder marked "St. Helena"; *Programul serbarii jubilare . . . parohia ortodoxǎ românǎ "Sfânta Maria" din Cleveland, Ohio* (Cleveland, 1929), pp. 6, 12-13; *Românul*, October 1, 1912; *Steaua noastrǎ*, December 25, 1912; *Solia*, July 19, 1936; *Calendarul America*, 1916, pp. 137-143. Minutes of USRA, July 5, 1912, March 16, 1913; minutes of Asociaţia Liga şi Ajutorul, July 4, 1916; Vasile Zdroba to George Marhǎo, April 29, 1923, folder marked "Aradanǎ, 1923." (All in USRA Collection.) Cf. USRA, *Rapoartele Pres. Gen. Paul D. Tomi . . . 1927* (Cleveland, 1927), pp. 1-10.

60. Minutes of Asociaţia Liga şi Ajutorul, July 3, 1919, July 3, 1927; USRA, *Proces verbal . . . 15-17 oct. 1922* (Cleveland, 1922), p. 7; USRA, *Procesele verbale . . . sept. 1923 pânǎ la 1 sept. 1924* (Cleveland, 1924), pp. 14, 24; Trifu Militariu to [unknown], March 23, 1931, folder marked "Banaţianǎ, 1931." (All in USRA Collection.)

61 *Calendarul America*, 1912, pp. 104-124; minutes of USRA, "Anex" to entry for December 16, 1912.

62. Minutes of Asociaţia Liga şi Ajutorul, 1913-28, especially July 3, 1916, July 3, 1917, July 3, 1918, January 13, July 3, 1924; minutes of Reuniunea de Cantări Traianǎ, May 25, 1913; John Ursu to Paul Tomy, July 16, 1926, folder marked "Ardeleana Ilasco, 1926"; Vasilie Vlad to Ţinerean, February 3, 1923, folder marked "Deşteaptǎ-te Române, 1923"; John Carpaţina to Paul Tomy, July 8, 1924, folder marked "Woodrow Wilson, 1924"; Dionisie Niculescu to Paul Tomy, June 1, 1926, folder marked "Dorobantul Român, 1926." (All in USRA Collection.)

63. USRA, *Procesele verbale . . . 1 sept. 1923 pânǎ la 1 sept. 1924*, p. 4; USRA, *Proces verbale, 1924-25* (Cleveland, 1925), pp. 40-41; Liga Societǎţilor Române Americane, *Procesul verbal luat in Congresul de Unire* (Youngstown, 1924); minutes of Asociaţia Liga şi Ajutorul, December 7, 1924, USRA Collection.

64. Minutes of Asociaţia Liga şi Ajutorul, December 19, 1926, USRA Collection; USRA, *Proces verbal . . . 1928-1929* (Cleveland, 1929), pp. 1-76; USRA, *Raportul funcţionarilor generali . . . 1928* (Cleveland, 1928).

CHAPTER 5   FATHERS AND SONS: TRENDS IN SOCIAL MOBILITY

1. W. G. Runciman, "Class, Status, and Power?" in John A. Jackson, ed., *Social Stratification*, vol. 1, *Sociological Studies* (Cambridge, 1968), p. 55; cf. Leonard Reissman, *Class in American Society* (Glencoe, Ill., 1959),

pp. 158-159. The best introduction to the literature on class is in Reinhard Bendix and Seymour Martin Lipset, eds., *Class, Status, and Power*, 2d ed. (New York, 1966).

2. See Appendix tables B-E for a crude ranking of occupations.

3. Cf. Paul K. Hatt, "Occupational and Social Stratification," *American Journal of Sociology*, 55 (1950), 539; Stephan Thernstrom, "Notes on the Historical Study of Social Mobility," *Comparative Studies in Society and History*, 10 (1967-68), 168.

4. Stephan Thernstrom, personal communication; Natalie Rogoff, *Recent Trends in Occupational Mobility* (Glencoe, Ill., 1953).

5. Throughout this and the following chapter I employ two conventions that require some explanation. First, I have judged twenty years long enough to determine the career mobility of both the fathers and the sons; this is what I call sometimes the "long run." The long run includes the job experience of an immigrant from his earliest appearance in the sources — city directories, marriage records, school records, and interviews — through the next twenty years. Second, I use the terms "first job" and "last job" to describe the course of an occupational career. These are not literal descriptions, of course, since I could not administer a questionnaire to these men. "First job" means here the earliest employment a man is known to have held, so long as he held it before age thirty. "Last job" means the last employment held in Cleveland according to available records, so long as it was held after age thirty. For the sample members who died before age fifty or sixty I used the occupation entered on the death certificate to describe the last job. The choice of thirty as the age of settling down to lifelong employment was based on information in this and other studies, which show a marked slowing of occupational mobility for men thirty and older. Cf. Stephan Thernstrom, "Immigrants and WASP: Ethnic Differences in Occupational Mobility in Boston, 1890–1940," in Thernstrom and Richard Sennett, eds., *Nineteenth-Century Cities: Essays in the New Urban History* (New Haven, 1969), p. 162, n. 3.

6. Cf. Gerhard E. Lenski, "Trends in Inter-generational Occupational Mobility in the United States," *American Sociological Review*, 23 (1958), 521.

7. The measure of association is the statistic gamma, of which an admirable exposition is Leo A. Goodman and William H. Kruskal, "Measures of Association for Cross Classifications," *Journal of the American Statistical Association*, 49 (1954), 732-764.

8. The village background of the Italians suggests one source of this stability. Eighty percent of the skilled among the small sample of Italians ($N = 71$) which I discussed in the first part of this chapter had artisan or proprietarial fathers. The continuity of village background and urban occupation is noted in several instances in *Inchiesta parlamentare sulle condizioni dei contadini nelle provincie meridionali e nella Sicilia*, 15 vols. (Rome, 1909-11), VI, fasc. 1, pp. 337, 368, and passim.

9. Max Weber, *The Theory of Social and Economic Organization* (New York, 1947), p. 425.

10. Merle Curti, *The Making of an American Community: A Case Study of Democracy in a Frontier County* (Stanford, 1959), pp. 176-192; Stephan Thernstrom, *Poverty and Progress: Social Mobility in a Nineteenth Century City* (Cambridge, Mass., 1964), pp. 115-137. Cf. Walter Firey, *Land Use in Central Boston* (Cambridge, Mass., 1947), pp. 214-217; Peter Roberts, *Anthracite Coal Communities* (New York, 1904), pp. 41-44, 133-135; Giuseppe Tuoti, "La proprietà immobiliare italiana in New York," in *Gli italiani negli Stati Uniti d'America* (New York, 1906), pp. 145-152.

11. Oscar Handlin, *The Newcomers: Negroes and Puerto Ricans in a Changing Metropolis* (Cambridge, Mass., 1959), p. 26.

12. Cf. Stephan Thernstrom, "Poverty in Historical Perspective," in Daniel P. Moynihan, ed., *On Understanding Poverty* (New York, 1969), pp. 170-171.

13. For suggestive treatments of these issues, see Otis Dudley Duncan and Stanley Lieberson, "Ethnic Segregation and Assimilation," *American Journal of Sociology*, 64 (1959), 364-374; Sam Bass Warner, Jr., and Colin Burke, "Cultural Change and the Ghetto," *Journal of Contemporary History*, 4 (1969), 181-182; Stanley Lieberson, *Ethnic Patterns in American Cities* (Glencoe, Ill., 1963), pp. 98-100; and Ely Chinoy, *Automobile Workers and the American Dream* (New York, 1955), pp. 125-126.

14. Thernstrom, *Poverty and Progress*, p. 137.

15. See chapter 7.

16. See, for example, Herbert J. Gans, *The Urban Villagers: Group and Class in the Life of Italian-Americans* (New York, 1962).

17. Cf. John Porter, *The Vertical Mosaic: An Analysis of Social Class and Power in Canada* (Toronto, 1965), pp. 63-64, 70-73.

18. Stephan Thernstrom, *The Other Bostonians: Poverty and Progress in the American Metropolis, 1880-1970* (Cambridge, Mass., 1973), pp. 122-124.

CHAPTER 6   SOURCES OF MOBILITY: FAMILY AND EDUCATION

1. The method of presentation and the mode of analysis are drawn from Stephan Thernstrom, *Poverty and Progress: Social Mobility in a Nineteenth Century City* (Cambridge, Mass., 1964), pp. 138-165.

2. As in chapter 5, these sketches are based on reconstitutions of families, city directories, school records, tax lists, and interviews.

3. This statement appears to contradict the amount of movement into the skilled occupations which I uncovered in chapter 5. But the statement must be made in this form because of a limitation in the method employed here to analyse different forms of mobility. As I point out later on, many of the brothers of young men gaining nonmanual status moved into skilled occupations. Hence chapter 5 is a better guide to the *volume* of movement into skilled occupations. My concern here, again, is to distinguish characteristic *forms* of movement and to suggest some sources of social mobility.

4. S. M. Miller and Frank Riessman develop a persuasive rationale

for the term "stable working class" in "The Working Class Subculture: A New View," *Social Problems*, 9 (1961), 86-97, and in *Social Class and Social Policy* (New York, 1968), pp. 35-51.

5. This evidence lends little support to Stephan Thernstrom's interesting hypothesis that the sons of prosperous Newburyport laborers did not enjoy superior career prospects because their education was generally sacrificed to the family's acquisition of property (*Poverty and Progress*, pp. 155-157). Thernstrom's more recent study of Boston qualifies his earlier study and lends support to my own findings (*The Other Bostonians: Poverty and Progress in the American Metropolis, 1880-1970* [Cambridge, Mass., 1973]), pp. 170-175.

6. The classic statement of this hypothesis is by Charles F. Westoff, "The Changing Focus of Differential Fertility Research: The Social Mobility Hypothesis," *Milbank Memorial Fund Quarterly*, 21 (1953), 24-38.

7. Cf. Clyde V. Kiser, *Group Differences in Urban Fertility* (Baltimore, 1942), pp. 443-468, who shows that completed families of the higher-status groups were either similar in size to or at times larger than the families of status groups immediately below them — the same pattern which appears here among the Rumanians.

8. The analysis here owes a good deal to David Goldberg, "The Fertility of Two-Generational Urbanites," *Population Studies*, 12 (1959), 214-222, and "Another Look at the Indianapolis Fertility Data," *Milbank Memorial Fund Quarterly*, 38 (1960), 23-36; and to the excellent summary of Ronald Freedman, "American Studies of Family Planning and Fertility: A Review of Major Trends and Issues," in Clyde V. Kiser, ed., *Research in Family Planning* (Princeton, 1962), pp. 211-227.

9. I have drawn heavily here on Gösta Carlsson, *Social Mobility and Class Structure* (Lund, 1958), pp. 121-137; C. Arnold Anderson, "A Skeptical Note on Education and Mobility," *American Journal of Sociology*, 66 (1961), 560-570; Samuel Bowles, "Towards Equality of Educational Opportunity?" *Harvard Educational Review*, 38 (1968), 89-99.

10. Gamma = 0.58.

11. Lájos Ambrozy to Ladislaus von Hengelmüller, November 14, 1908, MOL, K-26/1909/XXII/1937.

12. See Marc A. Fried, "The Role of Work in a Mobile Society," in Sam Bass Warner, Jr., ed., *Planning for a Nation of Cities* (Cambridge, Mass., 1966), pp. 88-89, 91.

13. Cf. David F. Aberle and Kaspar D. Naegele, "Middle-class Fathers' Occupational Roles and Attitudes toward Children," in Norman F. Bell and Ezra F. Vogel, ed., *A Modern Introduction to the Family* (Glencoe, Ill., 1960), pp. 126-136; Richard M. Titmuss, *Essays on 'The Welfare State,'* 2d ed. (London, 1963), pp. 108, 112-113.

14. The best summary of the literature on family and mobility is by Colin Rosser and Christopher Harris, *The Family and Social Change: A Study of Family and Kinship in a South Wales Town* (London, 1965), pp. 18-32. Four studies have been especially useful in my approach to the family: Marvin B. Sussman, "The Help Pattern in the Middle Class Family," *American Sociological Review*, 18 (1953), 22-28; "The Isolated

Nuclear Family: Fact or Fiction," *Social Problems*, 6 (1958-59), 333-340; Eugene Litwak, "Occupational Mobility and Extended Family Cohesion," *American Sociological Review*, 25 (1960), 9-21; and Virginia Yans McLaughlin, "Patterns of Work and Family Organization: Buffalo's Italians," *Journal of Interdisciplinary History*, 2 (1971), 299-314.

15. Cf. Natalie Rogoff, "Local Social Structure and Education," in A. H. Halsey, Jean Floud, and C. Arnold Anderson, eds., *Education, Economy, and Society* (New York, 1961), pp. 241-251; Seymour Martin Lipset and Reinhard Bendix, *Social Mobility in Industrial Society* (Berkeley, 1959), pp. 203-226.

16. Recent sociological literature on this problem shows, however, that there is no negative relationship between Roman Catholic parochial education and educational and occupational achievement: Andrew M. Greeley, *Religion and Career* (New York, 1963), pp. 99-109; Seymour Warkov and Greeley, "Parochial School Origins and Educational Achievement," *American Sociological Review*, 31 (1966), 406-414; Greeley and Peter H. Rossi, *The Education of Catholic Americans* (Chicago, 1966), pp. 138-157. The conclusions of these studies, nonetheless, apply to contemporary American society, and thus they leave open the possibility that only recently has Catholic education borne any positive relationship to social mobility.

17. James S. Coleman emphasizes the importance of local social context in Coleman et al., *Equality of Educational Opportunity* (Washington, D.C., 1966), pp. 302-312.

18. The reader may be surprised to discover this assertion, in view of the conclusion reached in chapter 5 that there is little evidence of an ordered relationship between father's origins and son's career mobility. The point in the preceding chapter was that the ethnic groups in the *aggregate* did not find themselves confined to particular occupational strata. Here, once again, the task is to circumscribe particular forms of mobility (as in this instance, the striking movement of second-generation Rumanians into the professions), and to identify the sources of movement.

19. Cf. Thernstrom, *The Other Bostonians*, pp. 145-175.

CHAPTER 7   THE EMERGENCE OF THE SECOND GENERATION

1. Quoted in Jozef Paučo, *75 rokov Prvej Katolickej Slovenskej Jednoty* (Cleveland, 1965), p. 11.

2. Štefan Furdek, "Z Ameriky," *Tovaryšstvo* (Ružomberok), 1 (1893), 235; *Jednota*, May 12, 1891; *Jednota kalendár*, 1899, p. 37.

3. *Slovák v Amerike*, March 19, 1896.

4. *Jednota kalendár*, 1898, pp. 109-110, 1900, p. 136, 1911, pp. 97-98, 1914, pp. 193-196; Štefan Furdek, "Všeličo z Ameriky," *Tovaryšstvo* (Ružomberok), 3 (1900), 299; *Jednota*, November 29, 1902, February 22, 1905, April 12, 1911; Karl von Giskra to Ladislaus von Hengelmüller, March 18, 1904, MOL, K-26/1904/XX/226/2447.

5. Pastoral letter of the Third Plenary Council (1884), in Peter Guilday,

The National Pastorals of the American Hierarchy (1792-1919) (Westminster, Md., 1954), pp. 246-247; Robert D. Cross, "Origins of the Catholic Parochial School in America," *American Benedictine Review*, 16 (1965), 206-209.

6. On German Catholicism, see *Cleveland und sein Deutschtum* (Cleveland, 1897-98); on the founding of St. Wendelin, see Ferenz Toth to Konzul Wein, November 25, 1904, MOL, K-26/1905/XX/85/ad1846a; and *Catholic Universe*, July 18, 1905.

7. *Jednota kalendár*, 1900, p. 136; *Jednota*, July 1, 1908, July 7, 1909, July 6, 1910, February 22, March 19, 1911, August 14, 1912, April 30, July 30, 1913; "Annual Report of the Neighborhood Visitor . . . 1909," box 29, Hiram House Records, Western Reserve Historical Society.

8. *Jednota*, April 30, July 30, 1913.

9. Paučo, *75 rokov Prvej Katolickej Slovenskej Jednoty*, p. 39; *Jednota*, June 13, 1906, March 27, 1907, February 5, November 25, 1908, September 25, 1912; *Jednota kalendár*, 1911, p. 68; *Catholic Universe*, January 18, 1907; *Národné noviny*, January 26, 1911.

10. Juraj Hudačko to Michal Senko, March 17, 1915, folder 427; Vendelin Hurban to Senko, March 10, 1919, folder 12; Imre Hiznay to Senko, June 12, 1922, and Senko to "Drahí bratia," June 14, 1922, folder 530; František Uhlarik to Senko, October 15, 1923, folder 57; Michal Čusma to Senko, March 1, 1925, folder 1. (All in Secretary's Files, IKSJ Papers.

11. *Noviny*, November 8, 17, 1894, June 11, 1895, June 7, 1900; *Slovák v Amerike*, September 7, 1900, July 4, 1903; *Jednota*, November 15, 1905, October 15, 1902; Lájos Ambrozy to Ladislaus von Hengelmüller, December 21, 1908, MOL, K-26/1910/XXIV/331/1967; Ambrozy to von Hengelmüller, January 16, 1909, ibid., K-26/1910/XXIV/2720.

12. Cf. Georg Timpe, "Karl Adams, Lehrer und Organist," in Timpe, ed., *Katolisches Deutschtum in den Vereinigten Staaten* (Freiburg im Breisgau, 1937), pp. 146-154; Ocyp Stetkevuich, "Ukraïns'ke shkil'nptšvo v Amerytsi," *Jubilee Book of the Ukrainian National Association . . . Fortieth Anniversary* (Jersey City, 1936), pp. 325-342; M. Nastasivs'kyi, *Ukraïns'ka imihratsiia v Spoluchenyk Dershavakh* (New York, 1934), pp. 73-74; Mark Zborowski and Elizabeth Herzog, *Life Is with People: The Jewish Little-Town of Eastern Europe* (New York, 1955), pp. 88-104.

13. *Jednota*, October 15, 1919; *Jednota kalendár*, 1900, pp. 135-136; *Slovák v Amerike*, July 20, 1900.

14. *Noviny*, February 8, June 14, 1894, November 21, 1895, December 30, 1897; *Jednota*, September 7, 21, 1904, September 6, 1905, December 26, 1906, January 20, February 17, March 3, April 14, May 12, June 16, July 7, 1909; *Národné noviny*, August 4, 1910, September 28, 1911.

15. *Jednota*, March 3, July 7, 1909, February 16, August 31, 1910, August 30, 1911, August 14, 1912, April 30, 1913, July 22, August 19, 1914.

16. Ibid., September 3, 1902, May 11, July 27, 1904, December 25, 1907, August 19, 1908, June 2, 1909, August 3, 1910; *Národné noviny*, June 9, August 4, 18, 1910; *Hlas*, March 15, 1926; "Report of the Neighbor-

hood Visitor, 1911," box 29, Hiram House Records; John Lutian to Michal Senko, November 25, 1915, folder 384, Secretary's Files, IKSJ Papers.

17. *Noviny*, October 15, 1895, April 3, 1910; *Jednota*, September 27, 1905, January 27, September 1, 1909; "Report of Girls' Work for 1908-1909," box 8, Hiram House Records; *Národné noviny*, August 17, 1911; *Národný kalendár*, 1912, pp. 60-62.

18. *La voce*, May 1, September 18, 25, October 23, 1909, April 27, 1912, June 21, 1913; *Catholic Universe*, November 11, 1905; Humberto Rocchi to John P. Farrelly, August 5, 1914, Diocese of Cleveland Archives, Parish Files, folder marked "St. Anthony"; "The Settlement and Its Neighborhood, 1924," pp. 48-50, Hiram House Records, box 3.

19. Ignaz Horstmann to Joseph Militello, December 16, 1907, and Militello to Stefan Furdek, April 1, 1908, Diocese of Cleveland Archives, Parish Files, folder marked "Holy Rosary"; Cleveland *Plain Dealer*, July 29, 1908; *La voce*, July 14, 1917. Cf. *La Trinacria*, July 1, 1921, January 19, 1923; *Il corriere del popolo*, January 21, June 6, 1916; *L'avvenire*, August 27, September 3, 10, 1904.

20. *La voce*, January 22, 1910.

21. *Central High School Annual* (Cleveland), 1905, 1906, 1910, 1913, 1915; *La voce*, July 3, 1910.

22. *La voce*, October 2, 1909; cf. a similar letter from a Cleveland laborer in *La fiaccola*, September 25, 1909.

23. *La voce*, June 19, November 6, 1909, January 22, 1910, February 22, 1919, November 6, 1920; George Bellamy to Samuel Mather, March 19, 1919, Hiram House Records, box 1.

24. *Proceedings of the Cleveland Board of Education*, 1910, p. 31, 1911, pp. 148, 272, 311; C. W. Hadden to George Bellamy, March 21, 1909, Hiram House Records, box 8; *La voce*, October 12, 1911, October 18, 1913. Cf. *Venticinque anni di missioni fra gl'immigrati di Boston, Mass., 1888-1913* (Milan, 1913), p. 160; *La luce*, June 1, 1912; *Il corriere del popolo*, January 9, 1917.

25. *Românul*, February 25, 1906; *America*, August 1, 8, 1909.

26. *Calendarul America*, 1922, pp. 22-27; *America*, August 22, 1909.

27. Minutes of Reuniunea de Cântări Traiană, June 25, September 15, 1909, October 6, 1912, USRA Collection; *America*, December 15, 1909, January 1, 1911; *Românul*, February 19, 1911, August 15, October 13, 1912; *Calendarul America*, 1927, p. 41; minutes of Asociația Romîna Americană Liga și Ajutorul, July 1, 22, 1925, USRA Collection.

28. *Calendarul America*, 1922, pp. 46-48; *America*, January 28, June 10, 1909, April 10, 1910.

29. *Românul*, January 9, 1910, September 1, 1912; *Programul serbarii jubilare . . . parohia ortodoxă română "Sfta Maria" din Cleveland, Ohio* (Cleveland, 1929), pp. 6, 12-13.

30. Minutes of Reuniunea de Cântări Traiană, May 25, 1913, USRA Collection; *Calendarul America*, 1916, pp. 137-143; USRA, *Proces verbal*

... *24 oct. 1920* (Cleveland, 1920), p. 6; *Calendarul America*, 1922, p. 26; USRA, *Proces verbal ... 15-17 oct. 1922* (Cleveland, 1922), p. 7; USRA, *Procesele verbale și rapoartele funcționarilor generali ... 1 sept. 1923 până la 1 sept. 1924* (Cleveland, 1924), pp. 14, 24. Vasile Vlad to Gheorghe Ținerean, February 3, 1923, folder marked "Deșteaptă-te Române, 1923", and minutes of Asociația Romîna Americană, July 3, 1927. (Both in USRA Collection.)

31. *America*, February 7, October 9, 1909; *Steaua noastră*, September 11, 1912; *Românul*, August 8, 1912.

32. *America*, December 15, 1907.

33. *Românul*, August 30, 1912; *Jubileul de aur al bisericii ortodoxe Române "Sfânta Maria"* (Cleveland, 1954), pp. 54-59; Aureliu Hațiegan to John P. Farelly, June 25, 1916, and John Vanca to Joseph Schrember, September 16, 1922, Diocese of Cleveland Archives, Parish Files, folder marked "Most Holy Trinity." Minutes of Reuniunea de Cântări Traiană, August 8, 1924; Trifu Militariu to Paul D. Tomy, January 9, February 27, March 23, 1931, folder marked "Banațiană, 1931." (Both in USRA Collection.) *Solia*, October 25, 1936, March 7, 1937.

34. The files of work permits in the Cleveland Board of Education show that children in my sample who left school at age sixteen invariably already held a full-time job or were promised one. This does not mean, of course, that some did not continue their education in night school. But the records of night schools are so poor that I could not follow these people through them.

35. Robert K. Merton, "Intermarriage and Social Structure: Fact and Theory," *Psychiatry*, 4 (1941), 361-374. See chapter 3, note 19, for a consideration of the difficulties of intermarriage statistics.

36. Ruby Jo Reeves Kennedy, "Single or Triple Melting Pot? Intermarriage Trends in New Haven, 1870-1940," *American Journal of Sociology*, 49 (1943-44), 331-339; Kennedy, "Single or Triple Melting Pot? Intermarriage in New Haven, 1870-1950," ibid., 58 (1952-53), 56-59; Milton L. Barron, *People Who Intermarry: Intermarriage in a New England Industrial Community* (Syracuse, 1946). These two studies do not, of course, exhaust the list which could be cited, but they are the only studies to employ enough controls to permit comparisons. For an excellent bibliography of American studies of intermarriage, see Joan Aldous and Reuben Hill, *International Bibliography of Research in Marriage and the Family, 1900-1964* (Minneapolis, 1967).

37. Kennedy, "Intermarriage Trends in New Haven, 1870-1940," pp. 334-335, 339.

38. Will Herberg, *Protestant, Catholic, Jew: An Essay in American Religious Sociology*, rev. ed. (Garden City, N.Y., 1960): Gerhard Lenski, *The Religious Factor*, rev. ed. (Garden City, N.Y., 1963).

CONCLUSION

1. J. C. Hronský, *Chlieb* (Turčiansky Sv. Martin, 1931), chap. XIII.

2. Ignazio Silone, *Fontamara* (Milan, 1930), preface.

3. I hope to document this view more fully in a forthcoming study of family life in a nineteenth-century Calabrian village.

4. Oscar Handlin, "The Social System," in Lloyd Rodwin, ed., *The Future Metropolis* (New York, 1961), p. 24.

5. John Higham, "Immigration," in C. Vann Woodward, ed., *The Comparative Approach to American History* (New York, 1968), pp. 91–103.

6. Cf. Charles Tilly, "Race and Migration to the American City," in James Q. Wilson, ed., *The Metropolitan Enigma* (Cambridge, Mass., 1968), pp. 135–157. Stephan Thernstrom's *The Other Bostonians: Poverty and Progress in the American Metropolis, 1880–1970* (Cambridge, Mass., 1973), develops this theme in a wholly new way.

Index

215